Knitted

tanks
& tunics

Knitted

tanks
& tunics

Angela Hahn

STACKPOLE
BOOKS

Guilford, Connecticut

Published by Stackpole Books
An imprint of The Rowman & Littlefield Publishing
Group, Inc.
4501 Forbes Blvd., Ste. 200
Lanham, MD 20706

Distributed by
NATIONAL BOOK NETWORK
800-462-6420

Copyright © 2018 by Angela Hahn

Photography: Tom Moore Studios (model photos) and
Angela Hahn (technique photos)

British Library Cataloguing in Publication Information
Available
Library of Congress Cataloging-in-Publication Data

Names: Hahn, Angela, author.
Title: Knitted tanks & tunics : 21 crisp, cool designs for
sleeveless tops / Angela Hahn.
Other titles: Knitted tanks and tunics
Description: Guilford, Connecticut : Stackpole Books,
2018.
Identifiers: LCCN 2017055454 (print) | LCCN
2017060327 (ebook) | ISBN 9780811767545 (e-book) |
ISBN 9780811717977 (pbk. : alk. paper)
Subjects: LCSH: Knitting--Patterns. | Women's
clothing.
Classification: LCC TT825 (ebook) | LCC TT825
.H25626 2018 (print) | DDC
   746.43/2--dc23
LC record available at https://lccn.loc.gov/2017055454

☉™ The paper used in this publication meets the
minimum requirements of American National Standard
for Information Sciences—Permanence of Paper for
Printed Library Materials, ANSI/NISO Z39.48-1992.

Printed in the United States of America

Contents

Patterns

Astoria **10**   Atlanta **16**

Bellingham **22**   Bethel **28**

Beverly **34**   Charlotte **40**

Introduction

An entire sweater can be a daunting project, especially for a novice knitter. The sheer amount of knitting, combined with the need for shaping and fitting, can be discouraging. Even an experienced knitter may hesitate to begin a sweater pattern that uses a fine gauge yarn, a complicated allover stitch or color pattern, or complex shaping (or all three)—no matter how appealing the design may be.

That is one reason I love sleeveless knits: without the sleeves, a sweater suddenly seems like a much more manageable project. A sleeveless top may actually be less knitting than a scarf, and no more complicated than a hat. Use a medium or bulky weight yarn, and you may be surprised by how fast your work progresses.

On the other hand, the fact that a sleeveless top requires less knitting than a complete sweater means that it is a great way to try out sport or fingering weight yarns, stitch patterns like cables or lace, or just-for-fun short row shaping, without committing to a weeks- or months-long knitting odyssey.

Another reason that I love sleeveless knits is that they are versatile to wear: they can be dressy or casual, sexy or sedate, and worn by themselves, layered over another top, or used as a shell under a cardigan or jacket. Although these patterns are geared toward warm weather knitting, and mostly use cotton or cotton-blend yarns, some of these designs could instead be worked in an extrafine merino, silk, or cashmere blend, and be equally at home in the office or at a holiday party.

A word of caution: There is nothing more disappointing than spending the time to knit a garment, only to find out that it doesn't fit. So please take the time to read the section on "Making Sure Your Knits Fit," and don't skip the gauge swatch, especially if you are substituting yarns!

I've used many different types and weights of yarns, and included a wide range of styles, fits, and knitting techniques, within the 21 designs in this book. The patterns also range in difficulty from Beginner to Experienced, with most falling in the Easy to Intermediate range. The many settings in which the models were photographed, from shore to garden to village to city, demonstrate the versatility of sleeveless tops, and inspired the pattern names (all are American towns of various sizes and locations).

I had a lot of fun creating these designs, and I hope you enjoy knitting them!

Making Sure
YOUR KNITS FIT

It's frustrating to spend a lot of time knitting something and then realize that it doesn't fit very well—especially when it's a garment that (like most of the designs in this book) is intended to fit fairly closely to the body. Patterns are written to fit a limited number of "standard" sizes, but these are averages for different body dimensions, and only a lucky few knitters will actually be a "standard" size.

How Patterns Are Sized

The Craft Yarn Council has published a chart of women's sizes that is often used as a basis for sizing knitting patterns. The bust circumference is used as the index measurement, and starts at 28–30"/71–76 cm for X-Small (XS) and increases by 4"/10 cm for each subsequent size: Small (S) is 32–34"/81–86 cm, Medium (M) is 36–38"/91.5–96.5 cm, Large (L) is 40–42"/101.5–106.5 cm, Extra Large (1X) is 44–46"/111.5–117 cm, 2X Large (2X) is 48–50"/122–127 cm, 3X Large (3X) is 52–54"/132–137 cm, 4X Large (4X) is 56–58"/142–147 cm, and 5X Large (5X) is 60–62"/152–158 cm. These measurements refer to body dimensions, not garment measurements (for more on this, see the section below on "Ease").

But there are many other body dimensions that can be equally important when fitting a garment, such as waist circumference, hip circumference, back waist length (length from the base of the neck to the natural waist), cross back (shoulder to shoulder width), upper arm circumference, and sleeve length (length

from armpit to cuff)—and the more of these measurements you consider, the less likely it will be that you fit one of the standard sizes perfectly. That is why, to get a well-fitted hand knit, you need to understand 1) how to choose the best pattern size for you, 2) how to make any changes to the pattern, preferably *before* you start knitting, to alter the finished dimensions to best fit your body, and 3) how to ensure that the dimensions of the finished garment match those specified in the pattern (original or with your changes).

Choosing the Best Pattern Size for You

To choose the right pattern size, you need to know your body measurements and the amount of ease that you want in your finished garment.

Measuring Your Body

Use a flexible tape measure and make sure it lies flat. When measuring circumferences, draw the tape so it is snug but not tight.

Bust: Measure around the fullest part of the bust, keeping the tape at the same level under the arms and across the back. If you normally wear a bra or other undergarment, wear it when you measure your bust.

Underbust: Measure the circumference just under the bust, at the level of the bra band.

Waist: With your hand on the side of your waist, bend sideways toward your hand; the point where you bend should be your natural waist. Measure your waist circumference at this point.

Low waist/high hip: Measure this circumference at the level of your belly button and just above the top of your front hipbones. Although this measurement is not usually included as such in pattern information, it is useful to know; for instance, the hems of tops that are slightly cropped will fall somewhere between this point and the widest part of your hips. In addition, for some women this might be wider than the hip measurement.

Hip: Measure around the lower part of your hips and over the largest part of your buttocks, *not* over the tops of your front hipbones. Most women have a larger hip than bust circumference, and the Craft Yarn Council charts reflect this, so the garments in this book with waist shaping have larger hip than bust measurements unless they are cropped in length and end above the widest part of the hips.

Cross back: This is the width across the top of your shoulders. Feel at the junction of your arm and shoulder, at the back, for a bony prominence; this is the acromion. Measure across your back from one acromion to the other. For sleeveless garments, the cross back measurement, sometimes called back width, is often smaller than this body measurement. On a sleeveless garment, the back width is usually measured across the back of the garment at the upper part of the armholes (after armhole shaping is completed). If the armholes are angled or cut out, this may be measured in a different place (which will be indicated on the garment schematic).

Armhole depth: Measure from the top outside edge of the shoulder down to the armpit. This measurement will give you at best a general idea of whether a garment armhole depth will suit you, because it is *not* the armhole circumference, which takes into account the width of the armhole front to back. Garment armhole depths are measured before armhole edging is added, and the edging will always make the armhole depth and circumference smaller.

Back waist length: This is difficult to measure without a helper: it is the distance from the

prominent bone at the center back of the base of the neck to the level of the natural waist.

All of the above body dimensions are included on the Craft Yarn Council's Woman Size Charts (www.craftyarncouncil.com/womansize.html), which I use as a guide when grading my patterns. Grading refers to the process of creating a range of sizes for a garment while maintaining the same look (shape, fit, and balance of details) across all of them.

This would be simple if all body dimensions changed by the same amount for each size, like bust circumference—but they don't. For instance, changes in hip and waist circumferences track changes in bust measurements fairly closely, but upper arm circumference increases relatively slowly from X-Small to Large (an average of ¾"/2 cm per size), and then more rapidly from Large to 5X Large (an average of 1½"/4 cm per size).

Ease

Ease is the difference between your body circumferences and the finished garment circumferences. It is rarely used when considering horizontal dimensions such as back and shoulder width, and doesn't really apply to vertical dimensions such as length or neck drop. A garment can have positive ease, meaning it is larger than your body; negative ease, meaning that it is smaller than your body; or no ease, meaning that body and garment measurements are the same. The greater the positive ease, the looser the garment will be, and the greater the negative ease, the tighter it will be.

Many knitters prefer different amounts of ease depending on the type of garment: a favorite Aran sweater or a flowing tunic might have 4–6"/10–15 cm positive ease, while a summer tank might have zero ease. The best way to decide how much ease you prefer for a particular type of garment is to measure a similar item that fits you well, and determine how much ease that garment has, not just at the bust but also in other areas. You may find that you prefer less ease at the bust than at the hip, for instance. Once you know how much ease you prefer in each body area, you can add this amount to your body dimensions,

and find a pattern size that is generally appropriate for you.

Although you can determine how much ease a pattern will have in multiple body areas by looking at the schematic measurements, suggested ease is given in pattern descriptions in this book for bust measurement only, *not* because ease in other parts of the garment doesn't matter (it does!), but because the amount of ease will not be the same for every part of the garment. For instance, a sweater might have negative ease at the bust, but positive ease at the waist.

So that you can see the appearance of the garment when worn with a particular amount of ease at the bust, every pattern in this book states how much ease the garment has in the photos. At the beginning of each pattern, at the end of the "Finished Measurements" section, there are a couple of sentences similar to this: "Shown in size S with ¾"/2 cm ease. Intended to fit with -1"/2.5 cm to +3"/7.5 cm ease." This means that the bust measurement of the garment is ¾"/2 cm larger than the bust measurement of the model in the photo, and that I designed the garment to be worn from

one inch smaller to three inches larger than the body, *at the bust*.

The total range of suggested ease in the above example is 4"/10 cm, which is the difference between standard bust sizes on the Craft Yarn Council charts; this means that all bust dimensions within the pattern range should be included in the suggested ease for one of the pattern sizes. However, you still need to decide how much ease you are most comfortable with, and whether that particular garment will suit you, based on both suggested ease and your usual preferences. Using the above example, if you happen to fall at the end of the suggested ease range, you have to decide whether to knit a garment with three inches of positive ease, or one inch of negative ease.

Choosing a pattern size carefully, based on your bust measurement and your preferred ease, is an important step toward creating a well-fitting garment. If the garment does not have waist shaping, or has an A-line shape, then usually there will already be enough ease built into the lower part of the garment for the waist and hips. Although the cross back measurement is also important, it is tricky to change without also altering the dimensions of the upper chest, back, and shoulders. However, if the garment does have waist shaping (the waist is narrower than the bust and hips), there are three other garment measurements that are usually fairly simple to change, and are also very important in determining whether a piece will fit well: hip circumference, waist circumference, and back waist length.

How to Alter a Pattern to Improve Fit

Use your body dimensions, along with the measurements on the pattern schematic, to decide whether you want to improve the fit of the finished garment. Again, this information is most relevant for garments with waist shaping.

Hem (hip) Circumference

In a garment worked from the bottom up, the number of stitches cast on will determine the hem circumference; look at the garment length to see if the hem will fall below, at, or above the widest part of the hips. Ensure that more or fewer stitches will not affect any special stitch patterns; for instance, an allover lace pattern would make it difficult to change the number of stitches cast on.

Make any changes in increments of four stitches, because you can easily compensate for these stitches by increasing or decreasing the number of waist shaping decreases (each four stitches). Decide how many inches you want to add or subtract, multiply this by the stitch gauge to get roughly how many stitches to add or subtract, and then round this to a number divisible by four.

To keep the garment the same length, you will need to recalculate the frequency of waist decreases.

EXAMPLE:

If the pattern calls for the first decrease on the 8th round after cast on, and then five more waist decreases spaced six rounds apart, the decreases will take 38 rounds: 8 + (5 x 6). If you want to cast on eight additional stitches, but keep the waist circumference the same, then you will need to add two waist decreases of four stitches each, which means fitting eight decreases instead of six into the same 38 rounds. There is more than one way to do this, of course; one possibility is to work the first decrease on the 6th round after cast on, then two decreases spaced six rounds apart, then five decreases spaced four rounds apart: 6 + (2 x 6) + (5 x 4) = 38.

Note: If the waist decrease frequency changes, it looks best to space the decreases farther apart closer to the hem, and then closer together as you approach the waist. (By the way, when working in the round, don't be afraid to work decreases or increases an odd number of rounds apart, if that seems to be the best solution).

If you want to increase the hip circumference *and* add length to the garment, you may be able to keep the decrease frequency the same, depending on how many stitches and how much length you would like to add. Always read that pattern's "Customizing Fit" section first, to see whether length must be changed in fixed increments (usually due to a stitch pattern continuing unbroken from the hem to upper part of the garment).

In a garment worked from the top down, change the hip circumference by changing the number of increases worked after the waist; if necessary, change the frequency of these increases as described above.

Waist Circumference

Decide how many stitches to add or subtract from the waist as described above, again in increments of four stitches. To keep the garment hip and bust dimensions unchanged, you will need to change the number of waist shaping decreases and increases by the same amount: for instance, if you want to do one extra waist decrease, you will need to add an extra waist increase. This holds true whether you are working from the bottom up or the top down. You will also need to change the frequency of increases and decreases.

EXAMPLE:

Part 1 (waist decreases): Starting with the same pattern example as above, you could change the number of waist decreases from six to seven, while keeping the number of rounds used for decreases the same, as follows: work the first decrease on the 6th round after cast on, then four decreases spaced six rounds apart, then two decreases spaced four rounds apart: 6 + (4 x 6) + (2 x 4) = 38.

Part 2 (waist increases): If the original pattern calls for the first increase to be worked on the 14th round after the last decrease and then three additional increases spaced 14 rounds apart, then the total number of rounds needed for increases is 14 + (3 x 14) = 56.

Option 1: To fit one additional waist increase into the same number of rounds, you could work the first increase as instructed, followed by three increases spaced ten rounds apart, then one spaced 12 rounds after the previous one: 14 + (3 x 10) + 12 = 56.

Option 2: Usually there is an area of the garment that is worked even after the last waist increase and before reaching the armholes; it may be possible to extend the waist increases slightly into this area. If the pattern calls for 18 rounds to be worked even before starting the armholes, then you could work the increases as follows: the first increase on the 12th round after the last decrease, followed by four additional increases spaced 12 rounds apart: 12 + (4 x 12) = 60 rounds. Since this is four more rounds than called for in the original pattern, compensate by working four fewer rounds even (14 instead of 18) before starting the armholes.

Note: If the waist increase frequency changes, it looks best to space the increases closer together near the waist, and then farther apart as you approach the bust.

Back Waist Length

I use the back waist length to decide where to place waist shaping: I find waist shaping to be most flattering when the narrowest part of the garment waist falls at or slightly above the natural waist. So it is helpful to know your back waist length, because if you have a long or short torso, your back waist length will be longer or shorter than the standard, and you may want to adjust the positioning of waist shaping accordingly.

On a garment, the back waist length is measured from the center of the narrowest part of the waist to a line drawn horizontally between the highest points of the shoulders. Since the top edge of the back neck of a garment is often lower than this point (unless it has been raised with short rows or a collar), this gives a consistent measurement that can be compared to the back waist length of the body.

The prominent bone at the base of the neck is usually slightly above the highest point of the garment shoulder, meaning that the garment back waist length should be a little shorter than the back waist length of the body. In this book, patterns with waist shaping include the garment back waist length on the schematic so that you can compare the garment measurement to your body measurement. If the garment back waist length is ½–1½"/1.5–4 cm less than your back waist measurement, then the garment waist should fall at or just above your natural waist. If it is 1½–3"/4–7.5 cm less than your back waist measurement, then the garment waist should fall an inch or two above your natural waist.

If your back waist length is shorter—or over three inches longer—than the garment waist length, then a garment with waist shaping will fit you better if you adjust the position of the waist shaping accordingly. To do this, you must change the frequency of the waist shaping decreases and increases to either raise or lower the narrowest part of the garment waist. First, decide how much length you want to add or subtract from the garment back waist length, and then convert this length into rounds; for instance, if you want to lengthen the back waist length by 2"/5 cm and the row/round gauge is six rounds to 1"/2.5 cm, then you will want to lower the narrowest part of the waist by 12 rounds.

EXAMPLE:

Part 1 (waist decreases): Using the same pattern example as above, 38 rounds are used for six waist shaping decreases; to lower the waist by 12 rounds, you will need to complete the waist decreases in 38 - 12 rounds, or 26 rounds. One way this could be done is by working the first decrease round on the 6th round after cast on, and then five more decreases spaced four rounds apart: 6 + (5 x 4) = 26.

Part 2 (waist increases): The four waist increases in the original pattern are worked over 56 rounds; to keep the garment length unchanged while lowering the garment waist, the 12 rounds subtracted from the waist decrease section now need to be added back above the waist: 56 + 12 = 68 rounds.

Option 1: To work four waist increases over 68 rounds, you could work the first increase as instructed, followed by three increases spaced 18 rounds apart: 14 + (3 x 18) = 68.

Option 2: You could also adjust the number of rounds worked even between the last waist increase and the armholes. If the pattern calls for 18 rounds to be worked even before starting the armholes, then you could work the increases as follows: the first increase on the 16th round after the last decrease, followed by three additional increases spaced 16 rounds apart: 16 + (3 x 16) = 64 rounds. Since this is four fewer rounds than called for in the original pattern, compensate by working four more rounds even (22 instead of 18) before starting the armholes.

Note: In this example, the length of the garment from hem to waist is shortened by two inches. If you want keep this portion of the garment the same length while changing the back waist length, then work the waist increases as instructed in the original pattern and add length as in Part 2 above; again, first read that pattern's "Customizing Fit" section to see whether length must be changed in fixed increments (usually due to a stitch pattern continuing unbroken from the hem to the upper part of the garment).

Ensuring That the Garment Dimensions Match Those Given in the Pattern

It doesn't matter how accurate your body measurements are if your stitch gauge doesn't match the pattern gauge! So work a gauge swatch *and* block it using the same method that you will use to block the finished garment; blocking often changes stitch gauge significantly (especially with lace, cabled, or ribbed stitch patterns), and may also change row gauge. Check both row and stitch gauges; if these don't match the gauges given in the pattern, then try again using a different size needle (larger if there were too many stitches and/or rows per inch or smaller if there were too few). Yes, this will take an hour or two, but it is worth it! What may seem a small difference in gauge can translate to a significant difference in the dimensions of the finished garment. For example, if the finished garment bust circumference should be 40"/101.5 cm, but you work the pattern with a gauge of 5.5 stitches instead of 5 stitches to 1"/2.5, your finished garment will instead have a bust circumference of 36¼"/92 cm.

If the stitch gauge matches but the row gauge is off, consider whether the difference is large enough that you need to add or subtract rows or rounds; in garments with a stockinette stitch body, this can easily be done, but if the body is worked in a different stitch, changing the number of rows or rounds might need to be done in whole or half multiples of the stitch pattern.

Remember that the dimensions shown on the schematic include the main garment pieces only; they do not include any edgings added during finishing. Armhole edgings will decrease the armhole depth and increase the shoulder and back width; neck edgings will decrease the neck depth and back neck width, and increase the shoulder width.

Working with PLANT-ORIGIN YARNS

I enjoy knitting with wool and wool-blend yarns for many reasons: they tend to be soft and springy, which makes them a tactile pleasure to handle; wool holds dyes well, which means that many gorgeous colorways are available; and the ends of non-superwash wool (or other animal-origin fiber) yarns can be joined by felting them, which means fewer ends to work in during the finishing of a garment.

However, some wearers find wool fabrics itchy if worn next to the skin, and wool and other animal fibers generally insulate too well (unless blended with other types of fibers) to make comfortable warm-weather garments. This is why the sleeveless tanks and tunics in this book utilize yarns made from plant-origin fibers such as cotton and linen, which absorb and release perspiration quickly, allowing the fabric to "breathe."

Cotton and linen both have high tensile strength, meaning that even thin yarns made from these fibers can be quite durable. They also lack resilience, or spring, which can mean a knitted cotton or linen fabric has increased drape, but can also mean it is more likely to stretch out and lose its shape. Often a synthetic fiber such as nylon or acrylic, or an animal-origin fiber, is blended with cotton or linen to increase its resilience.

A cotton or linen blend yarn can have enough resilience and softness that it feels much like a wool yarn when working with it, but if the yarn is mostly cotton or linen, it may feel harsh and unyielding during knitting, which can decrease the pleasure of the knitting process. Some cotton or linen yarns (and some silk or synthetic yarns) can be slippery, which can make it difficult to rip back stitches without dropping them, and in extreme cases can cause balls wound from these yarns to collapse and tangle. Finally, since plant-origin fibers don't stick to each other like many animal-origin fibers, some cotton or linen yarns tend to split easily.

To get the most out of working with cotton and linen yarns:

- Choose needles carefully. If the yarn splits easily, try needles with rounder or sharper points to see which tends to split the yarn less. If it is slippery, then wooden or synthetic needles or needle tips may be a better choice than metal.

- If yarn is slippery, use care when winding skeins into balls, and check the ball periodically as it is being used; if it appears about to collapse, it may be worth rewinding into a smaller ball, to keep the yarn from tangling. If any stitches need to be ripped back, go slowly and gently so that stitches in previous rounds or rows aren't accidentally pulled out.

- If the yarn lacks resilience and/or feels harsh, avoid hand fatigue by taking frequent breaks to stretch your fingers and wrists.

- Check yarn care instructions: some cotton and linen yarns can be machine-dried as well as machine-washed. If the label states the yarn can be machine-dried, try this on a swatch before throwing your finished garment in the dryer: machine drying can restore shape to a garment that has become

stretched out, but can also cause severe shrinkage! Machine drying can also soften linen fabrics.

- Since plant-based yarns cannot be joined by felting the yarn ends, pay attention to where you start a new ball of yarn. If working in the round, start a new ball either at the side of the garment or within a textured pattern stitch, such as the edge of a rib, at the back cross of a cable, or along a column of decreases (but not in the middle of an open area of lace). If you are working flat and the side edges will be seamed, join a new ball of yarn at the edge of the piece. Conversely, if the edge is self-finished, stay at least a few stitches away from the edge.

- Keep yarn ends to a minimum by leaving a long yarn tail when binding off or when preparing for three-needle bind-off: use the yarn tail for seaming or working the bind-off. I like to leave all of the yarn tails long in case I cut one short by accident or decide to do the three-needle bind-off starting from the shoulder instead of the neck edge (or vice versa). If you are working flat pieces that will

be joined with side seams, also leave a long yarn tail when casting on.

- Weave in ends on the wrong side using duplicate stitch if the yarn is fine to medium weight and the fabric is not open.

- Weave in ends on the wrong side using the skimming technique if the yarn is medium to bulky weight or if the end is a different color than the main color of the knitting.

- Medium to bulky weight yarn ends can also be separated into two or more plies, which can be woven in using either duplicate stitch or skimming.

- If fabric is open, use the skimming technique and choose the path of the yarn end carefully so it doesn't show on the right side.

- Ends near a seam can be woven up and down along the seamed selvage edges. Similarly, ends near the ridge that is left on the wrong side along a row of picked up stitches can be woven up and down through this ridge.

- When trimming yarn ends after weaving, do not cut them at the fabric surface; leave about ½"/1–1.5 cm to keep the ends from working free to the right side of the garment.

Astoria

The focal point of this tunic is the wide, face-framing collar, which combines with the A-line shaping and inverted box pleat to create a vintage feel. This project knits up quickly using Aran weight yarn worked at a loose gauge.

SKILL LEVEL

Intermediate: Skills include short rows, sturdy knitted cast-on method for casting on stitches, decreases, and increases. See Techniques section beginning on page 146 for photo tutorials on working short rows and the sturdy knitted cast-on.

SIZES

Women's XS (S, M, L, 1X, 2X, 3X)

FINISHED MEASUREMENTS

Bust: 32 (35½, 40, 43½, 48, 51½, 56)"/81.5 (90, 101.5, 110.5, 122, 130.5, 142) cm. *Shown in size S with 1½"/4 cm ease. Intended to fit with 0"/0 cm to +4"/10 cm ease at bust.*

YARN

530 (590, 660, 730, 830, 900, 990) yd/490 (550, 610, 670, 760, 830, 910) m medium weight #4 yarn; shown in #3105 Cream, Schachenmayr Catania Grande; 100% cotton; 68 yd/63 m per 1¾ oz/50 g skein, 8 (9, 10, 11, 13, 14, 15) skeins

NEEDLES

US 10"/6.0 mm 24–40"/60–100 cm circular needle, depending on selected garment size, for Body; 20"/50 cm circular needle, for Collar; double-pointed needles (dpns), 2 for pleat. *Adjust needle size if necessary to obtain correct gauge.*

NOTIONS

- Stitch markers
- Stitch holders
- Tapestry needle

GAUGE

14 sts and 20 rnds in St st = 4"/10 cm square, blocked

PATTERN NOTES

- Worked in the round to armholes
- Short rows shape the front and back to the collar
- Collar is also worked in the round
- A-line shaping
- Edges are self-finished except for collar

CUSTOMIZING FIT

Length can be changed as desired; to maintain A-line shaping, add or subtract four stitches to number of stitches cast on *and* add or subtract one decrease round for every 14 rounds added or subtracted.

SPECIAL STITCHES

SSE (Slipped Stitch Edge, worked over 3 sts and 2 rows):
RS: K1, sl st with yarn in front, k1.
WS: Sl st with yarn in front, k1, sl st with yarn in front.
Sturdy Knitted Cast-on: Turn work to RS; stitches just worked are now on left-hand needle. *Insert right-hand needle tip between first two stitches on left-hand needle, draw loop of working yarn through, and place loop on left-hand needle, taking care to keep it loose: 1 st cast on. Rep from * until required number of sts has been cast on.
LT (Left Twist, worked over 2 sts):
RS: Knit 2nd stitch on the left-hand needle through the back loop, leaving it on the needle, then knit first stitch and drop both stitches off needle.
RT (Right Twist, worked over 2 sts):
RS: Knit 2nd stitch on the left-hand needle, leaving it on the needle, then knit first stitch and drop both stitches off needle.

Body

Using longer circular needle, CO 132 (144, 160, 172, 188, 200, 216) sts. Pm and join for working in the rnd, taking care not to twist sts.

Set-up rnd: K66 (72, 80, 86, 94, 100, 108), pm for right side, k66 (72, 80, 86, 94, 100, 108).

Cont to work in St st for 14 more rnds.

Dec rnd: *K3, k2tog, work to 5 before m, ssk, k3; rep from * to end—4 sts dec.

Rep Dec rnd every 14th rnd 4 more times—112 (124, 140, 152, 168, 180, 196) sts.

Work even for 12 more rnds, stopping one st before end of final rnd; piece should measure approx 16¾"/42.5 cm from CO.

Next rnd: Work RT with last st of previous rnd and first st of new rnd, replacing m between 2 sts just worked; work to one st before right side m; work LT with sts before and after m, replacing m between 2 sts just worked; work to end.

Divide for Front and Back/Shape Armholes

Armhole Dec row (RS): SSE, k2tog, k to 5 sts before right-side marker, ssk, SSE, remove m—2 sts dec'd. Turn and continue to work rem 54 (60, 68, 74, 82, 88, 96) Front sts only (place 56 [62, 70, 76, 84, 90, 98] Back sts on holder).

Armhole Dec row (WS): SSE, ssp, p to 5 sts before left-side marker, p2tog, SSE, remove m—2 sts dec'd.

Rep these two rows 0 (0, 0, 1, 2, 4, 7) more times, then rep RS dec row 1 (3, 6, 6, 8, 7, 5) more times (work even in patt on WS rows), ending after last RS dec row—50 (52, 54, 56, 56, 56, 56) sts.

Work even for 9 (7, 3, 3, 1, 1, 1) more rows, continuing SSE at armhole edges, and ending after a WS row.

Next row (RS): Est fold st columns: Work in patt for 20 (21, 22, 23, 23, 23, 23) sts, p1, k8, p1, work in patt to end.

Next row (WS): Work in patt for 20 (21, 22, 23, 23, 23, 23) sts, k1, p8, k1, work in patt to end.

Work 2 more rows in patt as est.

Short row (SR) shaping, left neckline (cont SSE at armhole edge):

SR 1 (RS): Work 11 sts in patt, W&T.

SRs 2, 4, 6, 8, and 10 (WS): Work in patt to end.

SRs 3, 5, 7, and 9 (RS): Work in patt to 2 sts before last wrapped st, W&T.

Next row (RS): Work in patt to end, picking up 5 wraps and working tog with wrapped sts.

Short row shaping, right neckline (cont SSE at armhole edge):

SR 1 (WS): Work 11 sts in patt, W&T.

SRs 2, 4, 6, 8, and 10 (RS): Work in patt to end.

SRs 3, 5, 7, and 9 (WS): Work in patt to 2 sts before last wrapped st, W&T.

Next row (WS): Work in patt to end, picking up 5 wraps and working tog with wrapped sts.

Pleat row (RS):

Work 11 (12, 13, 14, 14, 14, 14) sts in patt.

Right fold: Place next 5 sts on dpn, place next 5 sts on 2nd dpn (last st should be fold st), and fold work so that 2nd dpn is behind and parallel to first dpn (see figure below). *Use right-hand needle to knit first st on front dpn tog with first st on back dpn; rep from * 4 more times, then place next 8 sts on holder.

Left fold (not shown in sketch): Place next 5 sts (first st should be fold st) on dpn and fold work so that dpn is rotated 180 degrees and is behind and parallel to left-hand needle. *Use right-hand needle to knit first st on left-hand needle tog with first st on dpn; rep from * 4 more times, then work rem 11 (12, 13, 14, 14, 14, 14) sts in patt—10 sts dec'd, 8 sts on holder, 32 (34, 36, 38, 38, 38, 38) sts rem.

Next row (WS): Work 12 (13, 14, 15, 15, 15, 15) sts in patt; place 8 held sts on dpn and hold in front of work; *use right-hand needle to purl first st on left-hand needle tog with first st on dpn; rep from * 7 more times; work in patt to end—8 sts dec'd. Turn to RS and CO 16 (14, 12, 16, 16, 16, 16) sts using sturdy knitted cast-on. Break yarn and place 48 (48, 48, 54, 54, 54, 54) sts on holder.

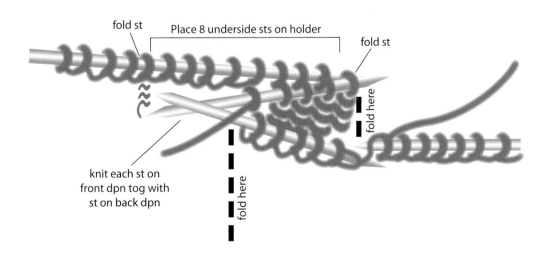

fold st

Place 8 underside sts on holder

fold st

fold here

fold here

knit each st on front dpn tog with st on back dpn

Back

Place 56 (62, 70, 76, 84, 90, 98) Back sts on needle and join yarn to work RS.

Armhole Dec row (RS): SSE, k2tog, k to 5 sts before end of row, ssk, SSE—2 sts dec'd.

Armhole Dec row (WS): SSE, ssp, p to 5 sts before end of row, p2tog, SSE—2 sts dec'd.

Rep these two rows 1 (2, 3, 4, 6, 7, 10) more times, then rep RS dec row 6 (6, 8, 8, 8, 10, 8) more times (work even in patt on WS rows), then rep RS dec row every 4th row 2 (2, 1, 1, 1, 0, 0) more times—32 (34, 36, 38, 38, 38, 38) sts. Work 1 more row (WS) even in patt.

Shape right back neckline with short rows (cont SSE at armhole edge):

SR 1 (RS): Work 11 sts in patt, W&T.

SRs 2, 4, 6, 8, and 10 (WS): Work in patt to end.

SRs 3, 5, 7, and 9 (RS): Work in patt to 2 sts before last wrapped st, W&T.

Next row (RS): Work in patt to end, picking up 5 wraps and working tog with wrapped sts.

Finished Measurements

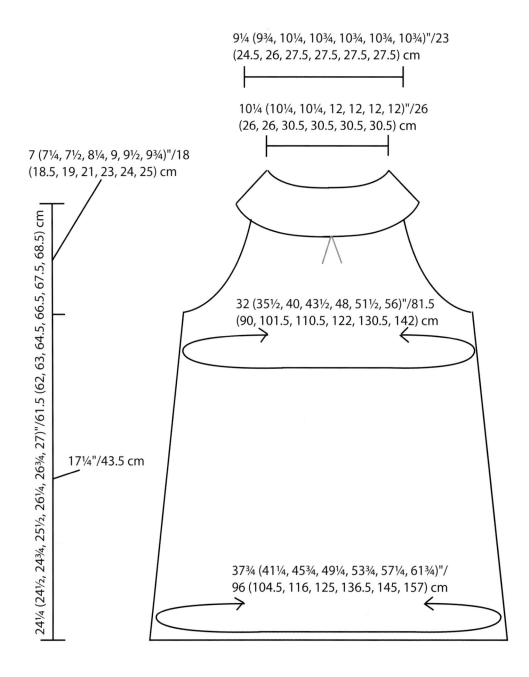

9¼ (9¾, 10¼, 10¾, 10¾, 10¾, 10¾)"/23 (24.5, 26, 27.5, 27.5, 27.5, 27.5) cm

10¼ (10¼, 10¼, 12, 12, 12, 12)"/26 (26, 26, 30.5, 30.5, 30.5, 30.5) cm

7 (7¼, 7½, 8¼, 9, 9½, 9¾)"/18 (18.5, 19, 21, 23, 24, 25) cm

32 (35½, 40, 43½, 48, 51½, 56)"/81.5 (90, 101.5, 110.5, 122, 130.5, 142) cm

24¼ (24½, 24¾, 25½, 26¼, 26¾, 27)"/61.5 (62, 63, 64.5, 66.5, 67.5, 68.5) cm

17¼"/43.5 cm

37¾ (41¼, 45¾, 49¼, 53¾, 57¼, 61¾)"/ 96 (104.5, 116, 125, 136.5, 145, 157) cm

Shape left back neckline with short rows (cont SSE at armhole edge):

SR 1 (WS): Work 11 sts in patt, W&T.

SRs 2, 4, 6, 8, and 10 (RS): Work in patt to end.

SRs 3, 5, 7, and 9 (WS): Work in patt to 2 sts before last wrapped st, W&T.

Next row (WS): Work in patt to end, picking up 5 wraps and working tog with wrapped sts. Turn to RS and CO 16 (14, 12, 16, 16, 16, 16) sts using sturdy knitted cast-on. Leave sts on needle and do not break yarn.

Collar

Turn work inside out. Place held Front sts on needle. With working yarn and needle and with WS facing, knit Front sts including knitted-on sts, then Back sts including knitted-on sts—96 (96, 96, 108, 108, 108, 108) sts. Pm for beg of rnd. Knit 4 more rnds.

SIZES XS, S, AND M ONLY

Dec rnd 1: K6 (7, 8, -, -, -, -), ssk, [k2tog, k12, ssk] 5 times, k2tog, k6 (5, 4, -, -, -, -)—12 sts dec'd, 84 sts rem. Work 4 rnds even in patt.

Dec rnd 2: K5 (6, 7, -, -, -, -), ssk, [k2tog, k10, ssk] 5 times, k2tog, k5 (4, 3, -, -, -, -)—12 sts dec'd, 72 sts rem. Work 6 rnds even in patt.

Inc rnd 1: K5 (6, 7, -, -, -, -), M1R, [k2, M1L, k10, M1R] 5 times, k2, M1L, k5 (4, 3, -, -, -, -)—12 sts inc'd, 84 sts. Work 5 rnds even in patt.

Inc rnd 2: K5 (6, 7, -, -, -, -), M1R, [k4, M1L, k10, M1R] 5 times, k4, M1L, k5 (4, 3, -, -, -, -)—12 sts inc'd, 96 sts.

SIZES L, 1X, 2X, AND 3X ONLY

Dec rnd 1: K8, ssk, [k2tog, k14, ssk] 5 times, k2tog, k6—12 sts dec'd, 96 sts rem. Work 4 rnds even in patt.

Dec rnd 2: K7, ssk, [k2tog, k12, ssk] 5 times, k2tog, k5—12 sts dec'd, 84 sts rem. Work 6 rnds even in patt.

Inc rnd 1: K7, M1R, [k2, M1L, k12, M1R] 5 times, k2, M1L, k5—12 sts inc'd, 96 sts. Work 5 rnds even in patt.

Inc rnd 2: K7, M1R, [k4, M1L, k12, M1R] 5 times, k4, M1L, k5—12 sts inc'd, 108 sts.

ALL SIZES

BO all sts knitwise. Break yarn, leaving 48"/120 cm long tail, and use tapestry needle and yarn tail to join beg and end of BO rnd so that BO edge appears unbroken. Leave yarn tail long (will use to sew edges of collar).

Finishing

Fold Collar to RS of garment. Use long yarn tail and tapestry needle to *whipstitch free CO and BO edges of Collar across right shoulder; stitch CO Collar edge to junction of Back and Collar by passing needle under every other st just below first row (purled) of Collar (see top photo below) and then through loop on WS of Collar just below every other BO st (see bottom photo below); rep from * across left shoulder and Front (at center front, may also stitch through all layers at center of pleat to reinforce, taking care that these sts do not show on RS).

Weave in ends and block to finished measurements.

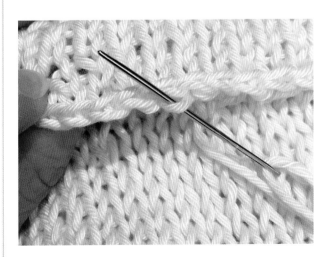

Atlanta

This tank is a great project for the novice knitter who would like to move on from simple scarves and washcloths: the body is worked in the round in stockinette stitch, and the upper front and back are worked flat in garter stitch, which is knitted on every row. The body is shaped without decreases or increases by changing needle size.

SKILL LEVEL
Easy: Skills include knitting in the round and knitting flat (no purling), decreases, binding off stitches in center of row, and sewing seams. Optional: Three-needle bind-off.

SIZES
Women's XS (S, M, L, 1X, 2X, 3X)

FINISHED MEASUREMENTS
Bust: 31 (34, 38, 42, 45, 49, 52)"/78.5 (86.5, 96.5, 106.5, 114.5, 124.5, 132) cm. *Shown in size S with 0"/0 cm ease. Intended to fit with -2"/5 cm to +2"/5 cm ease at bust.*

YARN
420 (470, 530, 590, 640, 700, 760) yd/390 (435, 490, 545, 590, 645, 700) m medium weight #4 yarn; shown in #026 light blue, Lily Sugar 'n Cream; 100% cotton; 120 yd/109 m per 2½ oz/71 g skein, 4 (5, 5, 6, 6, 7, 7) skeins

NEEDLES
US 9/5.5 mm, US 8/5.0 mm, and US 7/4.5 mm 24–40"/60–100 cm circular needles, depending on selected garment size, for Body; US 8/5.0 mm circular or straight needles, for upper Front and Back. *Adjust needle sizes if necessary to obtain correct gauge.*

NOTIONS
- Stitch markers
- Stitch holders
- Tapestry needle

GAUGE

Using large needle, 15 sts and 22 rnds in St st = 4"/10 cm square, blocked

Using medium needle, 16 sts and 23 rnds in St st = 4"/10 cm square, blocked

Using small needle, 17 sts and 24 rnds in St st = 4"/10 cm square, blocked

PATTERN NOTES

- Worked in the round to the armholes
- Decreases shape front and back garter stitch panels
- Straps can be sewn at shoulder or joined using three-needle bind-off

CUSTOMIZING FIT

Body length can be easily changed but remember to move waist shaping (rounds worked with smaller needles) as needed.

Body

Using large circular needle, CO 124 (136, 152, 168, 180, 196, 208) sts. Pm and join for working in the rnd, taking care not to twist sts.

Set-up rnd: *Work in St st (knit) for 62 (68, 76, 84, 90, 98, 104) sts**, pm for left side, rep from * to **.

Work in patt as est for 13 (13, 13, 13, 13, 13, 15) more rnds.

Switch to medium circular needle and work in patt for 12 (12, 14, 14, 14, 14, 16) rnds.

Switch to small circular needle and work in patt for 14 rnds.

Switch to medium circular needle and work in patt for 46 (46, 44, 44, 44, 44, 40) rnds, or until piece measures just under 15"/38 cm from CO, stopping 3 (4, 5, 6, 7, 8, 9) sts before end of final rnd.

Divide for Front and Back/Shape Armholes

*BO 6 (8, 10, 12, 14, 16, 18) sts (remove m)**, work in patt to 3 (4, 5, 6, 7, 8, 9) sts before m, rep from * to **, work in patt to end. Turn and cont to work 56 (60, 66, 72, 76, 82, 86) rem Front sts only (place rem 56 [60, 66, 72, 76, 82, 86] Back sts on holder).

Front (est Garter st patt):
Dec row (WS): K1, ssk, knit to 3 sts before end, k2tog, k1—2 sts dec'd.
Next row (RS): Knit.
Rep Dec row every WS row 7 (8, 10, 12, 13, 15, 17) more times—40 (42, 44, 46, 48, 50, 50) sts rem.
Next row (RS): Knit.
Next row (WS): K8 (8, 9, 9, 10, 11, 11), BO next 24 (26, 26, 28, 28, 28, 28) st, k8 (8, 9, 9, 10, 11, 11). Turn and cont to work Front Left Strap sts only (place Front Right Strap sts on holder).

Front left strap:
Continue to work in Garter st (knit every row) for 24 (24, 24, 22, 22, 20, 20) more rows, ending after a WS row.

If sewing shoulder seams:
Next row: BO all sts, then break yarn, leaving 24"/60 cm long tail.
If joining shoulder using three-needle bind-off:
Place sts on holder and break yarn, leaving 24"/60 cm long tail.

Front right strap:
Place held sts on medium needle and join yarn to work RS. Work as for Front Left Strap.

Back

Place 56 (60, 66, 72, 76, 82, 86) held Back sts on medium needle and join yarn to work WS.

Est Garter st patt:
Dec row (WS): K1, ssk, knit to 3 sts before end, k2tog, k1—2 sts dec'd, 54 (58, 64, 70, 74, 80, 84) sts rem.

SIZES M, L, 1X, 2X, AND 3X ONLY
Next row (RS): Knit.
Rep Dec row every WS row - (-, 2, 5, 6, 9, 11) more times— - (-, 60, 60, 62, 62, 62) sts rem.

ALL SIZES
Work even in Garter st (knit every row) for 3 rows, then work Dec row—2 sts dec'd. Rep these 4 rows 6 (7, 7, 6, 6, 5, 5) more times—40 (42, 44, 46, 48, 50, 50) sts rem.
Next row (RS): Knit.
Next row (WS): K8 (8, 9, 9, 10, 11, 11), BO next 24 (26, 26, 28, 28, 28, 28) sts, k8 (8, 9, 9, 10, 11, 11). Turn and cont to work Back Right Strap sts only (place Back Left Strap sts on holder).

Back right strap:
Continue to work in Garter st (knit every row) for 10 (8, 8, 8, 8, 8, 8) more rows, ending after a WS row.

If sewing shoulder seams:
Next row: BO all sts, then break yarn, leaving 24"/60 cm long tail.
If joining shoulder using three-needle bind-off:
Place sts on holder and break yarn, leaving 24"/60 cm long tail.

Back left strap:
Place held sts on medium needle and join yarn to work RS. Work as for Back Right Strap.

Finishing

If sewing shoulder seams: With right sides facing, use one of long yarn tails and tapestry needle to sew BO edge of Front Right Strap to BO edge of Back Right Strap. Repeat for Left Straps. Weave in ends and block to finished measurements.

Finished Measurements

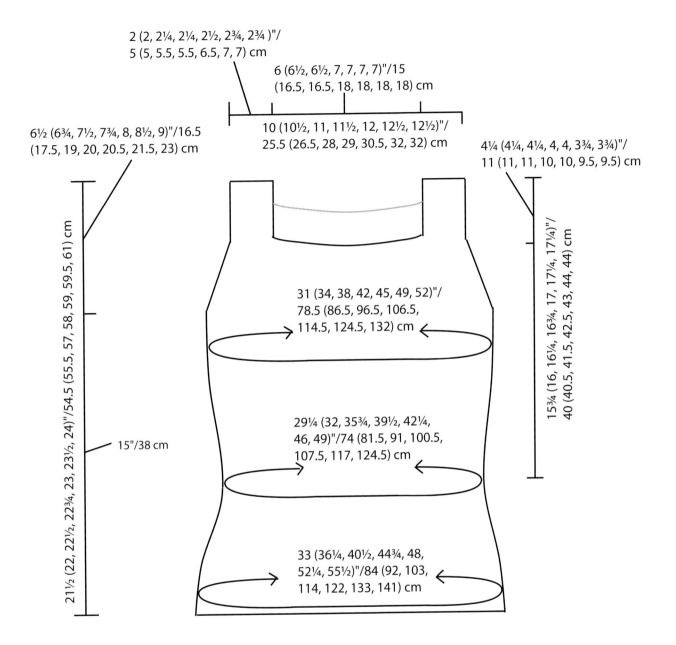

2 (2, 2¼, 2¼, 2½, 2¾, 2¾)"/
5 (5, 5.5, 5.5, 6.5, 7, 7) cm

6 (6½, 6½, 7, 7, 7, 7)"/15
(16.5, 16.5, 18, 18, 18, 18) cm

6½ (6¾, 7½, 7¾, 8, 8½, 9)"/16.5
(17.5, 19, 20, 20.5, 21.5, 23) cm

10 (10½, 11, 11½, 12, 12½, 12½)"/
25.5 (26.5, 28, 29, 30.5, 32, 32) cm

4¼ (4¼, 4¼, 4, 4, 3¾, 3¾)"/
11 (11, 11, 10, 10, 9.5, 9.5) cm

21½ (22, 22½, 22¾, 23, 23½, 24)"/54.5 (55.5, 57, 58, 59, 59.5, 61) cm

15"/38 cm

31 (34, 38, 42, 45, 49, 52)"/
78.5 (86.5, 96.5, 106.5,
114.5, 124.5, 132) cm

29¼ (32, 35¾, 39½, 42¼,
46, 49)"/74 (81.5, 91, 100.5,
107.5, 117, 124.5) cm

33 (36¼, 40½, 44¾, 48,
52¼, 55½)"/84 (92, 103,
114, 122, 133, 141) cm

15¾ (16, 16¼, 16¾, 17, 17¼, 17¼)"/
40 (40.5, 41.5, 42.5, 43, 44, 44) cm

If joining shoulders using three-needle bind-off: Turn garment inside out. Place Front Right Strap sts on medium needle and Back Right Strap sts on 2nd medium needle. Insert a third needle into first st on each of these 2 needles and knit these 2 sts together, using long yarn tail. *Knit next st on each needle the same way, then pass first st on right-hand needle over second st—1 st bound off. Repeat from * until 1 st is left on the right-hand needle, then pull yarn tail through last st.

Repeat for left shoulder. Weave in ends and block to finished measurements.

Bellingham

From the front this tank appears to have a simple A-line shape, but in fact the flared "skirt" wraps around the sides and then flows into elongated wings that cross over the back, joining the front at the opposite shoulder. A linen blend yarn ensures that the skirt drapes gracefully. This tank can be worn on its own or over another layer; try wearing it backwards if you are feeling adventurous!

SKILL LEVEL
Intermediate: Skills include picking up stitches, short rows, and three-needle bind-off. See Techniques section beginning on page 146 for photo tutorials on picking up stitches and working short rows.

SIZES
Women's XS (S, M, L, 1X)

FINISHED MEASUREMENTS
Bust (approx.): 32 (35, 38½, 44½, 48)"/81.5 (89.5, 97.5, 114, 122) cm. *Shown in Size S with +1 "/2.5 cm ease. Intended to fit with -2"/5 cm to +2"/5 cm ease at bust.*

YARN
490 (540, 600, 650, 680) yd/450 (500, 555, 600, 625) m medium weight #4 yarn; shown in #114 Mystic, Fibra Natura Good Earth Solids; 53% cotton, 47% linen; 170 yd/155 m per 3½ oz/100 g skein, 3 (4, 4, 4, 5) skeins

NEEDLES
US 9/5.5 mm 40"/100 cm or longer circular needle, to accommodate large number of stitches. *Adjust needle size if necessary to obtain correct gauge.*

NOTIONS
- Stitch markers
- Stitch holders
- Tapestry needle

GAUGE
15 sts and 23 rows in St st = 4"/10 cm square, blocked

PATTERN NOTES

- Center piece is worked first
- Stitches are picked up along lower sides of center piece for side pieces
- Center and sides are joined at the opposite shoulders, causing the side pieces to overlap
- All edges are self-finished

CUSTOMIZING FIT

Because of the unusual construction, many of the standard garment measurements are approximate. Side pieces are constructed so that they can be lengthened if necessary to adjust the fit.

SPECIAL STITCHES

M1L (worked from WS to create M1L on RS):
With left needle tip, lift strand between needles from front to back. Purl lifted loop through back, twisting created stitch.

M1R (worked from WS to create M1R on RS):
With left needle tip, lift strand between needles from back to front. Purl lifted loop through front, twisting created stitch.

Center

The Center is made up of 4 wedges that are shaped by regular decreases and are worked equally to the underarms; underarm shaping is then worked in each side wedge, while the shaping of the 2 center wedges continues uninterrupted to the neck.

Shaping rows occur every 5th row, alternating RS and WS. Since different sizes have different numbers of shaping rows, any given shaping row may be on a RS row for one size and a WS row for another size. Therefore instructions for each type of shaping row are given for both RS and WS.

Main Dec row (RS): [K1, k2tog, work in patt to 3 sts before m, ssk, k1] 4 times—8 sts dec'd.

Main Dec row (WS): [P1, ssp, work in patt to 3 sts before m, p2tog, p1] 4 times—8 sts dec'd.

Underarm Dec row (RS): K1, k2tog, work even to last 3 sts, ssk, k1—2 sts dec'd.

Underarm Dec row (WS): P1, ssp, work even to last 3 sts, p2tog, p1—2 sts dec'd.

Center Dec row (RS): Work even to m, [k1, k2tog, work in patt to 3 sts before m, ssk, k1] twice, work even to end—2 sts dec'd in each center wedge.

Center Dec row (WS): Work even to m, [p1, ssp, work in patt to 3 sts before m, p2tog, p1] twice, work even to end—2 sts dec'd in each center wedge.

Inc/Dec row (RS): *K1, M1L, work to 1 st before m, M1R, k1**, [k1, k2tog, work in patt to 3 sts before m, ssk, k1] twice, rep from * to **—2 sts inc'd in each side wedge, 2 sts dec'd in each center wedge.

Inc/Dec row (WS): *P1, M1R, work to 1 st before m, M1L, p1**, [p1, ssp, work in patt to 3 sts before m, p2tog, p1] twice, rep from * to **—2 sts inc'd in each side wedge, 2 sts dec'd in each center wedge.

[CO 46 (48, 52, 56, 58) sts, pm] 3 times, CO 46 (48, 52, 56, 58) sts—184 (192, 208, 224, 232) sts. Do not join.

Work 4 rows in St st (knit RS rows, purl WS rows), beg with a RS row, then work Main Dec row (RS)—8 sts dec'd.

Rep Main Dec row every 5th row, alternating WS and RS versions, 12 (12, 13, 13, 13) more times—80 (88, 96, 112, 120) sts rem, 20 (22, 24, 28, 30) sts in each wedge.

Shape Underarms

Next row: Underarm Dec row—2 sts dec'd.
Rep Underarm Dec row every row for 3 more
  rows, alternating WS and RS versions—16 (18,
  20, 24, 26) sts rem in each side wedge.
Next row: Main Dec row—14 (16, 18, 22, 24) sts
  rem in each side wedge, 18 (20, 22, 26, 28) sts
  in each center wedge.

SIZES XS AND S ONLY
Work 4 rows even.

SIZES M, L, AND 1X ONLY
Rep Underarm Dec row every row for - (-, 2, 4,
  4) more rows— - (-, 16, 18, 20) sts rem in each
  side wedge.
Work (-, -, 2, 0, 0) more rows even.

ALL SIZES
Next row: Main Dec row—12 (14, 14, 16, 18) sts
  rem in each side wedge, 16 (18, 20, 24, 26) sts
  in each center wedge.

SIZES XS AND S ONLY
Work 4 rows even.

SIZES M, L, AND 1X ONLY
Rep Underarm Dec row every row for - (-, 0, 2,
  4) more rows— - (-, 14, 14, 14) sts rem in each
  side wedge.
Work (-, -, 4, 2, 0) more rows even.

SIZE 1X ONLY
Next row: Main Dec row—12 sts rem in each side
  wedge, 24 sts in each center wedge.
Work 4 more rows even.

ALL SIZES

Shape Upper Front

Next row: Center Dec row—2 sts dec'd in each
  center wedge.
Rep Center Dec row every 5th row 1 (2, 2, 3, 1)
  more times—48 (52, 56, 60, 64) sts rem, 12
  (12, 14, 16, 20) sts in each center wedge.
Work 4 rows even.
Next row: Inc/Dec row—2 sts inc'd in each side
  wedge, 2 sts dec'd in each center wedge.
Rep Inc/Dec row every 5th row 2 (2, 2, 2, 3)
  more times—18 (20, 20, 20, 20) sts in each
  side wedge, 6 (6, 8, 10, 12) sts in each center
  wedge (total st count unchanged).

Shape Shoulders and Neck:
Shoulder shaping begins on a RS row; if last
row worked was RS, then work 1 more row
even (WS).

Shape Right Shoulder:
Next row: Short row (SR) 1 (RS): Work in patt to
  last 2 sts of row, W/T.
SR 2 (WS): Work to 1 st before m between side
  and center wedges, W/T.
SRs 3, 4, and 5: Work to 2 sts before last
  wrapped st, W/T.
SR 6 (WS): Work to 1 (2, 2, 2, 2) sts before last
  wrapped st, W/T.
SR 7 (RS): Work to 2 sts before last
  wrapped st, W/T.
SR 8 (WS): Work to 1 st before last
  wrapped st, W/T.
SR 9 (RS): Work to 2 sts before last
  wrapped st, W/T.
SR 10 (WS): Work to 1 st before last
  wrapped st, W/T.
SR 11 (RS): Work to 1 (2, 2, 2, 2) sts before last
  wrapped st, W/T.

Shape Left Shoulder:
Next row: SR 1 (WS): Work to last 2 sts of row,
  picking up wraps and working them tog with
  wrapped sts, W/T.
SR 2 (RS): Work to 1 st before m between side
  and center wedges, W/T.
SRs 3, 4, and 5: Work to 2 sts before last
  wrapped st, W/T.
SR 6 (RS): Work to 1 (2, 2, 2, 2) sts before last
  wrapped st, W/T.
SR 7 (WS): Work to 2 sts before last
  wrapped st, W/T.
SR 8 (RS): Work to 1 st before last
  wrapped st, W/T.
SR 9 (WS): Work to 2 sts before last
  wrapped st, W/T.
SR 10 (RS): Work to 1 st before last
  wrapped st, W/T.
SR 11 (WS): Work to 1 (2, 2, 2, 2) sts before last
  wrapped st, W/T.
Next row (RS): Work to last end of row,
  picking up wraps and working them tog with
  wrapped sts.
Next row (WS): P10 (11, 11, 11, 11), purl into front
  and back of next st, place first 11 (12, 12, 12, 12)
  sts worked on holder for Right Front Shoulder;
  BO last st created and next 26 (28, 32, 36,
  40) sts purlwise; p11 (12, 12, 12, 12), picking
  up wraps and working tog with wrapped sts.

Break yarn, leaving 30"/75 cm long tail for three-needle bind-off, and place rem 11 (12, 12, 12, 12) sts on holder for Left Front Shoulder.

Left Side (crosses back from left hip to Right Back Shoulder)

With RS facing, pick up and knit 48 (50, 52, 52, 52) sts along side of Center, from CO edge to beg of underarm shaping (approx 3 sts for every 4 rows).

Short rows and bottom edge decreases are worked AT THE SAME TIME; read through entire section before continuing.

Short rows:
SR 1 (WS): Work in St st (purl).
SR 2 (RS): Work in patt to last 10 sts, W&T.
SR 3 (WS): Work in patt to end.
SR 4 (RS): Work in patt to end, picking up wrap and working tog with wrapped st.
SRs 5 and 6: Work in patt to end.
Rep these 6 rows 12 (13, 13, 13, 13) more times, for a total of 78 (84, 84, 84, 84) rows, then work back and forth to ends of all rows until dec are completed (see below).
AT THE SAME TIME, beg on 4th row, shape bottom edge:
Dec row (RS): K2, k2tog, work in patt to end—1 st dec'd.
Rep Dec row every 4th row 6 (7, 7, 7, 7) more times, then every RS row 30 (30, 32, 32, 32) more times, ending after a RS row—11 (12, 12, 12, 12) sts rem.
Break yarn, leaving 3 yd/3 m long tail in case piece needs to be lengthened (recommend winding yarn into bobbin), and place sts on holder for shoulder.

Right Side (crosses back from right hip to Left Back Shoulder)

With RS facing, pick up and knit 48 (50, 52, 52, 52) sts along side of Center, from beg of underarm shaping to CO edge (approx 3 sts for every 4 rows).

Short rows and bottom edge decreases are worked AT THE SAME TIME; read through entire section before continuing.

Short rows:
SR 1 (WS): Work in St st (purl).
SR 2 (RS): Work in St st (knit).
SR 3 (WS): Work in patt to last 10 sts, W&T.
SR 4 (RS): Work in patt to end.
SR 5 (WS): Work in patt to end, picking up wrap and working tog with wrapped st.
SR 6 (RS): Work in patt to end.
Rep these 6 rows 12 (13, 13, 13, 13) more times, for a total of 78 (84, 84, 84, 84) rows, then work back and forth to ends of all rows until dec are completed (see below).
AT THE SAME TIME, beg on 4th row, shape bottom edge:
Dec row (RS): Work in patt to last 4 sts, ssk, k2—1 st dec'd.
Rep Dec row every 4th row 6 (7, 7, 7, 7) more times, then every RS row 30 (30, 32, 32, 32) more times, ending after a RS row—11 (12, 12, 12, 12) sts rem.
Break yarn, leaving 3 yd/3 m long tail in case piece needs to be lengthened (recommend winding yarn into bobbin), and place sts on holder for shoulder.

Finishing

Weave in ends *except* for long yarn tails, and block to finished measurements.

Lay out work with WS up and fold Side pieces so they overlap, with their RS facing up. Decide which Side piece should fall on the outside. Pin shoulder seams and try on garment. If it is too snug across chest, across back, or under arms, work additional rows even on both Side pieces. Turn work inside out and place Right Front and Right Back Shoulder sts on two needles or on opposite ends of circular needle, with points of needle(s) at neck edge of shoulder. Trim yarn tails to workable length for three-needle bind-off.

Three-needle bind-off: Insert a third needle into first st on each of these 2 needles and knit these 2 sts together, using long yarn tail. *Knit next st on each needle the same way, then pass first st on right-hand needle over second st—1 st bound off. Repeat from * until 1 st is left on the right-hand needle, then pull yarn tail through last st.

Repeat for left shoulder, using long yarn tail and starting at armhole edge of shoulder.

Weave in remaining ends and block again as needed.

Finished Measurements

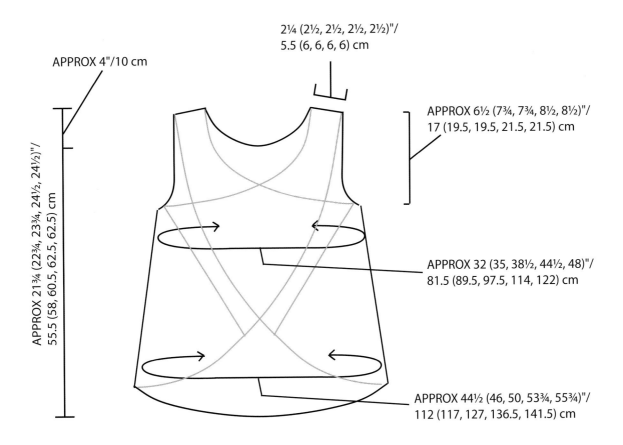

APPROX 4"/10 cm

2¼ (2½, 2½, 2½, 2½)"/
5.5 (6, 6, 6, 6) cm

APPROX 6½ (7¾, 7¾, 8½, 8½)"/
17 (19.5, 19.5, 21.5, 21.5) cm

APPROX 21¾ (22¾, 23¾, 24½, 24½)"/
55.5 (58, 60.5, 62.5, 62.5) cm

APPROX 32 (35, 38½, 44½, 48)"/
81.5 (89.5, 97.5, 114, 122) cm

APPROX 44½ (46, 50, 53¾, 55¾)"/
112 (117, 127, 136.5, 141.5) cm

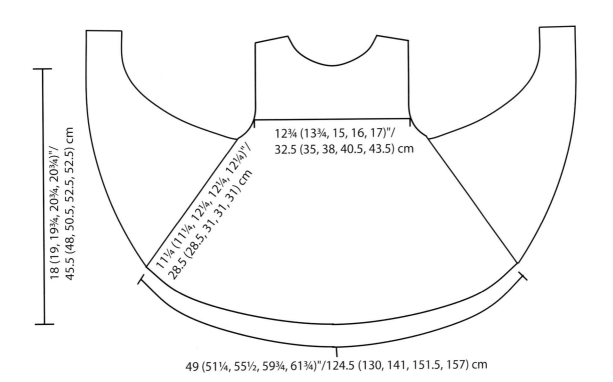

18 (19, 19¾, 20¾, 20¾)"/
45.5 (48, 50.5, 52.5, 52.5) cm

12¾ (13¾, 15, 16, 17)"/
32.5 (35, 38, 40.5, 43.5) cm

11¼ (11¼, 12¼, 12¼, 12¼)"/
28.5 (28.5, 31, 31, 31) cm

49 (51¼, 55½, 59¾, 61¾)"/124.5 (130, 141, 151.5, 157) cm

Bethel

The boldly colored stranded yoke is the focal point of this tank. In traditional Fair Isle fashion, only two colors are worked on each round, although a total of four different colors are used. Flattering cut-in armholes angle to meet the rounded yoke, suggesting a halter top but with more coverage. A narrow attached I-cord gives all garment edges a neat finish.

SKILL LEVEL
Intermediate to advanced: Skills include stranded knitting, following a color chart, knitting in the round, attached I-cord and grafting I-cord ends, picking up stitches, knitted cast-on, and short row shaping. See Techniques section beginning on page 146 for photo tutorials on attached I-cord and grafting I-cord ends, picking up stitches, knitted cast-on, and short row shaping.

SIZES
Women's XS (S, M, L, 1X, 2X, 3X)

FINISHED MEASUREMENTS
Bust: 29½ (32¾, 37, 41¼, 44¾, 48¾, 53)"/75 (83.5, 94, 105, 113.5, 124, 135) cm. *Shown in size S with -1¼"/3 cm ease. Intended to fit with -2"/5 cm to +2"/5 cm ease at bust.*

YARN
- **Color A:** 490 (540, 620, 690, 760, 840, 920) yd/455 (500, 570, 635, 700, 775, 850) m medium weight #4 yarn; shown in #CW-440 Spanish Olive, Brown Sheep Cotton Fleece; 80% cotton, 20% merino wool; 215 yd/197 m per 3½ oz/100 g skein, 3 (3, 3, 4, 4, 5, 5) skeins
- **Color B:** 50 (50, 50, 60, 60, 60, 60) yd /45 (45, 45, 55, 55, 55, 55) m medium weight #4 yarn; shown in #CW-844 Celery Leaves, Brown Sheep Cotton Fleece; 80% cotton, 20% merino wool; 215 yd/197 m per 3½ oz/100 g skein, 1 skein
- **Color C:** 20 (20, 20, 25, 25, 25, 25) yd/19 (19, 19, 23, 23, 23, 23) m medium weight #4 yarn; shown in #CW-452 Jubilant Jade, Brown Sheep Cotton Fleece; 80% cotton, 20%

merino wool; 215 yd/197 m per 3½ oz/100 g skein, 1 skein

- **Color D:** 10 (10, 10, 12, 12, 12, 12) yd/10 (10, 10, 11, 11, 11, 11) m medium weight #4 yarn; shown in #CW-555 Robin Egg Blue, Brown Sheep Cotton Fleece; 80% cotton, 20% merino wool; 215 yd/197 m per 3½ oz/100 g skein, 1 skein

Note: Wash in cold water! Darker colors of Brown Sheep Cotton Fleece may bleed slightly.

NEEDLES

US 7/4.5 mm 24–40"/60–100 cm circular needle, depending on selected garment size, for Body; 24"/60 cm circular needle for stranded yoke; 16–20"/40–50 cm circular needle or double-pointed needles (dpns), for armhole and neck edgings. *Adjust needle size if necessary to obtain correct gauge.*

NOTIONS

- Stitch markers
- Stitch holders
- Tapestry needle

GAUGE

19 sts and 26 rnds in St st = 4"/10 cm square, blocked; 21 sts and 26 rnds in stranded pattern = 4"/10 cm square, blocked

PATTERN NOTES

- Stranded yoke is worked first, from bottom up, in the round
- Stitches for front and back are picked up from bottom edge of yoke and worked down; short rows shape front and back to yoke
- After front and back are joined at underarms, body is worked down in the round
- Armhole edgings added during finishing

CUSTOMIZING FIT

Body length can be easily changed; side waist decrease and/or increase frequency may also need to be changed if changing body length. Since body is worked down, the garment can be tried on when partially completed, to check length.

SPECIAL STITCHES

Knitted Cast-on: Turn work to WS and, using working yarn, *k1 st, then return st to left-hand needle, taking care not to twist it: 1 st cast on. Rep from * until required number of sts has been cast on.

Yoke Chart

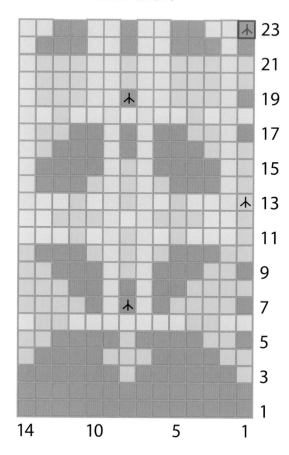

14   10   5   1

Key

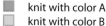

- knit with color A
- knit with color B
- knit with color C
- knit with color D
- s2kp with color shown
- no stitch
- s2kp with color shown on every OTHER rep (on rem reps, repeat chart Row 22).

Start at bottom of chart. Read all chart rows from right to left.

Yoke

Using 24"/60 cm circular needle and A, CO 168 (168, 168, 196, 196, 196, 196) sts. Pm and join for working in the rnd, taking care not to twist sts.
Rnd 1: Work Row 1 of chart 12 (12, 12, 14, 14, 14, 14) times to end of rnd.
Rnd 2: Work Row 2 of chart 12 (12, 12, 14, 14, 14, 14) times to end of rnd.
Work in patt as est, joining other colors as needed, until all 23 rows of chart have been completed—84 (84, 84, 98, 98, 98, 98) sts rem. Break Colors B, C, and D but do not break A.

Attached I-cord Neck Edging

Turn work to WS and CO 2 sts using knitted cast-on. *K1, ssk; return 2 sts just worked to left-hand needle. Take care not to pull yarn too tight; I-cord should be stretchy. Rep from * until all yoke sts have been worked and 2 sts rem. Do not BO sts; break yarn, leaving 12"/30 cm long tail, and use tail to graft rem 2 sts to beg of I-cord.

Front, Back, and Armholes

Pick up sts for front, back, and tops of armhole edgings:
Using 24"/60 cm circular needle and A, holding yoke upside down with **WS** facing, and starting at 1st (1st, 1st, 8th, 8th, 8th, 8th) st CO, pick up and knit 1 st for each CO st by passing needle through center of each st—168 (168, 168, 196, 196, 196, 196) sts. Leaving sts on needle, break yarn and tie loose ends snugly into square knot on RS (during finishing, these ends will be untied, passed to WS, and woven in).

Divide picked-up sts for front, back, and armholes:
Place the 15 (14, 13, 19, 18, 17, 16) sts on either side of tied ends (a total of 30 [28, 26, 38, 36, 34, 32] sts on holder for armhole). Place next 54 (56, 58, 60, 62, 64, 66) sts on 2nd holder for Back, ensuring that Stitch 1 from stranded chart is centered over Back sts (if not, move sections back or forward a stitch, as needed). Place next 30 (28, 26, 38, 36, 34, 32) sts on 3rd holder for other armhole. Rem 54 (56, 58, 60, 62, 64, 66) sts should also be centered around Stitch 1 from stranded chart. Cont to work these sts only for Front.

Front

Right front:
Join A to work RS and begin short row (SR) shaping:
SR 1 (RS): K3, W&T.
SRs 2, 4, 6, and 8 (WS): Purl to end.
SRs 3, 5, and 7: (RS): Knit to wrapped st, pick up wrap and knit it tog with wrapped st, k3, W&T.
SR 9 (RS): Knit to end of row, picking up wrap and knitting it tog with wrapped st.

Left front:
SR 1 (WS): P3, W&T.
SRs 2, 4, 6, and 8 (RS): Knit to end.
SRs 3, 5, and 7 (WS): Purl to wrapped st, pick up wrap and purl it tog with wrapped st, p3, W&T.
SR 9 (WS): Purl to end of row, picking up wrap and purling it tog with wrapped st.

Front continued:
Inc row (RS): K1, M1L, knit to last st, M1R, k1—2 sts inc'd. Rep Inc row every 4th row 3 (2, 1, 0, 0, 0, 0) more times, then every RS row 1 (4, 8, 12, 14, 15, 14) more times—64 (70, 78, 86, 92, 96, 96) sts.

SIZES 2X AND 3X ONLY

Inc row (WS): P1, M1R, purl to last st, M1L, p1—2 sts inc'd.
Next row: Inc row (RS)—2 sts inc'd.
Rep last 2 rows - (-, -, -, -, 0, 2) more times— - (-, -, -, -, 100, 108) sts.

ALL SIZES

Turn work to WS and CO 6 (8, 10, 12, 14, 16, 18) sts for underarm, using knitted cast-on. Break yarn.

Back

Place 54 (56, 58, 60, 62, 64, 66) held Back sts on longer circular needle and join A to work RS.
    Left Back: Work as for Right Front.
    Right Back: Work as for Left Front.
    Continue to work Back as for Front, but after casting on sts for underarm, do not break yarn. Turn work to RS.

Body

Join Front and Back (RS): Using working yarn and needle from Back, k64 (70, 78, 86, 92, 100, 108) Front sts, k3 (4, 5, 6, 7, 8, 9) underarm sts, pm for side, k3 (4, 5, 6, 7, 8, 9) underarm sts, k64 (70, 78, 86, 92, 100, 108) Back sts, k3 (4, 5, 6, 7, 8, 9) underarm sts, pm for side/beg of rnd, k3 (4, 5, 6, 7, 8, 9) underarm sts—140 (156, 176, 196, 212, 232, 252) sts. Working in St st (knit every rnd), work to the end of this rnd, then work 13 (13, 11, 9, 9, 7, 5) more rnds.

Dec rnd: *K3, k2tog, work to 5 sts before m, ssk, k3; rep from * to end of rnd—4 sts dec'd.
Rep Dec rnd every 12th rnd 3 more times—124 (140, 160, 180, 196, 216, 236) sts rem. Work 11 rnds even.
Inc rnd: *K3, M1R, work to 3 sts before m, M1L, k3; rep from * to end of rnd—4 sts inc'd.
Rep Inc rnd every 6th rnd 5 more times—148 (164, 184, 204, 220, 240, 260) sts.
Work 8 (8, 10, 10, 10, 10, 12) rnds even.
Attached I-cord hem edging: Work as for neck edging.

Finished Measurements

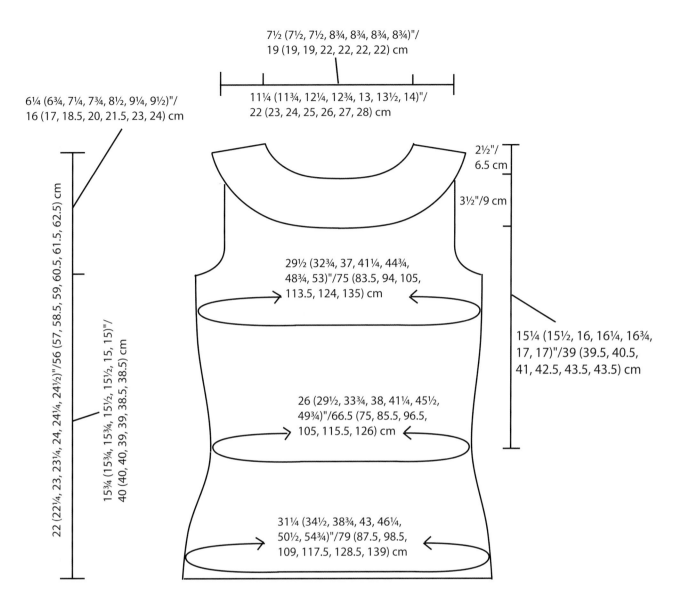

7½ (7½, 7½, 8¾, 8¾, 8¾, 8¾)"/
19 (19, 19, 22, 22, 22, 22) cm

11¼ (11¾, 12¼, 12¾, 13, 13½, 14)"/
22 (23, 24, 25, 26, 27, 28) cm

6¼ (6¾, 7¼, 7¾, 8½, 9¼, 9½)"/
16 (17, 18.5, 20, 21.5, 23, 24) cm

2½"/
6.5 cm

3½"/9 cm

29½ (32¾, 37, 41¼, 44¾,
48¾, 53)"/75 (83.5, 94, 105,
113.5, 124, 135) cm

15¼ (15½, 16, 16¼, 16¾,
17, 17)"/39 (39.5, 40.5,
41, 42.5, 43.5, 43.5) cm

22 (22¼, 23, 23¼, 24, 24¼, 24½)"/56 (57, 58.5, 59, 60.5, 61.5, 62.5) cm

15¾ (15¾, 15¾, 15½, 15½, 15, 15)"/
40 (40, 40, 39, 39, 38.5, 38.5) cm

26 (29½, 33¾, 38, 41¼, 45½,
49¾)"/66.5 (75, 85.5, 96.5,
105, 115.5, 126) cm

31¼ (34½, 38¾, 43, 46¼,
50½, 54¾)"/79 (87.5, 98.5,
109, 117.5, 128.5, 139) cm

Finishing

Untie square knot fastening yarn ends at base of stranded yoke. Using tapestry needle, pass ends to WS (making sure not to undo any sts) and weave in.

Armhole Edging

Place 30 (28, 26, 38, 36, 34, 32) held sts from yoke on shorter 16–20"/40–50 cm circular needle or dpns and join A to work RS. Pick up and knit 19 (21, 23, 26, 29, 32, 34) sts from yoke to CO underarm sts (approx 3 sts for every 4

rows); 1 st at transition to CO sts; 1 st for every CO underarm st; 1 st at transition from CO sts; 19 (21, 23, 26, 29, 32, 34) sts to yoke—76 (80, 84, 104, 110, 116, 120) sts.

Attached I-cord armhole edging: Work as for neck edging.

Weave in ends and block to finished measurements.

Beverly

Mosaic knitting uses two or more colors of yarn, but unlike stranded knitting, only one color is used on each row or round. This tank showcases mosaic panels on the upper chest and back.

SKILL LEVEL

Intermediate: Skills include reading a chart, decreases, increases, color knitting, sewing shoulder seams, and picking up stitches for edgings. See Techniques section beginning on page 146 for a photo tutorial on picking up stitches.

SIZES

Women's XS (S, M, L, 1X, 2X, 3X)

FINISHED MEASUREMENTS

Bust: 30½ (34½, 38½, 42½, 46½, 50½, 54½)"/77 (87.5, 97.5, 107.5, 118, 128, 138) cm. *Shown in size S with +½"/1.5 cm ease. Intended to fit with -1"/2.5 cm to +3"/7.5 cm ease at bust.*

YARN

- Color A: 500 (570, 630, 700, 770, 830, 890) yd/460 (525, 580, 645, 710, 765, 820) m light weight #3 yarn; shown in #318 Blackberry, Blue Sky Fibers Skinny Cotton; 100% organically grown cotton; 150 yd/137m per 2¼ oz/65 g skein, 4 (4, 5, 5, 6, 6, 7) skeins
- Color B: 100 (100, 110, 120, 120, 130, 130) yd/90 (90, 100, 105, 110, 120, 120) m light weight #3 yarn; shown in #304 Zinc, Blue Sky Fibers Skinny Cotton; 100% organically grown cotton; 150 yd/137 m per 2¼ oz/65 g skein, 1 skein
- Color C: 60 (60, 70, 70, 80, 80, 80) yd/55 (55, 60, 65, 70, 75, 75) m light weight #3 yarn; shown in #30 Birch, Blue Sky Fibers Skinny Cotton; 100% organically grown cotton; 150 yd/137 m per 2¼ oz/65 g skein, 1 skein

NEEDLES

US 7/4.5 mm 24–40"/60–100 cm circular needle, depending on selected garment size, for Body; 16–20"/40–50 cm circular needle or

double-pointed needles (dpns), for edgings. *Adjust needle size if necessary to obtain correct gauge.*

NOTIONS
- Stitch markers
- Stitch holders
- Tapestry needle

GAUGE
20 sts and 26 rnds in St st = 4"/10 cm square, blocked. 21 sts and 32 rows in Mosaic patt = 4"/10 cm square, blocked.

PATTERN NOTES
- Worked in the round to the armholes
- Neck and armhole edgings added during finishing

CUSTOMIZING FIT
Body length can be easily changed; side waist decrease and/or increase frequency may also need to be changed.

Body
Using longer circular needle and B, CO 160 (180, 200, 220, 240, 260, 280) sts. Pm and join for working in the rnd, taking care not to twist sts.

Garter st edging:
Rnd 1: Purl to end.
Rnd 2: Sl1 purlwise wyib, knit to end.
Rnd 3: K1, sl1 purlwise wyib, purl to end.
   Remove m, p2, pm for new beg of rnd. Break B and join A.
Set-up rnd: *K80 (90, 100, 110, 120, 130, 140) sts**, pm for side, rep from * to **. Work even in St st for 4 (4, 6, 8, 10, 12, 12) more rnds.
Dec rnd: *K3, k2tog, work to 5 sts before m, ssk, k3**, rep from * to **—4 sts dec'd.
Rep dec rnd every 6th rnd 4 more times—140 (160, 180, 200, 220, 240, 260) sts rem. Work even for 13 (13, 13, 13, 13, 11, 11) rnds.
Inc rnd: *K3, M1R, work to 3 sts before m, M1L, k3**, rep from * to **—4 sts inc'd.

If slipped st is first or last st of row, instead knit on RS/purl on WS with working color. If slipped st falls within 2 sts of edge and next row is a dec row, instead knit on RS/purl on WS.

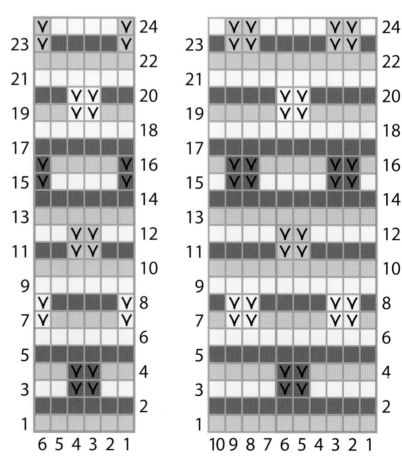

Sizes S and 1X
Sizes XS, M, L, 2X, and 3X

- ■ Color A: knit on RS, purl on WS
- ▨ Color B: knit on RS, purl on WS
- □ Color C: knit on RS, purl on WS
- Ⅴ Ⅴ Ⅴ Sl st purlwise wyib on RS, wyif on WS (color shown is slipped st, NOT working yarn)
- □ patt rep

Rep inc rnd every 14th (14th, 14th, 14th, 14th, 14th, 12th) rnd 2 more times—152 (172, 192, 212, 232, 252, 272) sts.

Work even for 23 (23, 21, 19, 17, 15, 15) more rnds, stopping 3 (4, 5, 6, 7, 8, 9) sts from end of last rnd; piece should measure 15 (15, 15, 15, 15, 14¾, 14¼)"/38.5 (38.5, 38.5, 38.5, 38.5, 37.5, 36) cm from CO.

Divide for front and back/shape armholes:
*BO 6 (8, 10, 12, 14, 16, 18) sts (remove m)**; work to 3 (4, 5, 6, 7, 8, 9) sts before m; rep from * to **; work to end. Turn and cont to work 70 (78, 86, 94, 102, 110, 118) rem Back sts only (place rem 70 [78, 86, 94, 102, 110, 118] Front sts on holder).

Back

SIZE XS ONLY

WS: Work 1 row even in St st (purl).
Armhole Dec row (RS): K1, k2tog, work in patt to 3 sts before end, ssk, k1—2 sts dec'd. Rep these 2 rows 2 more times—64 sts rem.

SIZES S, M, L, 1X, 2X, AND 3X ONLY

Armhole Dec row (WS): P1, ssp, purl to 3 sts before end, p2tog, p1—2 sts dec'd.
Armhole Dec row (RS): K1, k2tog, work in patt to 3 sts before end, ssk, k1—2 sts dec'd.
Rep these 2 rows - (1, 3, 3, 5, 6, 8) more times, then rep RS dec row - (2, 0, 1, 0, 0, 0) more times (work even in patt on WS rows), ending after a RS row— - (66, 70, 76, 78, 82, 82) sts rem.

ALL SIZES

Next row (WS): Beg Mosaic patt for your size as follows:

SIZES XS, M, L, 2X, AND 3X ONLY

Row 1 (WS): Using Row 1 of chart FOR YOUR SIZE, join B (do not break A) and work Sts 10–7 once, then work Sts 6–1, 10 (-, 11, 12, -, 13, 13) times to end of row.
Row 2 (RS): Using Row 2 of chart FOR YOUR SIZE and A (do not break B), work Sts 1–6, 10 (-, 11, 12, -, 13, 13) times, then work Sts 7–10 once.

SIZES S AND 1X ONLY

Row 1 (WS): Using Row 1 of chart FOR YOUR SIZE, join B (do not break A) and work Sts 6–1 - (11, -, -, 13, -, -) times to end of row.
Row 2 (RS): Using Row 2 of chart FOR YOUR SIZE and A (do not break B), work Sts 1–6 - (11, -, -, 13, -, -) times to end of row.

ALL SIZES

Join C for next row (do not break A or B). Cont to work Mosaic patt as est for 43 (43, 47, 49, 51, 53, 53) more rows, ending after a WS row.

Shape shoulders:

Note: When BO sts, do not work slipped sts as charted; instead knit on RS/purl on WS with working yarn before binding st off.

Next 2 rows: BO 4 (4, 4, 5, 5, 6, 6), work in mosaic patt to end.
Next 2 rows: BO 5 (5, 5, 5, 5, 6, 6), work in mosaic patt to end.
Next row: BO all rem sts. Break yarn, leaving 30"/75 cm long tail.

Front

Place 70 (78, 86, 94, 102, 110, 118) held Front sts on needle and join yarn to work WS. Work as for Back until 25 (25, 29, 31, 33, 35, 35) rows of Mosaic patt have been completed, ending after a WS row.

Shape neck:
Next row (RS): Work 25 (25, 26, 27, 28, 30, 30) sts in mosaic patt, BO 14 (16, 18, 22, 22, 22, 22), work 25 (25, 26, 27, 28, 30, 30) sts in mosaic patt. Turn and cont to work Right Front only (place Left Front sts on holder).

Right Front

Next row (WS): Work even in mosaic patt.
Next row (RS): BO 3, work in mosaic patt to end.
Rep last 2 rows one more time—19 (19, 20, 21, 22, 24, 24) sts rem.
Next row (WS): Work even in mosaic patt.
Dec row (RS): K1, k2tog, work in mosaic patt to end—1 st dec'd. Rep Dec row every RS row 4 more times, then every 4th row one more time—13 (13, 14, 15, 16, 18, 18) shoulder sts rem.

Shape shoulders:

Next row (WS): BO 4 (4, 4, 5, 5, 6, 6), work in mosaic patt to end.

Next row (RS): Work even in mosaic patt.

Next row (WS): BO 5 (5, 5, 5, 5, 6, 6), work in mosaic patt to end.

Next row (RS): Work even in mosaic patt.

Next row (WS): BO rem 4 (4, 5, 5, 6, 6, 6) shoulder sts. Break yarn, leaving 30"/75 cm long tail.

Left Front

Place held Left Front sts on needle and join yarn to work WS.

Next row (WS): BO 3, work in mosaic patt to end.

Next row (RS): Work even in mosaic patt.

Rep last 2 rows one more time—19 (19, 20, 21, 22, 24, 24) sts rem.

Next row (WS): Work even in mosaic patt.

Dec row (RS): Work in mosaic patt to last 3, ssk, k1—1 st dec'd. Rep Dec row every RS row 4 more times, then every 4th row one more time—13 (13, 14, 15, 16, 18, 18) shoulder sts rem.

Next row (WS): Work even in mosaic patt.

Shape shoulders:

Next row (RS): BO 4 (4, 4, 5, 5, 6, 6), work in mosaic patt to end.

Next row (WS): Work even in mosaic patt.

Next row (RS): BO 5 (5, 5, 5, 5, 6, 6), work in mosaic patt to end.

Next row (WS): BO rem 4 (4, 5, 5, 6, 6, 6) shoulder sts. Break yarn, leaving 30"/75 cm long tail.

Finishing

Use yarn tails to sew shoulder seams. Weave in ends and block to finished measurements.

Armhole Edging

Using shorter circular needle or dpns and B, and starting at center underarm, pick up and knit 3 (4, 5, 6, 7, 8, 9) sts (1 for each BO st); 1 st at end of BO sts; 5 (6, 9, 11, 13, 15, 18) sts along solid color part of armhole (approx 3 sts for every 4 rows); 30 sts along mosaic panel to shoulder seam (approx 2 sts for every 3 rows); 30 sts along mosaic panel; 5 (6, 9, 11, 13, 15, 18) sts along solid color part of armhole; 1 st at beg of BO sts; 3 (4, 5, 6, 7, 8, 9) sts along BO sts—78 (82, 90, 96, 102, 108, 116) sts. Pm and join.

Finished Measurements

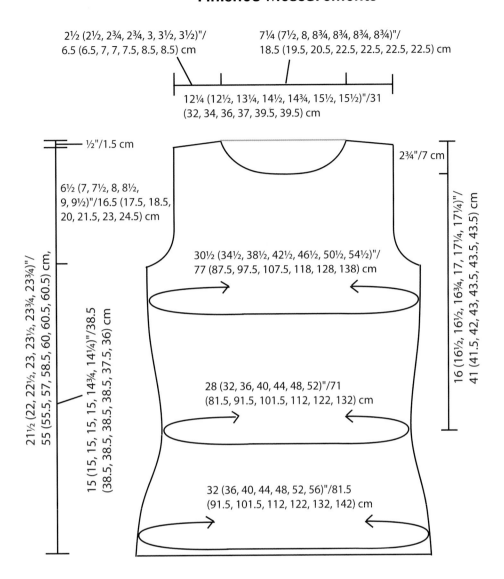

2½ (2½, 2¾, 2¾, 3, 3½, 3½)"/
6.5 (6.5, 7, 7, 7.5, 8.5, 8.5) cm

7¼ (7½, 8, 8¾, 8¾, 8¾, 8¾)"/
18.5 (19.5, 20.5, 22.5, 22.5, 22.5, 22.5) cm

12¼ (12½, 13¼, 14½, 14¾, 15½, 15½)"/31
(32, 34, 36, 37, 39.5, 39.5) cm

½"/1.5 cm

2¾"/7 cm

6½ (7, 7½, 8, 8½,
9, 9½)"/16.5 (17.5, 18.5,
20, 21.5, 23, 24.5) cm

30½ (34½, 38½, 42½, 46½, 50½, 54½)"/
77 (87.5, 97.5, 107.5, 118, 128, 138) cm

16 (16½, 16½, 16¾, 17, 17¼, 17¼)"/
41 (41.5, 42, 43, 43.5, 43.5, 43.5) cm

21½ (22, 22½, 23, 23½, 23¾, 23¾)"/
55 (55.5, 57, 58.5, 60, 60.5, 60.5) cm,

15 (15, 15, 15, 15, 14¾, 14¼)"/38.5
(38.5, 38.5, 38.5, 38.5, 37.5, 36) cm

28 (32, 36, 40, 44, 48, 52)"/71
(81.5, 91.5, 101.5, 112, 122, 132) cm

32 (36, 40, 44, 48, 52, 56)"/81.5
(91.5, 101.5, 112, 122, 132, 142) cm

Rnd 1: P2 (3, 4, 5, 6, 7, 8), p2tog, purl to last 4 (5, 6, 7, 8, 9, 10) sts, p2tog, purl to end—2 sts dec'd.

Rnd 2: Sl1 purlwise wyib, knit to end.

Rnd 3: K1, sl1 purlwise wyib, purl to end, dec'ing 5 (5, 6, 6, 7, 7, 8) sts evenly spaced—71 (75, 82, 88, 93, 99, 106) sts rem.

Rnd 4: P2, then BO all sts knitwise.

Neck Edging

Using shorter circular needle and B, and starting at right shoulder seam, pick up and knit 38 (40, 42, 44, 46, 46, 46) sts across back neck (1 st for every BO st); 19 sts between shoulder seam and center front BO sts; 14 (16, 18, 20, 22, 22, 22) sts across center front (1 st for every BO st); 19 sts to shoulder seam—90 (94, 98, 102, 106, 106, 106) sts. Pm and join.

Rnd 1: Purl across back neck sts, dec'ing 4 (4, 4, 5, 5, 5, 5) sts evenly spaced; purl to center front sts; purl across center front sts, dec'ing 2 (3, 3, 4, 4, 4, 4) sts evenly spaced; purl to end—84 (87, 91, 93, 97, 97, 97) sts rem.

Rnd 2: Sl1 purlwise wyib, knit to end.

Rnd 3: K1, sl1 purlwise wyib, purl to end.

Rnd 4: P2, then BO all sts knitwise.

Weave in rem ends and block again as needed.

Charlotte

This close-fitting tank is accented by a braided cable; extra rows on each cable cross give the cable added depth. A demure high neck in front is contrasted by a deeply cut out upper back; hem sits just above the hip. This top can be worn backwards if you are feeling adventurous!

SKILL LEVEL

Intermediate: Skills include reading charts, cables, and short rows. See Techniques section beginning on page 146 for a photo tutorial on working short rows.

SIZES

Women's XS (S, M, L, 1X, 2X, 3X)

FINISHED MEASUREMENTS

Bust: 29¼ (32½, 36¾, 41, 45¼, 49½, 52¾)"/74 (82.5, 93.5, 104, 115, 125.5, 134) cm. *Shown in size S with -1½"/4 cm ease. Intended to fit with -2"/5 cm to +2"/5 cm ease at bust.*

YARN

530 (580, 670, 740, 840, 920, 980) yd/490 (535, 620, 680, 775, 850, 905) m medium weight #4 yarn; shown in #5910 Cornsilk, Berroco Weekend; 75% acrylic, 25% Peruvian cotton; 205 yd/189 m per 3½ oz/100 g skein, 3 (3, 4, 4, 5, 5, 5) skeins

NEEDLES

US 7/4.5 mm 24–40"/60–100 cm circular needle, depending on selected garment size, for Body; straight or double-pointed needles, for cabled straps. *Adjust needle size if necessary to obtain correct gauge.*

NOTIONS

- Stitch markers
- Cable needle
- Tapestry needle

GAUGE

19 sts and 26 rnds in St st = 4"/10 cm square, blocked

PATTERN NOTES

- Worked in the round to the armholes; short rows shape front neckline
- All edgings are self-finished
- Instructions for cable stitch patterns are given in written and chart form
- Because the number of decreases required to shape the cutout back increases with each size, in larger sizes the end of the braided cable falls higher on the back, meaning that the front takes on more of a halter silhouette

CUSTOMIZING FIT

- Changing the length of the straps will adjust their angle; increasing their length will decrease the halter effect somewhat, but will also increase the armhole depth and neck drop.
- Body length can be changed in increments of 12 rounds (one full repeat of Main Cable pattern); side waist decrease and/or increase frequency may need to be changed if changing body length.

SPECIAL STITCHES

LT (Left Twist, worked over 2 sts):

RS: Knit 2nd stitch on the left-hand needle through the back loop, leaving it on the needle, then knit first stitch and drop both stitches off needle.

RT (Right Twist, worked over 2 sts):

RS: Knit 2nd stitch on the left-hand needle, leaving it on the needle, then knit first stitch and drop both stitches off needle.

Main Cable (worked over 17 sts and 12 rnds or rows):

Rnds or Rows 1, 3, 7, and 9 (RS): P1, k15, p1.

Rnd or Row 5 (RS): P1, sl 5 sts to cn and hold in back; k5, turn work and purl same 5 sts, turn work and knit same 5 sts; k5 from cn, k5, p1.

Rnd or Row 11 (RS): P1, k5, sl 5 sts to cn and hold in front, k5; k5 from cn; turn work and purl same 5 sts, turn work and knit same 5 sts; p1.

All even-numbered rnds (RS): Knit.

All even-numbered rows (WS): Purl.

Strap cables (worked over 10 sts and 8 rows): See Strap sections.

Body

Using circular needle, CO 158 (174, 194, 214, 254, 270) sts. Pm for side/beg of rnd and join, taking care not to twist sts.

Set-up rnd: *K31 (35, 40, 45, 50, 55, 59), pm for beg cable, p1, k15, p1, pm for end cable, k31 (35, 40, 45, 50, 55, 59)**; pm for side; rep from * to **.

Est patt: *Knit to beg cable m, work Main Cable Row 1 (1, 1, 1, 7, 1, 1) over 17 sts, knit to side m; rep from * to end of rnd.

SIZES XS, S, M, L, 2X, AND 3X ONLY

Work Main chart Rows 2–12 as est on subsequent rnds; work other sections in St st.

SIZE 1X ONLY

Work Main chart Rows 8–12 as est on subsequent rnds; work other sections in St st.

ALL SIZES

Cont to work patts as est, using Main chart Rows 1–12.

AT THE SAME TIME, on 10th (8th, 10th, 10th, 12th, 12th, 12th) rnd after CO, work Dec rnd: *K3, k2tog, work in patt to 5 sts before side m, ssk, k3; rep from * to end of rnd—4 sts dec'd.

Rep Dec rnd every 6th rnd 5 more times—134 (150, 170, 190, 210, 230, 246) sts. Work even for 11 more rnds.

Inc rnd: *K3, M1R, work in patt to 3 sts before side m, M1L, k3; rep from * to end of rnd—4 sts inc'd.

Rep Inc rnd every 12th (12th, 12th, 10th, 10th, 10th, 8th) rnd 3 more times—150 (166, 186, 206, 226, 246, 262) sts.

Work even for 9 (7, 9, 11, 11, 9, 11) more rnds, stopping 1 st before end of final rnd; piece should measure approx 15 (14¼, 15, 14¼, 14½, 14¼, 13¾)"/38 (36.5, 38, 36.5, 37, 36.5, 35) cm from CO.

Divide for front and back:

RT, (remove and replace m), *ssk, work to 3 sts before side m, k2tog**, LT (remove and replace m); rep from * to **, k1—4 sts dec'd. Turn and cont to work 73 (81, 91, 101, 111, 121, 129) rem Front sts only (remove side m and place rem 73 [81, 91, 101, 111, 121, 129] sts on holder for Back).

Main

12

3 rows

3 rows

17

1

Right Strap

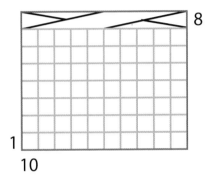

Left Strap

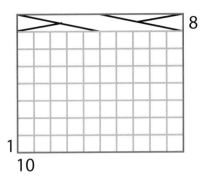

8

1

10

Key

☐ knit on RS, purl on WS

· purl on RS, knit on WS

sl 5 sts to cn and hold in back, k5, turn work and p5, turn work and k5, k5 from cn

sl 5 sts to cn and hold in front, k5, k5 from cn, turn work and p5, turn work and k5

☐ patt repeat

sl 5 sts to cn and hold in front, k5, k5 from cn

sl 5 sts to cn and hold in back, k5, k5 from cn

When working in the round, read all chart rows from right to left. When working flat, read odd (RS) rows from right to left and even (WS) rows from left to right.

Front

Cont armhole shaping (AND cont to follow chart as est):

Dec row (WS): P1, p2tog, work in patt to last 3 sts, ssp, p1—2 sts dec'd.

Dec row (RS): K1, ssk, work in patt to last 3 sts, k2tog, k1—2 sts dec'd.

Rep last 2 rows 0 (1, 1, 1, 3, 6, 8) times, then rep Dec row (RS) on every RS row 2 (3, 5, 7, 9, 9, 9) times, then every 4th row 0 (0, 1, 3, 2, 1, 1) times, then every 6th row 2 (2, 1, 0, 0, 0, 0) times—61 (63, 69, 73, 73, 73, 73) sts rem. Work 5 (5, 5, 3, 3, 3, 3) rows even.

Begin short row (SR) shaping (Left Front):

SR 1 (RS): K1, ssk, work 22 sts in patt, W&T—1 st dec'd.

SR 2 (WS): Work in patt to end.

SR 3 (RS): Work in patt to 2 sts before last wrapped st, W&T.

SR 4 (WS): Work in patt to end.

Rep last 2 rows 6 more times.

Next row (RS): Work in patt to last 3 sts of row, picking up wraps and working tog with wrapped sts; k2tog, k1—1 st dec'd.

Short row shaping (Right Front):

SR 1 (WS): Work 24 sts in patt (work even at armhole edge), W&T.

SR 2 (RS): Work in patt to end.

SR 3 (WS): Work in patt to 2 sts before last
wrapped st, W&T.
SR 4 (RS): Work in patt to end.
Rep last 2 rows 6 more times.
Next row (WS): Work in patt to end cable
m, picking up wraps and working tog with
wrapped sts; k1, p4 (cont to pick up wraps
and work tog with wrapped sts as needed),
p2tog, p3, ssp, p4, k1; work in patt to end—2
sts dec'd.
Next row (RS): BO all sts in patt. Break yarn,
leaving 24"/60 cm long tail.

Back

Place 73 (81, 91, 101, 111, 121, 129) held Back sts
on needle and join yarn to work WS of Back.

*Cont armhole shaping (AND cont to follow
chart as est):*
Dec row (WS): P1, p2tog, work in patt to last 3
sts, ssp, p1—2 sts dec'd.
Dec row (RS): K1, ssk, work in patt to last 3 sts,
k2tog, k1—2 sts dec'd.
Rep last 2 rows 12 (14, 15, 18, 21, 22, 24) more
times, then rep Dec row (WS) once more—19
(19, 25, 23, 21, 27, 27) sts rem.

SIZES M, L, 1X, 2X, AND 3X ONLY
Rep Dec row (RS) on every RS row - (-, 3, 2, 1, 4,
4) more times—19 sts rem.
Work one more row even (WS).

ALL SIZES
Last row worked should be Main chart Row 4.
Next row (RS): K1, sl 6 sts to cn and hold in
back; k5, turn work and purl same 5 sts, turn
work and knit same 5 sts; [k2tog, k4] from cn,
k4, ssk, k1—2 sts dec'd.

Note: I recommend working straps to suggested
length (see below), then trying on garment to
assess fit; lengthen or shorten straps as needed
before sts are BO. Remember that straps will
stretch slightly when garment is worn.

Divide for Straps/Left Strap

Next row (WS): P11; turn and cont to work these
sts only for Left Strap (place rem 6 sts on
holder for Right Strap).
Work 2 rows in St st.

Next row (RS): Sl 5 sts to cn and hold in front,
k4, k2tog; k5 from cn, [turn work and purl
same 5 sts, turn work and knit same 5 sts]
twice—1 st dec'd, 10 sts rem.
Work 7 rows in St st, beg and ending
on WS row.
Next row (RS): Sl 5 sts to cn and hold in front,
k5, k5 from cn.
Rep last 8 rows for patt. Work until strap
measures 4¾ (5, 5½, 5¾, 5¾, 5¾, 5¾)"/12.5
(13, 13.5, 14.5, 14.5, 14.5, 14.5) cm long or to
preferred length, then BO all sts in patt. Break
yarn, leaving 24"/60 cm long tail.

Right Strap

Place held Right Strap sts on needle. Using 2nd
needle and wyif, pick up and purl 5 sts from WS
of first rep of Left Strap, 1 st away from edge,
by inserting needle into purl bumps (see photo
below), then purl held sts—11 sts. Work 2 rows in
St st, starting with a knit (RS) row.

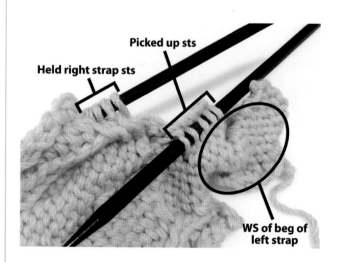

Picked up sts

Held right strap sts

WS of beg of
left strap

Next row (RS): Sl 6 sts to cn and hold in back;
k5, turn work and purl same 5 sts, turn work
and knit same 5 sts; [k2, k2tog, k2] from cn—1
st dec'd, 10 sts rem.
Work 7 rows in St st, beg and ending on WS row.
Next row (RS): Sl 5 sts to cn and hold in back,
k5, k5 from cn.
Rep last 8 rows for patt. Work until strap
measures 4¾ (5, 5½, 5¾, 5¾, 5¾, 5¾)"/12.5
(13, 13.5, 14.5, 14.5, 14.5, 14.5) cm long or to
preferred length, then BO all sts in patt. Break
yarn, leaving 24"/60 cm long tail.

Finished Measurements

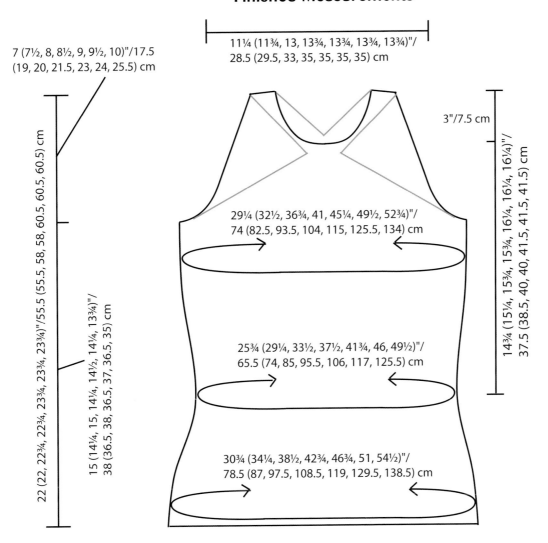

11¼ (11¾, 13, 13¾, 13¾, 13¾, 13¾)"/
28.5 (29.5, 33, 35, 35, 35, 35) cm

7 (7½, 8, 8½, 9, 9½, 10)"/17.5
(19, 20, 21.5, 23, 24, 25.5) cm

3"/7.5 cm

29¼ (32½, 36¾, 41, 45¼, 49½, 52¾)"/
74 (82.5, 93.5, 104, 115, 125.5, 134) cm

22 (22, 22¾, 22¾, 23¾, 23¾, 23¾)"/55.5 (55.5, 58, 58, 60.5, 60.5, 60.5) cm

14¾ (15¼, 15¾, 16¼, 16¼, 16¼)"/
37.5 (38.5, 40, 41.5, 41.5, 41.5) cm

25¾ (29¼, 33½, 37½, 41¾, 46, 49½)"/
65.5 (74, 85, 95.5, 106, 117, 125.5) cm

15 (14¼, 15, 14½, 14¼, 13¾)"/
38 (36.5, 38, 36.5, 37, 36.5, 35) cm

30¾ (34¼, 38½, 42¾, 46¾, 51, 54½)"/
78.5 (87, 97.5, 108.5, 119, 129.5, 138.5) cm

Finishing

Weave in ends except for long yarn tails rem from BO. Block to finished measurements. With right sides facing, pin end of Right Strap to last 10 sts of Right Front; pin end of Left Strap to first 10 sts of Left Front. Ensure that cable crosses lie properly and that strap lengths provide the proper fit, then sew strap ends to fronts using long yarn tails and invisible horizontal seam method (see photos on page 152). Weave in rem ends and block again as needed.

Galena

An unusual lace pattern makes the yoke the centerpiece of this tank. The yoke is worked sideways and shaped using short rows.

SKILL LEVEL
Intermediate to advanced: Skills include following a lace chart, grafting using the contrast color duplicate stitch method, knitting in the round, short rows, picking up stitches, and sturdy knitted cast-on. See Techniques section beginning on page 146 for photo tutorials on grafting using the contrast color duplicate stitch method, working short rows, picking up stitches, and the sturdy knitted cast-on.

SIZES
Women's XS (S, M, L, 1X, 2X, 3X)

FINISHED MEASUREMENTS
Bust: 29½ (33, 37½, 41½, 45, 49½, 53)"/75 (84, 95, 105.5, 114.5, 125.5, 135) cm. *Shown in size S with -1"/2.5 cm ease. Intended to fit with -2"/5 cm to +2"/5 cm ease at bust.*

YARN
530 (610, 680, 760, 830, 920, 1000) yd/490 (565, 625, 700, 765, 850, 920) m light weight #3 or fine weight #2 yarn; shown in #710 Dinghy, Quince & Co. Willet; 100% California Cleaner Cotton; 160 yd/146 m per 1¾ oz/50 g skein, 4 (4, 5, 5, 6, 6, 7) skeins

NEEDLES
US 6/4.0 mm 24–40"/60–100 cm circular needle, depending on selected garment size, for Body; US 5/3.75 mm needles for Yoke. *Adjust needle size if necessary to obtain correct gauge.*

NOTIONS
- Contrast color waste yarn of the same weight as main yarn
- Stitch markers
- Removable marker
- Stitch holders
- Tapestry needle

GAUGE

22 sts and 28 rnds in St st = 4"/10 cm square, blocked

PATTERN NOTES

- Yoke is worked sideways, shaped with short rows, and ends grafted
- Stitches for front and back are picked up from bottom edge of yoke and worked down; short rows shape front and back to yoke
- After front and back are joined at underarms, body is worked down in the round

CUSTOMIZING FIT

Body length can be easily changed; side waist decrease and/or increase frequency may also need to be changed if changing body length. Since body is worked down, the garment can easily be tried on when partially completed, to check length.

SPECIAL STITCHES
Double Increase:

1. Insert tip of right-hand needle into the back of the stitch below first stitch on left-hand needle, and knit.

2. Knit first stitch on needle (not pictured).

3. Use tip of left-hand needle to lift left strand of stitch worked in step 1 (stitch below stitch just knit), and knit through the back.

M1P (worked from WS): With left needle tip, lift strand between needles from front to back. Knit lifted loop through the back, twisting the created stitch (creates purl stitch on RS).

Sturdy Knitted Cast-on: Turn work to WS; stitches just worked are now on left-hand needle. *Insert right-hand needle tip between first two stitches on left-hand needle, draw loop of working yarn through, and place loop on left-hand needle, taking care not to twist it: 1 st cast on. Rep from * until required number of sts has been cast on.

Yoke

Note: When wrapping a stitch for working short rows in garter stitch, wrap stitch as if working from the RS of Stockinette stitch, but after turning work so WS is facing, bring yarn between needles and back to RS to work next row. Wraps in short row shaping of yoke do not have to be picked up because they are hidden by the garter stitch background.

Using smaller needle and waste yarn, loosely CO 19 sts. Work Rows 6 (WS) and 7 (RS) of chart across 19 sts. Break yarn and join main yarn.

Est patt (WS): Work Row 8 of chart across 19 sts.

Next row (RS): Work Row 9 of chart across 17 sts (last st should be W&T).

Yoke Chart

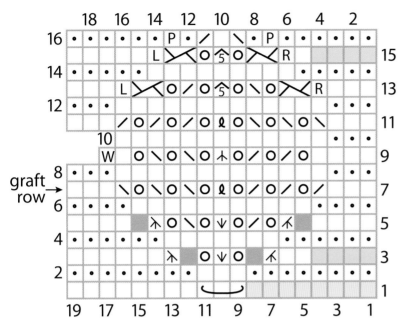

graft row →

Key

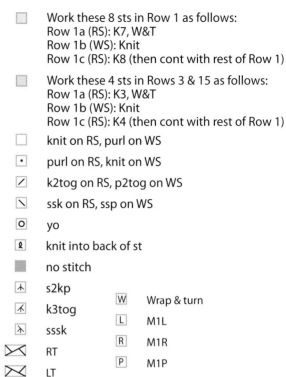

	Work these 8 sts in Row 1 as follows: Row 1a (RS): K7, W&T Row 1b (WS): Knit Row 1c (RS): K8 (then cont with rest of Row 1)
	Work these 4 sts in Rows 3 & 15 as follows: Row 1a (RS): K3, W&T Row 1b (WS): Knit Row 1c (RS): K4 (then cont with rest of Row 1)
	knit on RS, purl on WS
⋅	purl on RS, knit on WS
╱	k2tog on RS, p2tog on WS
╲	ssk on RS, ssp on WS
O	yo
ℓ	knit into back of st
	no stitch
⅄	s2pk
⅄	k3tog
⅄	sssk
⋈	RT
⋈	LT

W	Wrap & turn
L	M1L
R	M1R
P	M1P

↓	double inc: k1b in st in row below, k1b, k1b in left strand of st in row below
⌣	sl3 purlwise wyif, pass yarn to back, sl same 3 back to left-hand needle, k3
5	[sl1 knitwise] 3 times, *pass 2nd st on right-hand needle over 1st (center) st, sl center st back to left-hand needle and pass next st on left-hand needle over it**; sl center st back to right-hand needle and rep from * to **; purl center st- 4 sts dec'd

Cont to work charted patt as est through Row 16 of chart, then repeat Rows 1–16 of chart 15 (15, 15, 17, 17, 17, 17) more times. Work Rows 1–6 of chart once more, then break yarn, leaving a 24"/60 cm long tail. Join waste yarn and work Rows 7 and 8 of chart, then BO all sts and break yarn.

Graft ends of yoke:
With RS facing, fold yoke so BO edge and CO edges are parallel, with BO edge below CO edge and main yarn tail at lower right. You will be following path of waste yarn with yarn tail, using a tapestry needle, so good lighting and visibility is essential: use reading glasses or magnifier as needed. See photo tutorial on page 155 in addition to reading section below.

Fold waste yarn sections under so that junction of main and waste yarn rows is at fold of both ends. For CO edge, follow just top loops of waste yarn; for BO edge, follow just bottom loops of waste yarn. Avoid following waste yarn as it goes through other loops of waste yarn. Work from right to left along the rows where main and waste yarn are linked.

Pull stitches gently so you can see the path of the waste yarn clearly. You can also pull gently on the working yarn to review its path, and make sure you are neither repeating nor skipping stitches. Check your work as you proceed, to make sure yarn tension is correct, and to make sure the stitch pattern is lining up properly (any errors can be corrected by simply undoing stitches made by working yarn and redoing them). When you reach the left edge of the piece, you should end by passing the working yarn through a single loop of main yarn. Once you are satisfied with the appearance of the graft, start at one edge of piece and carefully cut loops of waste yarn that pass through loops of main yarn, freeing waste yarn from piece. Weave in ends and block to measurements.

Front

Use removable m to mark center Front on bottom edge of yoke at chart Row 1a (1a, 1a, 9, 9, 9, 9), on any rep of yoke. Turn work to WS and pass larger needle through purl bump of every other row just below edge (see photo below), picking up 29 (30, 32, 35, 36, 37, 37) sts before m, 1 (1, 1, 0, 0, 0, 0) sts at m, and 29 (30, 32, 35, 36, 37, 37) sts after m—59 (61, 65, 70, 72, 74, 74) sts. Ensure that these sts appear centered on yoke patt. Join yarn to work RS.

Short row (SR) and armhole shaping are worked AT THE SAME TIME; read through the following section completely before beginning.

Short row shaping, Right Front (worked in St st):

SR 1 (RS): K2, W&T.

SRs 2, 4, 6, 8, 10, 12, 14, 16, and 18 (WS): Purl to end.

SRs 3, 5, and 7 (RS): Work in patt to wrapped st, pick up wrap and knit it tog with wrapped st, k2, W&T.

SRs 9, 11, 13, 15, and 17 (RS): Work in patt to wrapped st, pick up wrap and knit it tog with wrapped st, k2 (2, 2, 2, 3, 3, 3), W&T.

Next row (RS): Work in patt to end, picking up wrap and knitting it tog with wrapped st.

AT THE SAME TIME, on SR 9 (9, 9, 5, 5, 5, 5), beg armhole shaping:

Inc row (RS): K2, M1L, work rem of row as instructed above—1 st inc'd. Rep Inc row every 4th row 1 (1, 1, 1, 1, 0, 0) more times, then every RS row 3 (3, 3, 5, 5, 7, 7) more times— 64 (66, 70, 77, 79, 82, 82) sts.

Short row shaping, Left Front:

SR 1 (WS): P2, W&T.

SRs 2, 4, 6, 8, 10, 12, 14, 16, and 18 (RS): Work in patt to end.

SRs 3, 5, and 7 (WS): Purl to wrapped st, pick up wrap and purl it tog with wrapped st, p2, W&T.

SRs 9, 11, 13, 15, and 17 (WS): Purl to wrapped st, pick up wrap and purl it tog with wrapped st, p2 (2, 2, 2, 3, 3, 3), W&T.

Next row (WS): Purl to end, picking up wrap and purling it tog with wrapped st.

AT THE SAME TIME, on SR 8 (8, 8, 4, 4, 4, 4), beg armhole shaping:

Inc row (RS): Work in patt to last 2 sts, M1R, k2—1 st inc'd.

Rep Inc row every 4th row 1 (1, 1, 1, 1, 0, 0) more times, then every RS row 3 (3, 3, 5, 5, 7, 7) more times—69 (71, 75, 84, 86, 90, 90) sts.

Next row: Inc row (RS): K2, M1L, work in patt to last 2 sts, M1R, k2—2 sts inc'd.

Rep Inc row every RS row 0 (3, 6, 4, 7, 8, 8) more times, ending after a RS row (work even in patt on WS rows).

Next row: Inc row (WS): P2, M1R, work in patt to last 2 sts, M1L, p2—2 sts inc'd.

Next row: Inc row (RS)—2 sts inc'd. Rep last 2 rows 0 (0, 0, 1, 1, 2, 4) more times—75 (83, 93, 102, 110, 120, 128) sts. Break yarn and place sts on holder.

Back

Use removable m to mark center Back on yoke directly opposite center Front. Pick up stitches as for Front. Ensure that free sections of yoke between Front and Back are identical.

Left Back: Work as for Right Front.

Right Back: Work as for Left Front.

Continue to work Back as for Front, but at end of last Inc row (RS), do not break yarn—75 (83, 93, 102, 110, 120, 128) sts.

Finished Measurements

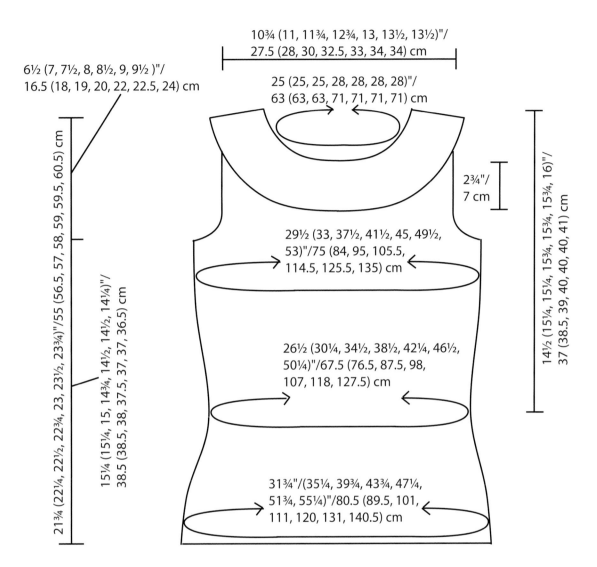

10¾ (11, 11¾, 12¾, 13, 13½, 13½)"/
27.5 (28, 30, 32.5, 33, 34, 34) cm

25 (25, 25, 28, 28, 28, 28)"/
63 (63, 63, 71, 71, 71, 71) cm

6½ (7, 7½, 8, 8½, 9, 9½)"/
16.5 (18, 19, 20, 22, 22.5, 24) cm

2¾"/
7 cm

29½ (33, 37½, 41½, 45, 49½, 53)"/75 (84, 95, 105.5, 114.5, 125.5, 135) cm

26½ (30¼, 34½, 38½, 42¼, 46½, 50¼)"/67.5 (76.5, 87.5, 98, 107, 118, 127.5) cm

31¾"/(35¼, 39¾, 43¾, 47¼, 51¾, 55¼)"/80.5 (89.5, 101, 111, 120, 131, 140.5) cm

21¾ (22¼, 22½, 22¾, 23, 23½, 23¾)"/55 (56.5, 57, 58, 59, 59.5, 60.5) cm

15¼ (15¼, 15, 14¾, 14½, 14½, 14¼)"/ 38.5 (38.5, 38, 37.5, 37, 37, 36.5) cm

14½ (15¼, 15¼, 15¾, 15¾, 15¾, 16)"/ 37 (38.5, 39, 40, 40, 40, 41) cm

Body

Join Front and Back (RS): Using working yarn and needle from Back, turn to WS and *CO 3 (4, 5, 6, 7, 8, 9) sts using sturdy knitted cast-on**, pm for beg of rnd, rep from * to **, turn to RS, place 75 (83, 93, 102, 110, 120, 128) held Front sts on opposite end of needle and knit, turn to WS and rep from * to **, pm for side, rep from * to **, turn to RS and knit across Back sts to end of rnd—162 (182, 206, 228, 248, 272, 292) sts.

Working in St st (knit every rnd), work 12 (12, 10, 10, 12, 10, 8) more rnds.

Dec rnd: *K5, k2tog, work to 7 sts before m, ssk, k5; rep from * to end of rnd—4 sts dec'd.

Rep Dec rnd every 12th (12th, 12th, 12th, 10th, 10th, 10th) rnd 3 more times—146 (166, 190, 212, 232, 256, 276) sts rem. Work 11 rnds even.

Inc rnd: *K5, M1R, work to 5 sts before m, M1L, k5; rep from * to end of rnd—4 sts inc'd.

Rep Inc rnd every 6th rnd 6 more times—174 (194, 218, 240, 260, 284, 304) sts.

Work 8 (8, 8, 8, 10, 12, 12) rnds even. BO all sts knitwise.

Finishing

Weave in ends and block to finished measurements.

Greenville

Lace panels form the side sections of this fitted tank and cause the hem to curve gracefully. Binding off and then picking up stitches just below the bust creates an accent cord, above which gentle bust shaping and short rows create a flattering silhouette; in addition, these short rows allow the tops of the side panels to take their natural shape, clearly displaying the lace motif. The neck and hem are finished with an applied I-cord edging, while the armhole edges are self-finished.

SKILL LEVEL

Intermediate: Skills include reading charts, lace knitting, short rows, three-needle bind-off, attached I-cord, and grafting I-cord ends. See Techniques section beginning on page 146 for photo tutorials on working short rows, attached I-cord, and grafting I-cord ends.

SIZES

Women's XS (S, M, L, 1X, 2X, 3X)

FINISHED MEASUREMENTS

Bust: 28 (32, 36, 40, 44, 48, 52)"/71 (81.5, 91.5, 101.5, 112, 122, 132) cm. *Shown in size S with -2"/5 cm ease. Intended to fit with -2"/5 cm to +2"/5 cm ease at bust.*

YARN

440 (500, 570, 650, 730, 800, 870) yd/410 (460, 530, 600, 670, 740, 800) m medium weight #4 yarn; shown in #30 Ecru, Cascade Yarns Avalon; 50% cotton, 50% acrylic; 175 yd/160 m per 3½ oz/100 g skein, 3 (3, 4, 4, 5, 5, 6) skeins

NEEDLES

US 10/6.0 mm 24–40"/60–100 cm circular needle, depending on selected garment size, for Body; 20"/50 cm circular needle, for Neck edging. *Adjust needle size if necessary to obtain correct gauge.*

NOTIONS

- Stitch markers
- Stitch holders
- Tapestry needle

GAUGE

16 sts and 22 rnds in St st = 4"/10 cm
square, blocked

PATTERN NOTES

- Worked in the round to the armholes
- Neck and bottom edgings are added after shoulders are seamed
- Instructions for lace panels are given in chart form only

CUSTOMIZING FIT

This top is intended to fit closely; however, the lace panels are very stretchy, so that even with zero or negative ease, the fit is somewhat forgiving. Change the body length in increments of 10 rows only (full repeat of lace pattern). If length is increased, I recommend adding one or two waist decreases (and casting on 4 additional stitches to compensate for each additional waist decrease) at intervals of 6 to 8 rounds. This is because the hem circumference was calculated for a length that hits above the widest part of the hip.

SPECIAL STITCHES

SSE (Slipped Stitch Edge, worked over 3 sts and 2 rows):
RS: K1, sl st with yarn in front, k1.
WS: Sl st with yarn in front, k1, sl st with yarn in front.

LT (Left Twist, worked over 2 sts):
RS: Knit 2nd stitch on the left-hand needle through the back loop, leaving it on the needle, then knit first stitch and drop both stitches off needle.
RT (Right Twist, worked over 2 sts):
RS: Knit 2nd stitch on the left-hand needle, leaving it on the needle, then knit first stitch and drop both stitches off needle.

Body

Using longer circular needle, CO 132 (148, 164, 180, 196, 212, 228) sts. Pm and join for working in the rnd, taking care not to twist sts. Note that beg of rnd does not fall at side seam, but on left side of Back, at beg of left-side lace panel.
Set-up rnd: *K13, p2, k13, pm for end lace, k38 (46, 54, 62, 70, 78, 86)**; pm for beg right side lace panel; rep from * to **.
Rnd 1: *Work Row 1 of Lace Chart over 28 sts, k38 (46, 54, 62, 70, 78, 86); rep from * to end.
Rnd 2: *Work Row 2 of Lace Chart, k38 (46, 54, 62, 70, 78, 86); rep from * to end.
Cont patt as est for a total of 8 rnds.

Shape waist:
Dec rnd: *Work in patt to end lace m, k2, k2tog, work in patt to 4 sts before beg lace m, ssk, k2; rep from * to end—4 sts dec'd.

Lace Chart

BO/Dec Row

Key

	knit
	purl
	k3tog
	sssk
	yo
	pattern repeat
	k2tog
	ssk
	no stitch

Read all chart rows from right to left. Start at bottom row and work up.

Rep Dec rnd every 6th rnd 6 more times—104
(120, 136, 152, 168, 184, 200) sts rem.
Work even until 6 reps of Rows 1–10 of lace
chart have been completed.
Next rnd: *Work lace chart BO/Dec row (BO
each st after working it according to chart)**;
BO st to beg lace panel m; rep from * to **;
BO rem sts—4 sts dec in BO rnd. Break yarn
and use tail to graft last BO st with first, so
line of sts appears unbroken.

Accent cord:
Using longer needle, join yarn from RS and with
RS facing, beg at 2nd purl st in left-side lace
panel, and wyif.

1. Insert needle from WS to RS thru center
of st just below BO (shown in photo on St st,
not lace).

2. Wrap yarn around needle counterclockwise
and use needle tip to draw yarn from RS to WS:
one st picked up.

3. Cont picking up one st thru each st in
rnd below BO by inserting needle through
center of st from WS to RS, and drawing yarn
through to WS.

4. At end of rnd break yarn (weave ends into
WS during finishing).

100 (116, 132, 148, 164, 180, 196) sts picked up.
With RS facing, join yarn to WS of work at
first picked-up st.
Next rnd: *K50 (58, 66, 74, 82, 90, 98)**; pm
for right side; rep from * to **; pm for beg of
rnd/left side. Each m should fall at center of
lace panel.
Bust Inc rnd: Inc 10 sts evenly spaced across 50
(58, 66, 74, 82, 90, 98) Front sts, sm, k15, inc1,
knit to last 15 sts, inc1, knit to end—112 (128,
144, 160, 176, 192, 208) sts, 60 (68, 76, 84,
92, 100, 108) in Front, 52 (60, 68, 76, 84, 92,
100) in Back.

Front short rows:
RS: Work in St st to 13 sts before right
  side m, W&T.
Next row (WS): Work in St st (purl) to 13 sts
  before beg of rnd/left side m, W&T.
Next 6 rows (alternating RS and WS): Work in
  patt to wrapped st, pick up wrap and work
  tog with wrapped st, work 2 sts in patt, W&T.

Back short rows:
Next row (RS): Work in patt to 13 sts before
  beg of rnd/left side m, picking up wrap and
  working tog with wrapped st, W&T.
Next row (WS): Work to 13 sts before right
  side m, W&T.
Next 6 rows (alternating RS and WS): Work to
  wrapped st, pick up wrap and work tog with
  wrapped st, work 2 sts in patt, W&T.
Next row (RS): Resume working in the rnd,
  picking up wraps and working tog with
  wrapped st.
Cont to work in the round until a total of 3 (4,
  5, 6, 7, 7, 7) rnds have been worked above
  accent cord (not including short rows),
  stopping one st before end of final rnd.
Next rnd: Work RT with last st of previous rnd
  and first st of new rnd, replacing m between
  2 sts just worked; work to one st before right
  side m; work LT with sts before and after
  m, replacing m between 2 sts just worked;
  work to end.

Front, Back, and Armholes

Divide for Front and Back/shape armholes:
Armhole Dec row (RS): SSE, k2tog, k to 5 sts
  before right-side marker, ssk, SSE—2 sts
  dec'd. Turn and continue to work rem 58 (66,
  74, 82, 90, 98, 106) Front sts only (place 52
  [60, 68, 76, 84, 92, 100] Back sts on holder).
Armhole Dec row (WS): SSE, ssp, p to 5
  sts before left-side marker, p2tog, SSE—2
  sts dec'd.
Rep these two rows 1 (2, 3, 4, 5, 6, 7) times: 52
  (56, 60, 64, 68, 72, 76) sts rem.
Work even for 6 (6, 6, 8, 8, 8, 8) more rows,
  continuing SSE at armhole edges, and ending
  on a WS row.

Shape neckline (Left):
Dec row (RS): SSE, k14 (14, 16, 18, 19, 21, 23),
  ssk, k1—1 st dec'd. Turn and cont to work Left
  Front sts only (place rem Front sts on holder).
Dec row (WS): P1, ssp, work in patt to last 3 sts,
  SSE—1 st dec'd.
Dec row (RS): SSE, work in patt to last 3 sts,
  ssk, k1—1 st dec'd.
Rep last 2 rows 0 (0, 1, 1, 1, 1, 2) more time(s)—17
  (17, 17, 19, 20, 22, 22) sts.
Rep Dec row every RS row 3 (3, 2, 2, 3, 4, 4)
  times (work even on WS rows), then every 6th
  row 1 (1, 1, 1, 1, 1, 2) more time(s), then every
  8th row 1 (1, 1, 1, 1, 1, 0) more time(s)—12 (12, 13,
  15, 15, 16, 16) sts rem.
Work even for 10 (10, 10, 10, 8, 6, 6) more rows.

Shape shoulder with short rows:
WS: Work 6 (6, 6, 7, 7, 7, 7) sts in patt, W&T.
RS: Work in patt to end.
WS: Work in patt to end, picking up wrap and
  working it tog with wrapped st, then place all
  sts on holder. Break yarn, leaving 30"/75 cm
  long tail for three-needle bind-off.

Right front:
Leave 12 (16, 16, 16, 18, 18, 18) Center Front
  sts on holder and place 20 (20, 22, 24, 25,
  27, 29) Right Front sts on needle. Join yarn
  to work RS.
Dec row (RS): K1, k2tog, work in patt to last 3
  sts, SSE—1 st dec'd.
Dec row (WS): SSE, work in patt to last 3 sts,
  p2tog, p1—1 st dec'd.
Rep last 2 rows 0 (0, 1, 1, 1, 1, 2) more time(s),
  then rep Dec row (RS) 1 more time—17 (17, 17,
  19, 20, 22, 22) sts.
Rep Dec row every RS row 3 (3, 2, 2, 3, 4, 4)
  times (work even on WS rows), then every 6th
  row 1 (1, 1, 1, 1, 1, 2) more time(s), then every
  8th row 1 (1, 1, 1, 1, 1, 0) more time(s)—12 (12, 13,
  15, 15, 16, 16) sts rem.
Work even for 9 (9, 9, 9, 7, 5, 5) more rows.

Shape shoulder with short rows:
RS: Work 6 (6, 6, 7, 7, 7, 7) sts in patt, W&T.
WS: Work in patt to end.
RS: Work in patt to end, picking up wrap and
  working it tog with wrapped st. Work 1 more
  row (WS) in patt, then place all sts on holder.
  Break yarn.

Back/Armhole shaping:

Place 52 (60, 68, 76, 84, 92, 100) held Back sts on needle and join yarn to work RS. Immediately begin armhole shaping as for Front; Back armhole shaping is identical to Front—44 (48, 52, 56, 60, 64, 68) sts. Work even, continuing SSE at armhole edges, for 38 (38, 38, 40, 40, 40, 40) more rows.

Shape shoulders with short rows:

RS: *Work in patt to 6 (6, 6, 7, 7, 7, 7) sts before end, W&T**.

WS: Rep from * to **.

RS: *Work in patt to end of row, picking up wrap and working it tog with wrapped st**.

WS: Rep from * to **. Break yarn, leaving 30"/75 cm long tail for three-needle bind-off. Place first 12 (12, 13, 15, 15, 16, 16) sts worked on holder for Left shoulder, place next 20 (24, 26, 26, 30, 32, 36) sts on 2nd holder for back neck, and leave rem 12 (12, 13, 15, 15, 16, 16) sts on needle for Right shoulder.

Finishing

Turn work inside out and place Right Front shoulder sts on 2nd needle or on opposite end of circular needle, with points of needle(s) at armhole edge of shoulder.

Join shoulders using three-needle bind-off: Insert a third needle into first st on each of these 2 needles and knit these 2 sts together, using long yarn tail from Back. *Knit next st on each needle the same way, then pass first st on right-hand needle over second st—1 st bound off. Repeat from * until 1 st is left on the right-hand needle, then pull yarn tail through last st.

Repeat for Left shoulder, using long yarn tail from Left Front and starting at armhole edge of shoulder.

Neck Edging

Using shorter circular needle, starting at right shoulder seam, and with RS facing, work across back neck sts AT THE SAME TIME dec 1 (3, 5, 5, 5, 5, 7) sts evenly spaced; pick up and knit 30 sts (approx 4 sts for every 5 rows) between back neck and center front sts; work across center front sts AT THE SAME TIME dec 1 (3, 3, 3, 4, 4, 4) sts evenly spaced; pick up and knit

Finished Measurements

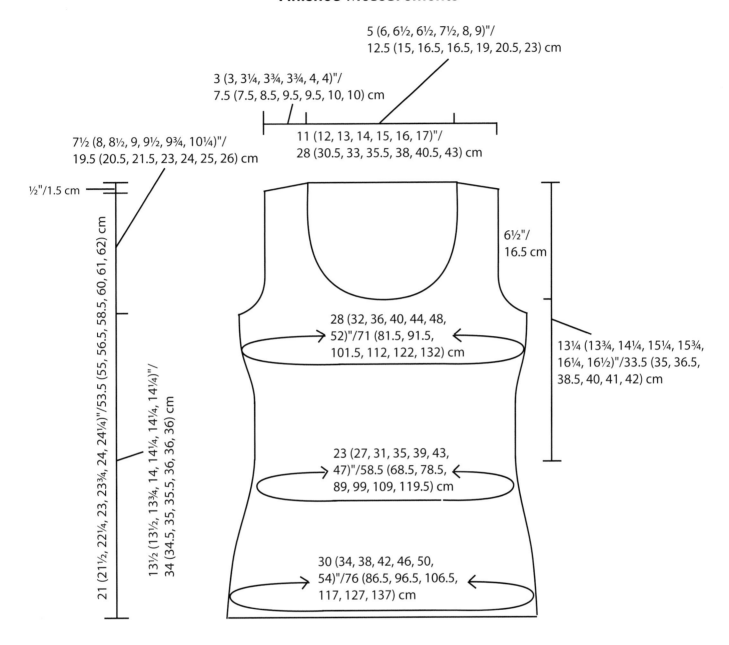

5 (6, 6½, 6½, 7½, 8, 9)"/
12.5 (15, 16.5, 16.5, 19, 20.5, 23) cm

3 (3, 3¼, 3¾, 3¾, 4, 4)"/
7.5 (7.5, 8.5, 9.5, 9.5, 10, 10) cm

11 (12, 13, 14, 15, 16, 17)"/
28 (30.5, 33, 35.5, 38, 40.5, 43) cm

7½ (8, 8½, 9, 9½, 9¾, 10¼)"/
19.5 (20.5, 21.5, 23, 24, 25, 26) cm

½"/1.5 cm

6½"/
16.5 cm

21 (21½, 22¼, 23, 23¾, 24, 24¼)"/53.5 (55, 56.5, 58.5, 60, 61, 62) cm

13½ (13½, 13¾, 14, 14¼, 14¼, 14¼)"/
34 (34.5, 35, 35.5, 36, 36, 36) cm

28 (32, 36, 40, 44, 48, 52)"/71 (81.5, 91.5, 101.5, 112, 122, 132) cm

13¼ (13¾, 14¼, 15¼, 15¾, 16¼, 16½)"/33.5 (35, 36.5, 38.5, 40, 41, 42) cm

23 (27, 31, 35, 39, 43, 47)"/58.5 (68.5, 78.5, 89, 99, 109, 119.5) cm

30 (34, 38, 42, 46, 50, 54)"/76 (86.5, 96.5, 106.5, 117, 127, 137) cm

30 sts between center front and back neck sts—90 (94, 94, 94, 99, 101, 103) sts.

Attached I-cord: Without breaking yarn, turn work, insert needle into last st as if to knit, and draw yarn thru to make new st; place new st back on left-hand needle and rep twice more—3 new sts. *K2, ssk, place 3 sts just worked back on left-hand needle; rep from * without turning work until all neck edging sts have been picked up and knit. Do not BO rem 3 sts; break yarn and use yarn tail to graft these sts to first row of I-cord.

Hem Edging

Using longer circular needle, starting just after side lace panel, and with RS facing, *pick up and knit 1 st for every st in St st panel; skip 1 st at beg and end of lace panel and pick up 1 st for every st in between; rep from * to end—128 (144, 160, 176, 192, 208, 224) sts. Work I-cord as directed above.

Weave in ends and block again as needed.

Haddonfield

Highly textured lace cables run from hem to neck of this
fitted tank, accentuating its figure-flattering lines.

SKILL LEVEL
Intermediate to advanced: Skills include reading
lace charts, working lace stitches on every
round or row, working two types of shaping
simultaneously, short rows, and three-needle
bind-off. See Techniques section beginning
on page 146 for a photo tutorial on working
short rows.

SIZES
Women's XS (S, M, L, 1X, 2X, 3X)

FINISHED MEASUREMENTS
Bust: 30½ (34½, 39, 42¾, 46½, 50½,
54¼)"/77.5 (87.5, 99, 108.5, 118.5, 128, 137.5) cm.
*Shown in size S with +½"/1.5 cm ease. Intended
to fit with -2"/5 cm to +2"/5 cm ease at bust.*

YARN
600 (670, 710, 880, 950, 1020, 1100) yd/555
(620, 655, 810, 875, 940, 1010) m medium
weight #4 yarn; shown in #1656 Napatree,
Berroco Modern Cotton; 60% pima cotton, 40%
modal rayon; 209 yd/191 m per 3½ oz/100 g
skein, 3 (4, 4, 5, 5, 5, 6) skeins

NEEDLES
US 6/4.0 mm 24–40"/60–100 cm circular
needle, depending on selected garment size,
for Body; 16–20"/40–50 cm circular needle, for
Armhole edging. *Adjust needle size if necessary
to obtain correct gauge.*

NOTIONS
- Stitch markers
- Cable needle
- Stitch holders
- Tapestry needle

GAUGE
21 sts and 27 rnds in St st = 4"/10 cm
square, blocked

PATTERN NOTES

- Worked in the round to the armholes; short rows shape shoulders
- Armhole and neck edgings are added after shoulders are joined
- Instructions for lace cable stitch pattern are given in chart form only
- Front and back are identical

CUSTOMIZING FIT

To simultaneously change armhole depth and neck drop, add or subtract strap rows before beginning short row shoulder shaping. Change body length in increments of 12 rounds only (½ repeat of lace cable pattern); side waist decrease and/or increase frequency may also need to be changed.

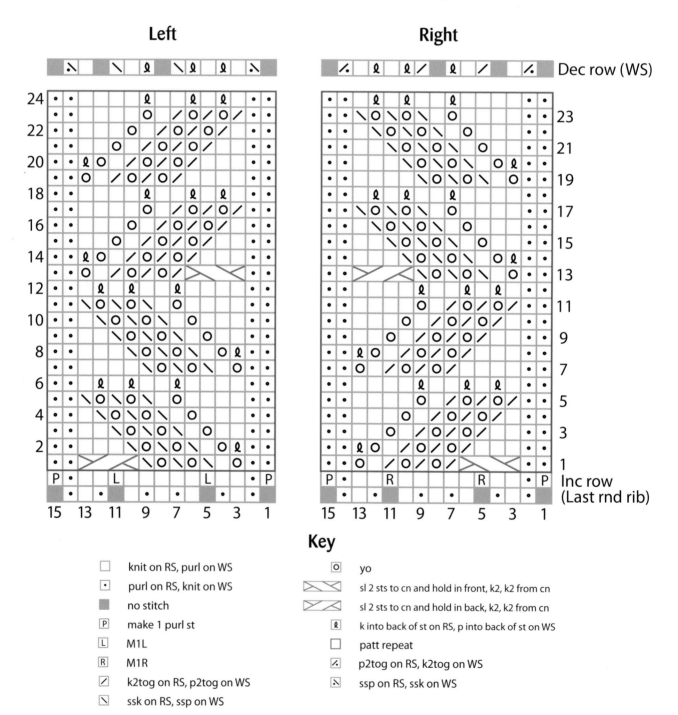

Left

Right

Key

☐	knit on RS, purl on WS	○	yo
・	purl on RS, knit on WS	⟋⟍	sl 2 sts to cn and hold in front, k2, k2 from cn
▨	no stitch	⟍⟋	sl 2 sts to cn and hold in back, k2, k2 from cn
P	make 1 purl st	ℓ	k into back of st on RS, p into back of st on WS
L	M1L	☐	patt repeat
R	M1R	⟋	p2tog on RS, k2tog on WS
⟋	k2tog on RS, p2tog on WS	⟍	ssp on RS, ssk on WS
⟍	ssk on RS, ssp on WS		

When working in the round, read all chart rows from right to left. When working flat, read odd (RS) rows from right to left and even (WS) rows from left to right.

Body

Using longer circular needle, CO 160 (180, 204, 224, 244, 264, 284) sts. Pm for beg of rnd and join, taking care not to twist sts.

Ribbing: [K1, p1] for 4 rnds.

Inc rnd: *K6 (9, 11, 13, 17, 21, 26), M1R, k7 (10, 12, 14, 18, 22, 27), pm for beg cable lace (CL) panel, M1P, p1, k2, M1R, k5, M1R, k2, p1, M1P, pm for end CL panel, k22 (24, 28, 31, 32, 33, 33), M1L, k23 (25, 29, 32, 33, 34, 34), pm for beg CL panel, M1P, p1, k2, M1L, k5, M1L, k2, p1, M1P**; pm for end CL panel; rep from * to **—20 sts inc'd, 14 (20, 24, 28, 36, 44, 54) sts in each side St st panel, 46 (50, 58, 64, 66, 68, 68) in each Front and Back St st panel, 15 sts in each CL panel, 180 (200, 224, 244, 264, 284, 304) total sts. *Note:* Beg of rnd falls at beg of side St st panel.

Est CL patt: *Knit to beg CL panel m, work Right chart Row 1 over 15 sts, knit to beg CL panel m, work Left chart Row 1 over 15 sts; rep from * to end of rnd.

Cont to work patts as est (work sts between CL panels in St st) and AT THE SAME TIME, beg waist shaping on 10th (8th, 10th, 10th, 10th, 8th, 8th) rnd from CO.

Dec rnd: Work in patt to end CL panel m, *ssk, work in patt to 2 sts before beg CL panel m, k2tog, work in patt across CL panel**; work side St st panel and CL panel in patt; rep from * to **—4 sts dec'd.

Rep Dec rnd every 8th rnd 1 (0, 4, 3, 3, 3, 3) more times, then every 6th rnd 5 (6, 2, 3, 3, 3, 3) more times—32 (36, 44, 50, 52, 54, 54) sts rem each in Front and Back St st panels, 152 (172, 196, 216, 236, 256, 276) total sts rem.

Work 11 rnds even.

Inc rnd: Work in patt to end CL panel m, *k1, M1R, work in patt to 1 st before beg CL panel m, M1L, k1, work in patt across CL panel**; work side St st panel and CL panel in patt; rep from * to **—4 sts inc'd.

Rep Inc rnd every 12th (12th, 12th, 12th, 10th, 10th, 10th) rnd 3 more times—40 (44, 52, 58, 60, 62, 62) sts each in Front and Back St st panels, 168 (188, 212, 232, 252, 272, 292) total sts.

Work even for 13 (13, 11, 9, 13, 11, 7) more rnds (last rnd worked should fall on even-numbered chart row).

Divide for Front and Back: *K4 (6, 7, 8, 11, 14, 18), BO next 6 (8, 10, 12, 14, 16, 18) sts, work in patt to side St st panel**; rep from * to **; work to end. Turn and cont to work 78 (86, 96, 104, 112, 120, 128) Back sts only (cont to follow charts as est).

Back

Armhole and accent shaping are worked AT THE SAME TIME; read through entire section before proceeding.

Armhole Dec row (WS): P1, ssp, work in patt to last 3 sts, p2tog, p1—2 sts dec'd.

Armhole Dec row (RS): K1, k2tog, work in patt to last 3 sts, ssk, k1—2 sts dec'd.

Rep these 2 rows 0 (0, 0, 0, 2, 2, 4) more times, then rep Armhole Dec row (RS) every RS row 0 (2, 3, 4, 3, 6, 6) more times (work even at armhole edges on WS rows)—2 (4, 5, 6, 9, 12, 16) sts dec'd at each armhole edge.

AT THE SAME TIME, on 4th row after dividing for Front and Back, beg Accent dec:

Accent Dec row (RS): Work in patt to end CL panel m, ssk, work in patt to 2 sts before beg CL panel m, k2tog, work in patt to end—2 sts dec'd in center St st panel.

Work 1 (3, 1, 1, 3, 3, 3) rows even at center St st panel (cont to work Armhole shaping dec).

Accent shaping row (RS): Work in patt to 1 st before beg CL panel m, M1R, k1, work in patt to end CL panel m, ssk, work in patt to 2 sts before beg CL panel m, k2tog, work in patt to 1 st after end CL panel m, M1L, work in patt to end—2 sts dec'd in center St st panel, 1 st inc'd in each side St st panel (not including any Armhole shaping dec worked at the same time).

Rep Accent shaping row every 4th row 0 (0, 0, 0, 0, 1, 3) more times, then every RS row 10 (11, 14, 16, 16, 16, 14) more times—16 (18, 20, 22, 24, 24, 24) sts rem in center St st panel.

After both Armhole dec and Accent shaping are completed, 13 (14, 17, 19, 19, 20, 20) sts rem in each side St st panel.

Next row (WS): Work to end CL panel m, work Dec row of Right (Right, Left, Left, Left, Left) chart, work to end CL panel m, work Dec row of Left (Left, Right, Right, Right, Right, Right) chart, work to end—4 sts dec'd in each CL panel.

Next row (RS): K13 (14, 17, 19, 19, 20, 20), place these sts on holder for Right strap, BO next 38 (40, 42, 44, 46, 46, 46) sts, knit to end.

Left strap:
Cont to work 13 (14, 17, 19, 19, 20, 20) Left strap sts only. Work 13 rows even in St st, ending on a WS row.

Beg short row (SR) shoulder shaping:
SR 1 (RS): Work in patt to last 3 (3, 3, 4, 4, 4, 4) sts, W&T.
SR 2, 4, 6, and 8 (WS): Work in patt to end.
SR 3, 5, and 7 (RS): Work in patt to 3 (3, 4, 4, 4, 4, 4) sts before last wrapped st, W&T.
Next row (RS): Work in patt to end, picking up wraps and working tog with wrapped sts.
Work 1 more row in patt (WS). Break yarn, leaving 30"/75 cm long tail for three-needle bind-off, and place sts on holder.

Right strap:
Place held Right strap sts on needle and join yarn to work WS of Right strap. Work 14 rows even in patt, ending on a RS row.

Beg short row shoulder shaping:
SR 1 (WS): Work in patt to last 3 (3, 3, 4, 4, 4, 4) sts, W&T.
SR 2, 4, 6, and 8 (RS): Work in patt to end.
SR 3, 5, and 7 (WS): Work in patt to 3 (3, 4, 4, 4, 4, 4) sts before last wrapped st, W&T.
Next row (WS): Work in patt to end, picking up wraps and working tog with wrapped sts. Break yarn, leaving 30"/75 cm long tail for three-needle bind-off, and place sts on holder.

Front

Join yarn to work WS of Front. Front is worked same as Back (note that Left and Right straps refer to Front sts with RS facing, not side of garment when worn).

Finishing

Turn garment inside out. Place Front and Back sts for right shoulder on 2 needles or 2 ends of circular needle.
Three-needle bind-off: Insert a third needle into first st on each of these 2 needles and knit these 2 sts together, using one of the long yarn tails. *Knit next st on each needle the same way, then pass first st on right-hand needle over second st—1 st bound off. Repeat from * until 1 st is left on the right-hand needle, then pull yarn tail through last st.
   Repeat for left shoulder.
   Weave in ends and block to finished measurements.

Armhole Edging

With RS facing, using shorter circular needle, and starting at beg of BO underarm sts, pick up and knit 1 st for each BO st (6 [8, 10, 12, 14, 16, 18] sts); 31 (34, 37, 40, 42, 45, 48) sts (approx 3 sts per 4 rows) to shoulder seam; 1 st at seam; 31 (34, 37, 40, 42, 45, 48) sts to BO underarm sts—69 (77, 85, 93, 99, 107, 115) sts. Pm and join.

Finished Measurements

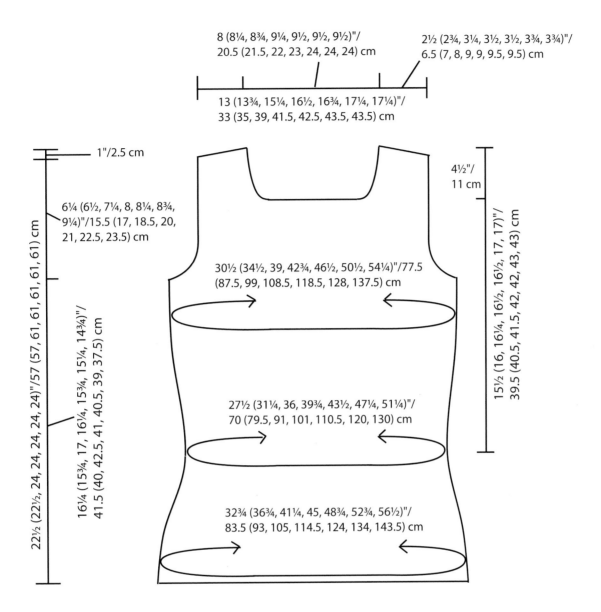

8 (8¼, 8¾, 9¼, 9½, 9½, 9½)"/
20.5 (21.5, 22, 23, 24, 24, 24) cm

2½ (2¾, 3¼, 3½, 3½, 3¾, 3¾)"/
6.5 (7, 8, 9, 9, 9.5, 9.5) cm

13 (13¾, 15¼, 16½, 16¾, 17¼, 17¼)"/
33 (35, 39, 41.5, 42.5, 43.5, 43.5) cm

1"/2.5 cm

4½"/
11 cm

6¼ (6½, 7¼, 8, 8¼, 8¾, 9¼)"/15.5 (17, 18.5, 20, 21, 22.5, 23.5) cm

30½ (34½, 39, 42¾, 46½, 50½, 54¼)"/77.5 (87.5, 99, 108.5, 118.5, 128, 137.5) cm

15½ (16, 16¼, 16½, 17, 17, 17)"/ 39.5 (40.5, 41.5, 42, 43, 43) cm

16¼ (15¾, 17, 16¼, 15¾, 15¼, 14¾)"/ 41.5 (40, 42.5, 41, 40.5, 39, 37.5) cm

22½ (22½, 24, 24, 24, 24, 24)"/57 (57, 61, 61, 61, 61, 61) cm

27½ (31¼, 36, 39¾, 43½, 47¼, 51¼)"/ 70 (79.5, 91, 101, 110.5, 120, 130) cm

32¾ (36¾, 41¼, 45, 48¾, 52¾, 56½)"/ 83.5 (93, 105, 114.5, 124, 134, 143.5) cm

Rnd 1: Work in k1, p1 rib, AT THE SAME TIME dec'ing 3 (3, 3, 3, 3, 5, 5) sts evenly spaced along underarm area—66 (74, 82, 90, 96, 102, 110) sts.

Work in rib as est for 2 more rnds, then BO all sts loosely in patt.

Neck Edging

With RS facing and starting at one shoulder seam, *pick up and knit 16 sts along strap edge (approx 2 sts per 3 rows); 1 st for each BO st (38 [40, 42, 44, 46, 46, 46] sts); 16 sts along strap edge; 1 st at shoulder seam**; rep from

* to **—142 (146, 150, 154, 158, 158, 158) sts. Pm and join.

Rnd 1: *[P1, k1] along strap edge and across CL panel, ending p1; ssk; cont to work in rib as est to last 2 center St st panel sts, AT THE SAME TIME dec'ing 1 (1, 1, 3, 3, 3, 3) sts evenly spaced; k2tog; [p1, k1] across CL panel and along strap edge, ending p1; k1 at shoulder seam**; rep from * to **—136 (140, 144, 144, 148, 148, 148) sts.

Work in rib as est for 2 more rnds, then BO all sts loosely in patt.

Weave in ends and block again as needed.

Livonia

Working a traditional lace pattern in a wide tape yarn gives this tank a modern edge. Even though the yarn is classified as bulky weight and works up quickly on large needles, the tape construction and fiber mix give it a wonderful drape.

SKILL LEVEL

Intermediate: Skills include reading charts, lace knitting, duplicate stitch grafting, picking up stitches, short rows, and three-needle bind-off. See Techniques section beginning on page 146 for photo tutorials on picking up stitches, duplicate stitch grafting, and working short rows.

SIZES

Women's XS (S, M, L, 1X, 2X, 3X)

FINISHED MEASUREMENTS

Bust: 32 (36, 40, 44, 48, 52, 56)"/81.5 (91.5, 101.5, 112, 122, 132, 142) cm. *Shown in size S with +2"/5 cm ease. Intended to fit with -1"/2.5 cm to +3"/7.5 cm ease at bust.*

YARN

440 (500, 560, 630, 690, 760, 820) yd/400 (460, 520, 580, 640, 700, 760) m bulky weight #5 yarn; shown in #375 Harebell, Rowan Cotton Lustre; 55% cotton, 35% modal, 10% linen; 87 yd/80 m per 1¾ oz/50 g skein, 6 (6, 7, 8, 9, 9, 10) skeins

NEEDLES

US 11/8.0 mm 24"/60 cm or longer circular needle for lace band; 24–40"/60–100 cm circular needle, depending on selected garment size, for Body; 20"/50 cm circular needle, for Neckband. *Adjust needle size if necessary to obtain correct gauge.*

NOTIONS

- Waste yarn, same approximate weight as main yarn but in a contrasting color, if using contrast color duplicate stitch method for grafting
- Stitch markers
- Stitch holders
- Tapestry needle

GAUGE

14 sts and 19 rows in St st = 4"/10 cm
square, blocked

PATTERN NOTES

- The lace band is worked sideways, the ends grafted, and then stitches for the bodice are picked up from one edge and worked in the round to the armholes
- Instructions are given for the contrast color duplicate stitch method of grafting on page 155, but the Kitchener stitch may also be used if preferred (instructions not included)
- Instructions for lace stitch pattern are given in chart and written form

CUSTOMIZING FIT

There is no waist shaping, so tank length is easily changed: add/subtract rows to stockinette stitch section before starting to shape armholes.

SPECIAL STITCHES

Lace Pattern (worked over 12 rows):
CO 24 sts.
Rows 1 and 5 (RS): Knit.
Rows 2, 6, and 10 (WS): Knit.
Row 3 (RS): K3, [k2tog, yo twice, k2tog, k1] 3 times, [k1, yo twice] 4 times, k2—8 sts inc'd, 32 sts.

Row 4 (WS): K1, [k2, p1] 4 times, [k4, p1] 3 times, k4.
Row 7 (RS): K3, [k2tog, yo twice, k2tog, k1] 3 times, k14.
Row 8 (WS): [K1, wrapping yarn 3 times around needle] 12 times, yo 3 times, k1, [k4, p1] 3 times, k4—3 sts inc'd (not including extra wraps on first 12 sts).
Row 9 (RS): K21, p1, k1; sl next 12 sts to right-hand needle, dropping extra wraps; replace these 12 elongated sts back on left-hand needle and k12tog—11 sts dec'd, 24 sts rem.
Row 11 (RS): K3, [k2tog, yo twice, k2tog, k1] 3 times, k6.
Row 12 (WS): K9, [p1, k4] 3 times.

SSE (Slipped Stitch Edge, worked over 3 sts and 2 rows):
RS: K1, sl st with yarn in front, k1.
WS: Sl st with yarn in front, k1, sl st with yarn in front.

LT (Left Twist, worked over 2 sts):
RS: Knit 2nd stitch on the left-hand needle through the back loop, leaving it on the needle, then knit first stitch and drop both stitches off needle.

RT (Right Twist, worked over 2 sts):
RS: Knit 2nd stitch on the left-hand needle, leaving it on the needle, then knit first stitch and drop both stitches off needle.

Lace Pattern Chart

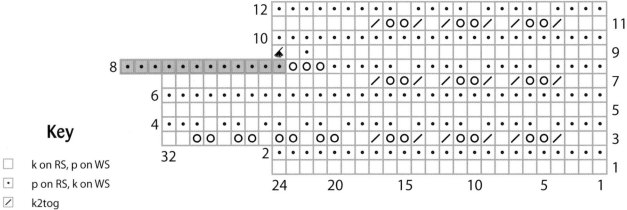

Key

☐	k on RS, p on WS
·	p on RS, k on WS
╱	k2tog
O	yo
▪	k, wrapping yarn 3 times
◢	sl 12 sts to right-hand needle, dropping extra loops, then sl sts back to left-hand needle and k12tog

Lace Band

Notes: If using the contrast color duplicate stitch method of grafting described below, a conventional long-tail CO may be used. However, if using Kitchener stitch to graft ends of band, use a provisional method of casting on.

Join new balls of yarn at right edge of RS of piece.

Using waste yarn and circular needle for Lace Band, CO 24 sts. Knit 1 row, then break yarn and join Main yarn.

Est lace patt (WS): Work Row 2 of Lace patt, following written instructions or chart.

Cont to work patt as est for patt Rows 3–12, then rep Rows 1–12 of patt 15 (17, 19, 21, 23, 25, 27) more times. Break yarn, leaving 36"/90 cm long tail.

Join waste yarn and knit 1 row (RS), then BO all sts knitwise.

Graft ends:

With RS facing, fold yoke so BO edge and CO edges are parallel, with BO edge below CO edge and main yarn tail at lower right. You will be following path of waste yarn with yarn tail, using a tapestry needle, so good lighting and visibility is essential: use reading glasses or magnifier as needed. See photo tutorial on page 155 in addition to reading section below.

Fold waste yarn sections under so that junction of main and waste yarn rows is at fold of both ends. For CO edge, follow just top loops of waste yarn; for BO edge, follow just bottom loops of waste yarn. Avoid following waste yarn as it goes through other loops of waste yarn. Work from right to left along the rows where main and waste yarn are linked. Pull stitches gently so you can see the path of the waste yarn clearly. You can also pull gently on the working yarn to review its path, and make sure you are neither repeating nor skipping stitches. Check your work as you proceed, to make sure yarn tension is correct, and to make sure the stitch pattern is lining up properly (any errors can be corrected by simply undoing stitches made by working yarn and redoing them). When you reach the left edge of the piece, you should end by passing the working yarn through a single loop of main yarn. Once you are satisfied with the appearance of the

graft, start at one edge of piece and carefully cut loops of waste yarn that pass through loops of main yarn, freeing waste yarn from piece. Weave in ends and block to measurements.

Bodice

Using longer circular needle, beg at graft and with RS facing, pick up and knit one st for every knit row—96 (108, 120, 132, 144, 156, 168) sts. Pm and join.

Inc rnd: [k3, yo, k3] 16 (18, 20, 22, 24, 26, 28) times to end of rnd—16 (18, 20, 22, 24, 26, 28) sts inc'd, 112 (126, 140, 154, 168, 182, 196) sts.

Next rnd: K56 (63, 70, 77, 84, 91, 98), pm for right side, k56 (63, 70, 77, 84, 91, 98).

Cont to work in St st as est for 21 more rnds, stopping one st before end of final rnd; piece should measure approx 13¾"/35 cm from lowest part of CO edge.

Next rnd: Work RT with last st of previous rnd and first st of new rnd, replacing m between 2 sts just worked; work in patt to one st before right side m; work LT with sts before and after m, replacing m between 2 sts just worked; work in patt to end.

Divide for Front and Back/shape armholes:

Armhole Dec row (RS): SSE, k2tog, k to 5 sts before right-side marker, ssk, SSE—2 sts dec'd. Turn and continue to work rem 54 (61, 68, 75, 82, 89, 96) Front sts only (place 56 [63, 70, 77, 84, 91, 98] Back sts on holder).

Armhole Dec row (WS): SSE, ssp, p to 5 sts before left-side marker, p2tog, SSE—2 sts dec'd.

Rep these two rows 0 (0, 1, 2, 4, 6, 8) more times, then rep RS dec row 6 (8, 8, 8, 7, 6, 5) more times (work even in patt on WS rows)—40 (43, 46, 49, 50, 51, 52) sts.

Work even for 11 (9, 9, 11, 11, 11, 11) more rows, continuing SSE at armhole edges and ending after a WS row.

Shape Front neck:

Next row (RS): Work 15 (16, 17, 18, 18, 18, 18) sts in patt, BO next 10 (11, 12, 13, 14, 15, 16) sts, work in patt to end. Place 15 (16, 17, 18, 18, 18, 18) Left Front sts on holder or leave on needle to work later.

Right Front

Next row (WS): Work in patt to end.
Next row (RS): BO 2 sts, work in patt to end.
Rep last 2 rows once more—11 (12, 13, 14, 14, 14, 14) sts rem.
Next row (WS): Work in patt to end.
Next row (RS): K1, k2tog, work in patt to end—1 st dec'd.
Rep last 2 rows once more—9 (10, 11, 12, 12, 12, 12) sts rem.
Next row (WS): Work in patt to end.

Beg short row (SR) shoulder shaping:
SR 1 (RS): Work in patt to last 4 (4, 4, 5, 5, 5, 5) sts, W&T.
SR 2 (WS): Work in patt to end.
SR 3 (RS): Work 2 (3, 3, 3, 3, 3, 3) sts in patt, W&T.
SR 4 (WS): Work in patt to end.
Next row (RS): Work in patt to end, picking up wraps and working tog with wrapped sts.
Next row (WS): P1, ssp, p 6 (7, 8, 9, 9, 9, 9). Break yarn and place rem 8 (9, 10, 11, 11, 11, 11) sts on holder.

Left Front

If Left Front sts are on holder, return to needle. Join yarn to work WS.
Next row (WS): BO 2 sts, work in patt to end.
Next row (RS): Work in patt to end.
Rep last 2 rows once more—11 (12, 13, 14, 14, 14, 14) sts rem.
Next row (WS): Work in patt to end.
Next row (RS): Work in patt to last 3 sts, ssk, k1—1 st dec'd.

Rep last 2 rows once more—9 (10, 11, 12, 12, 12, 12) sts rem.
Next 2 rows: Work in patt to end.

Beg short row shoulder shaping:
SR 1 (WS): Work in patt to last 4 (4, 4, 5, 5, 5, 5) sts, W&T.
SR 2 (RS): Work in patt to end.
SR 3 (WS): Work 2 (3, 3, 3, 3, 3, 3) sts in patt, W&T.
SR 4 (RS): Work in patt to end.
Next row (WS): Work in patt to last 3 sts, picking up wraps and working tog with wrapped sts; p2tog, p1. Break yarn, leaving 30"/75 cm long tail for three-needle bind-off, and place rem 8 (9, 10, 11, 11, 11, 11) sts on holder.

Back

Place 56 (63, 70, 77, 84, 91, 98) Back sts on needle and join yarn to work RS. Work armhole shaping as for Front, then work 21 (19, 19, 21, 21, 21, 21) rows even in patt, continuing SSE at armhole edges, and ending after a WS row.

Beg short row shoulder shaping:
SR 1 (RS): Work in patt to last 4 (4, 4, 5, 5, 5, 5) sts, W&T.
SR 2 (WS): Rep SR 1.
SR 3 (RS): Work to 3 (3, 4, 4, 4, 4, 4) sts before last wrapped st, W&T.
SR 4 (WS): Rep SR 3.

Finished Measurements

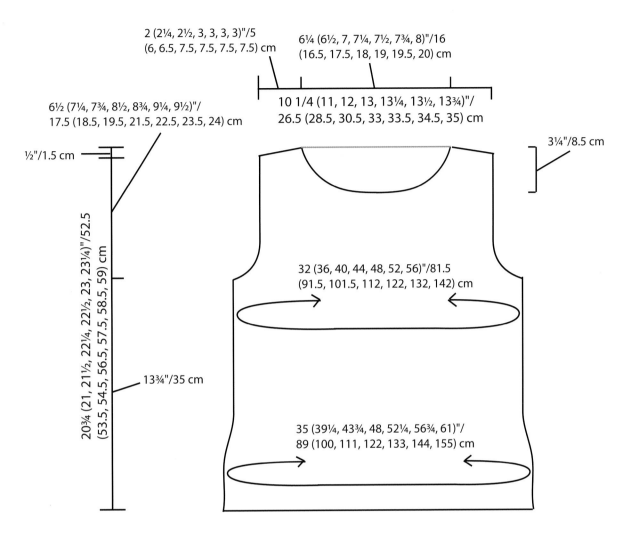

2 (2¼, 2½, 3, 3, 3, 3)"/5 (6, 6.5, 7.5, 7.5, 7.5, 7.5) cm

6¼ (6½, 7, 7¼, 7½, 7¾, 8)"/16 (16.5, 17.5, 18, 19, 19.5, 20) cm

10 1/4 (11, 12, 13, 13¼, 13½, 13¾)"/ 26.5 (28.5, 30.5, 33, 33.5, 34.5, 35) cm

6½ (7¼, 7¾, 8½, 8¾, 9¼, 9½)"/ 17.5 (18.5, 19.5, 21.5, 22.5, 23.5, 24) cm

3¼"/8.5 cm

½"/1.5 cm

20¾ (21, 21½, 22¼, 22½, 23, 23¼)"/52.5 (53.5, 54.5, 56.5, 57.5, 58.5, 59) cm

32 (36, 40, 44, 48, 52, 56)"/81.5 (91.5, 101.5, 112, 122, 132, 142) cm

13¾"/35 cm

35 (39¼, 43¾, 48, 52¼, 56¾, 61)"/ 89 (100, 111, 122, 133, 144, 155) cm

Next row (RS): Work in patt to end, picking up wraps and working tog with wrapped sts.

Next row (WS): P1, ssp, p 6 (7, 8, 9, 9, 9, 9); BO next 22 (23, 24, 25, 26, 27, 28) sts purlwise; purl to last 3 sts, picking up wraps and working tog with wrapped sts; p2tog, p1. Break yarn, leaving 30"/75 cm long tail for three-needle bind-off. Leave rem shoulder sts on needle.

Finishing

Turn garment inside out. Place Front sts for right shoulder on needle.

Three-needle bind-off: Insert a third needle into first st on each of these 2 needles and knit these 2 sts together, using long yarn tail from Back. *Knit next st on each needle the same way, then pass first st on right-hand needle over second st—1 st bound off. Repeat from * until 1 st is left on the right-hand needle, then pull yarn tail through last st.

Repeat for left shoulder, using long yarn tail from Left Front.

Weave in ends and block to finished measurements, stretching lace scallops well.

Neck Edging

With RS facing and starting at right shoulder seam, pick up and knit 2 sts across seam; 22 (23, 24, 25, 26, 27, 28) sts along Back Neck (one for each BO st); 2 sts across seam; 16 sts along Left Front; 10 (11, 12, 13, 14, 15, 16) sts along Center Front (one for each BO st); 16 sts along Right Front—68 (70, 72, 74, 76, 78, 80) sts. Purl one rnd, then BO all sts knitwise. Weave in ends and block again as needed.

Marietta

Twisted rib cables run up the center front and back of this slightly cropped tank, dividing in front to frame a striking textured inset.

SKILL LEVEL
Intermediate to advanced: Skills include cable knitting, reading a large chart with crossed stitches on wrong and right side rows, working in the round, and three-needle bind-off.

SIZES
Women's XS (S, M, L, 1X, 2X, 3X)

FINISHED MEASUREMENTS
Bust: 31 (34¾, 39, 42¾, 47, 50¾, 54¼)"/78.5 (88, 99, 108.5, 119.5, 128.5, 138) cm. *Shown in size S with +¾"/2 cm ease. Intended to fit with -1½"/4 cm to +2½"/6.5 cm ease at bust.*

YARN
530 (600, 670, 750, 840, 910, 990) yd/490 (555, 620, 690, 775, 840, 910) m light weight #3 yarn; shown in #231 Steppe, Rowan Softyak DK; 76% cotton, 15% yak, 9% nylon; 148 yd/135 m per 1¾ oz/50 g skein, 4 (5, 5, 6, 6, 7, 7) skeins

NEEDLES
US 7/4.5 mm 24–40"/60–100 cm circular needle, depending on selected garment size, for Body; dpns or 16–20"/40–50 cm circular needles, for armhole edgings; dpns or straight needles, for upper front and back. *Adjust needle size if necessary to obtain correct gauge.*

NOTIONS
- Stitch markers
- Stitch holders
- Cable needle, tapestry needle

GAUGE
22 sts and 31 rnds in St st = 4"/10 cm square, blocked; 26 sts and 31 rnds in textured inset patt = 4"/10 cm square, blocked

PATTERN NOTES

- Worked in the round to the armholes
- Waist is shaped with decreases and increases along sides
- Armhole edgings added during finishing
- Textured stitch patterns are given in chart form only

CUSTOMIZING FIT

Body can be lengthened in increments of 10 rows (one repeat of the twisted cable pattern). If body is lengthened by 10 rows, I recommend increasing the interval between waist decreases from 6 to 8 rounds, to keep the narrowest part of the waist just above the natural waist; work the rest of the pattern as written. For a more classic fit and length, increase the interval between waist decrease rounds from 6 to 8 rounds, increase the interval between waist increase rounds from 14 to 16 rounds, *and* add 6 more rounds worked even after the last waist increase and before beginning the Inset pattern. This tank may be worn backwards.

SPECIAL STITCHES

LT (Left Twist, worked over 2 sts):

RS: Knit 2nd stitch on the left-hand needle through the back loop, leaving it on the needle, then knit first stitch and drop both stitches off needle.

WS (creates Left Twist with knit sts on the RS): Purl 2nd stitch on the left-hand needle through the back loop, leaving it on the needle, then purl first stitch and drop both stitches off needle.

RT (Right Twist, worked over 2 sts):

RS: Knit 2nd stitch on the left-hand needle, leaving it on the needle, then knit first stitch and drop both stitches off needle.

WS (creates Right Twist with knit stitches on the RS): Purl 2nd stitch on the left-hand needle, leaving it on the needle, then purl first stitch and drop both stitches off needle.

Body

Using circular needle, *CO 42 (47, 53, 58, 64, 69, 74) sts, pm for beg cable, CO 11 sts, pm for end cable, CO 41 (46, 52, 57, 63, 68, 73) sts**, pm for left side, rep from * to **—188 (208, 232, 252, 276, 296, 316) sts. Pm for right side/beg of rnd and join for working in the rnd, taking care not to twist sts.

Note: Each side m is placed just before st that falls at side of garment.

Ribbing:

SIZES XS, L, 1X, AND 3X ONLY

*[P1, k1b] to beg cable m, work Row 1 of Cable chart over 11 sts, [k1b, p1] to 1 st before side m, k1b**, rep from * to **.

SIZES S, M, AND 2X ONLY

*[K1b, p1] to 1 st before beg cable m, k1b, work Row 1 of Cable chart over 11 sts, [k1b, p1] to side m**, rep from * to **.

ALL SIZES

Cont patt as est for 4 more rnds (working subsequent rows of Cable chart on each rnd).

Next rnd: *Work in St st (knit) to beg cable m, work Cable chart over 11 sts, work in St st to side m**, rep from * to **.

Work 1 more rnd in patt as est.

Dec rnd: *K6, k2tog, work in patt to 7 sts before side m, ssk, k5**, rep from * to **—4 sts dec'd.

Rep Dec rnd every 6th rnd 5 more times—164 (184, 208, 228, 252, 272, 292) sts rem.

Work even in patt for 13 rnds.

Inc rnd: *K6, M1R, work in patt to 5 sts before side m, M1L, k5**, rep from * to **—4 sts inc'd.

Rep Inc rnd every 14th rnd 2 more times—176 (196, 220, 240, 264, 284, 304) sts. Last rnd worked should have been Row 10 of Cable chart.

Work 2 more rnds even in patt.

Next rnd: Work in patt to left side m (cont to work Cable chart as est), work in patt to 22 sts before beg cable m, pm for beg Inset, work in patt to 22 sts after end cable m, pm for end Inset, work in patt to end.

Est Inset patt: Work in patt to beg Inset m, work Row 1 of Inset chart over next 55 sts (1 st dec'd), work in patt to end.

Cont to work in patt as est for 11 (9, 7, 7, 7, 7, 7) more rnds, stopping 3 (4, 5, 6, 7, 8, 9) sts before end of final rnd; next Inset chart row should be Row 13 (11, 9, 9, 9, 9, 9).

Divide for Front/Back: *BO next 7 (9, 11, 13, 15, 17, 19) sts (remove m)**, work in patt to 3 (4, 5, 6, 7, 8, 9) sts before side m, rep from * to **, work in patt to end—81 (89, 99, 107, 117, 125, 133) sts rem in Back, 80 (88, 98, 106, 116, 124, 132) sts rem in Front.

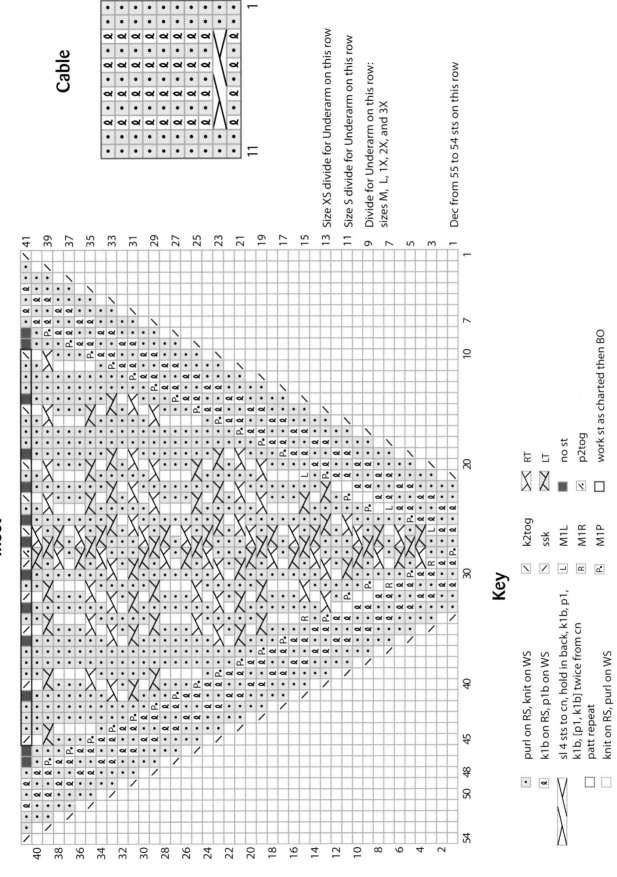

Cable

Inset

Size XS divide for Underarm on this row

Size S divide for Underarm on this row

Divide for Underarm on this row: sizes M, L, 1X, 2X, and 3X

Dec from 55 to 54 sts on this row

Key

•	purl on RS, knit on WS	⟋	k2tog
ℚ	k1b on RS, p1b on WS	⟍	ssk
⟋⟍	sl 4 sts to cn, hold in back, k1b, p1, k1b, [p1, k1b] twice from cn	L	M1L
		R	M1R
☐	patt repeat	P•	M1P
☐	knit on RS, purl on WS		

⟋	k2tog	⟋⟍	RT
⟍	ssk	⟍⟋	LT
L	M1L	■	no st
R	M1R	⸚	p2tog
P•	M1P	☐	work st as charted then BO

Front

Turn and cont to work Front sts only (place Back sts on holder).

Shape armholes:
Dec row (WS): P1, ssp, work in patt to last 3 sts, p2tog, p1—2 sts dec'd.
Dec row (RS): K1, k2tog, work in patt to last 3 sts, ssk, k1—2 sts dec'd.
Rep last 2 rows 0 (0, 0, 1, 1, 5, 7) more times, then rep Dec row (RS) every RS row 3 (5, 7, 7, 9, 5, 5) more times (work even on WS rows), then rep Dec row (RS) every 4th row 1 more time—68 (72, 78, 82, 88, 88, 88) sts rem.
Cont to work even in patt until 40 rows of Inset chart have been completed, ending after a WS row.
Next row (RS): Work in patt to beg Inset m, remove m, work Sts 1–7 of Row 41 of Inset chart; work Sts 10–48 of Row 41 *and* BO each st after working it according to chart, until 1 st rem at tip of right-hand needle; work in patt to end of row (remove m)—13 sts dec'd in Inset, 14 (16, 19, 21, 24, 24, 24) sts rem in Left and Right Front. Turn and cont to work Right Front only (place Left Front sts on holder).

Right Front

SIZES M, L, 1X, 2X, AND 3X ONLY
Next row (WS): Purl to last 6 sts, k2, [p1b, k1] twice.
Next row (RS): [P1, k1b] twice, p2, ssk, work in patt to end—1 st dec'd.
Rep last 2 rows - (-, 0, 0, 1, 1, 1) more times— - (-, 18, 20, 22, 22, 22) sts rem.

ALL SIZES
Next row (WS): Purl to last 6 sts, k2, [p1b, k1] twice.
Next row (RS): [P1, k1b] twice, p2, knit to end.
Rep last 2 rows 10 (11, 11, 13, 14, 15, 17) more times, then work one more row (WS) in patt. Break yarn, leaving 30"/75 cm long tail for three-needle bind-off, and place rem 14 (16, 18, 20, 22, 22, 22) sts on holder for right shoulder.

Left Front

Place held Left Front sts on straight needle or dpn and join yarn to work WS.

SIZES M, L, 1X, 2X, AND 3X ONLY
Next row (WS): [K1, p1b] twice, k2, purl to end.
Next row (RS): Work in patt to last 8 sts, k2tog, p2, [k1b, p1] twice—1 st dec'd.
Rep last 2 rows - (-, 0, 0, 1, 1, 1) more times— - (-, 18, 20, 22, 22, 22) sts rem.

ALL SIZES
Next row (WS): [K1, p1b] twice, k2, purl to end.
Next row (RS): Knit to last 6 sts, p2, [k1b, p1] twice.
Rep last 2 rows 10 (11, 11, 13, 14, 15, 17) more times, then work one more row (WS) in patt. Break yarn, leaving 30"/75 cm long tail for three-needle bind-off, and place rem 14 (16, 18, 20, 22, 22, 22) sts on holder for left shoulder.

Back

Place held Back sts on circular needle and join yarn to work WS.

Note: Armhole and back neck shaping are worked AT THE SAME TIME; read through entire section before continuing.

Armhole shaping:
Dec row (WS): P1, ssp, work in patt to last 3 sts, p2tog, p1—2 sts dec'd.
Dec row (RS): K1, k2tog, work in patt to last 3 sts, ssk, k1—2 sts dec'd.
Rep last 2 rows 0 (0, 0, 1, 1, 5, 7) more times, then rep Dec row (RS) every RS row 1 (2, 3, 2, 7, 3, 1) more times (work even on WS rows)— 75 (81, 89, 95, 95, 95, 99) sts rem.
Work 1 more row even (WS). Next row should be Row 2 (cable cross row) of Cable chart.

Divide for Left/Right Back:
RS: K1, k2tog, work in patt to 2 sts before beg cable m, k2tog, remove m, work Row 2 of Cable patt, ssk, work in patt to last 3 sts, ssk, k1—4 sts dec'd, 71 (77, 85, 91, 91, 91, 95) sts.
Next row (WS): Work to end cable m, remove m, k2, p1b, k1, p1b, M1L; turn and cont to work 36 (39, 43, 46, 46, 46, 48) Left Back sts only

(place rem 36 [39, 43, 46, 46, 46, 48] sts on holder for Right Back).

Left Back

Armhole/Neck Dec row (RS): [P1, k1b] twice, p2, ssk, work in patt to last 3 sts, ssk, k1—2 sts dec'd.

Next row (WS): Purl to last 6 sts, k2, [p1b, k1] twice.

Rep last 2 rows 0 (1, 2, 3, 0, 0, 2) more times—34 (35, 37, 38, 44, 44, 42) sts rem.

Neck Dec row (RS): [P1, k1b] twice, p2, ssk, knit to end—1 st dec'd.

Work 1 row even in patt (WS), then rep Armhole/Neck Dec row (RS)—2 sts dec'd, 31 (32, 34, 35, 41, 41, 39) sts rem.

Work 1 row even (WS) in patt, then work Neck Dec row (RS)—1 st dec'd.

Rep last 2 rows 16 (15, 15, 14, 18, 18, 16) more times—14 (16, 18, 20, 22, 22, 22) sts rem.

Work even in patt for 5 (7, 7, 11, 3, 5, 9) more rows, ending after a WS row. Break yarn, leaving 30"/75 cm long tail for three-needle bind-off, and place sts on holder for left shoulder.

Right Back

Place held Right Back sts on straight needle or dpn and join yarn to work WS.

Next row (WS): [K1, p1b] twice, k2, purl to end.

Armhole/Neck Dec row (RS): K1, k2tog, work in patt to last 8 sts, k2tog, p2, [k1b, p1] twice—2 sts dec'd.

Rep last 2 rows 0 (1, 2, 3, 0, 0, 2) more times—34 (35, 37, 38, 44, 44, 42) sts rem. Work 1 row even in patt (WS).

Neck Dec row (RS): Knit to last 8 sts, k2tog, p2, [k1b, p1] twice—1 st dec'd.

Work 1 row even in patt (WS), then rep Armhole/Neck Dec row (RS)—2 sts dec'd, 31 (32, 34, 35, 41, 41, 39) sts rem.

Work 1 row even (WS) in patt, then work Neck Dec row (RS)—1 st dec'd.

Rep last 2 rows 16 (15, 15, 14, 18, 18, 16) more times—14 (16, 18, 20, 22, 22, 22) sts rem.

Work even in patt for 5 (7, 7, 11, 3, 5, 9) more rows, ending after a WS row. Break yarn, leaving 30"/75 cm long tail for three-needle bind-off; leave sts on needle.

Finished Measurements

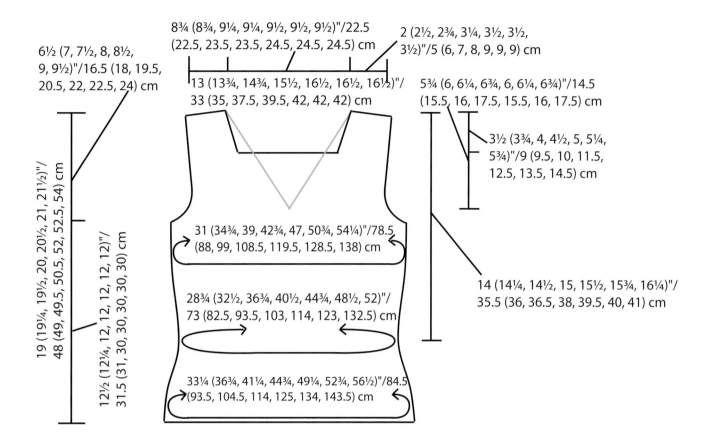

6½ (7, 7½, 8, 8½, 9, 9½)"/16.5 (18, 19.5, 20.5, 22, 22.5, 24) cm

8¾ (8¾, 9¼, 9¼, 9½, 9½, 9½)"/22.5 (22.5, 23.5, 23.5, 24.5, 24.5, 24.5) cm

2 (2½, 2¾, 3¼, 3½, 3½, 3½)"/5 (6, 7, 8, 9, 9, 9) cm

13 (13¾, 14¾, 15½, 16½, 16½, 16½)"/33 (35, 37.5, 39.5, 42, 42, 42) cm

5¾ (6, 6¼, 6¾, 6, 6¼, 6¾)"/14.5 (15.5, 16, 17.5, 15.5, 16, 17.5) cm

3½ (3¾, 4, 4½, 5, 5¼, 5¾)"/9 (9.5, 10, 11.5, 12.5, 13.5, 14.5) cm

19 (19¼, 19½, 20, 20½, 21, 21½)"/48 (49, 49.5, 50.5, 52, 52.5, 54) cm

12½ (12¼, 12, 12, 12, 12, 12)"/31.5 (31, 30, 30, 30, 30, 30) cm

31 (34¾, 39, 42¾, 47, 50¾, 54¼)"/78.5 (88, 99, 108.5, 119.5, 128.5, 138) cm

28¾ (32½, 36¾, 40½, 44¾, 48½, 52)"/73 (82.5, 93.5, 103, 114, 123, 132.5) cm

14 (14¼, 14½, 15, 15½, 15¾, 16¼)"/35.5 (36, 36.5, 38, 39.5, 40, 41) cm

33¼ (36¾, 41¼, 44¾, 49¼, 52¾, 56½)"/84.5 (93.5, 104.5, 114, 125, 134, 143.5) cm

Finishing

Turn garment inside out. Place held Right Front sts on 2nd needle.

Join shoulders using three-needle bind-off: Insert a third needle into first st on each of these 2 needles and knit these 2 sts together, using one of long yarn tails. *Knit next st on each needle the same way, then pass first st on right-hand needle over second st—1 st bound off. Repeat from * until 1 st is left on the right-hand needle, then pull yarn tail through last st.

Left shoulder: Place held Left Back and Left Front sts on 2 needles and join as for right shoulder.

Armhole Edging

Using shorter circular needle or dpns and starting at center of underarm, pick up and knit 4 (5, 6, 7, 8, 9, 10) sts (one for each BO st), *38 (41, 44, 47, 50, 52, 55) sts along armhole edge (approx 3 sts for every 4 rows)**, 1 st at shoulder seam; rep from * to **, pick up 3 (4, 5, 6, 7, 8, 9) sts (one for each BO st)—84 (92, 100, 108, 116, 122, 130) sts. Pm and join to work in the round.

Ribbing: [K1b, p1] to end of rnd.

Work in patt as est for 2 more rnds.

Next rnd: BO all sts loosely in patt.

Weave in ends and block to finished measurements.

Memphis

Columns of eyelets from hem to waist and narrow I-cord ties allow the sides of this tunic to be gathered, adjusting its length. The back is narrower than the front, which causes the front neck to drape after the shoulders are seamed. The yarn is worked at a loose gauge to create a lightweight fabric with lots of drape.

SKILL LEVEL
Easy: Skills include eyelets, decreases, and I-cord.

SIZES
Women's XS (S, M, L, 1X, 2X, 3X)

FINISHED MEASUREMENTS
Bust: 31 (35, 39, 43, 47, 51, 55)"/78.5 (89, 99, 109, 119.5, 129.5, 139.5) cm. *Shown in size S with +1"/2.5 cm ease. Intended to fit with 0"/0 cm to +4"/10 cm ease at bust.*

YARN
510 (580, 650, 730, 800, 880, 960) yd/470 (540, 600, 675, 740, 810, 885) m light weight #3 yarn; shown in #20 Bird of Paradise, Cascade Yarns Sunseeker Shade; 50% cotton, 50% acrylic; 246 yd/225 m per 3½ oz/100 g skein, 3 (3, 3, 4, 4, 4, 5) skeins

NEEDLES
US 10/6.0 mm 24–40"/60–100 cm circular needle, depending on selected garment size, for Body; double-pointed needles (dpns), for I-cord. *Adjust needle size if necessary to obtain correct gauge.*

NOTIONS
- Stitch markers
- Tapestry needle

GAUGE
16 sts and 21 rnds in St st = 4"/10 cm square, blocked

PATTERN NOTES
- Worked in the round to the armholes.

CUSTOMIZING FIT

Body is worked even after the last eyelet round to the underarms, so length can easily be changed by adding or subtracting rounds in this section. Width of shoulders can also be changed: simply include more or fewer stitches in each shoulder seam.

SPECIAL STITCHES

LT (Left Twist, worked over 2 sts):
RS: Knit 2nd stitch on the left-hand needle through the back loop, leaving it on the needle, then knit first stitch and drop both stitches off needle.

RT (Right Twist, worked over 2 sts):
RS: Knit 2nd stitch on the left-hand needle, leaving it on the needle, then knit first stitch and drop both stitches off needle.

Body

CO 140 (156, 172, 188, 204, 220, 236) sts. Pm and join for working in the rnd, taking care not to twist sts.

Set-up rnd: K70 (78, 86, 94, 102, 110, 118), pm, k70 (78, 86, 94, 102, 110, 118).

Cont to work in St st for 6 more rnds.

Eyelet rnd: K2, [k2tog, yo] twice, work in patt to 6 sts before m, [yo, ssk] twice, k2, sm, work in patt to end.

Work even in St st for 5 rnds.

Dec and Eyelet rnd: K2, [k2tog, yo] twice, k3, k2tog, work in patt to 11 sts before m, ssk, k3, [yo, ssk] twice, k2, sm, k9, k2tog, work in patt to 11 sts before m, ssk, k9—4 sts dec'd.

Work even in St st for 5 rnds.

Rep last 12 rnds 3 more times—124 (140, 156, 172, 188, 204, 220) sts rem.

Work even for 45 more rnds, stopping 1 st before end of final rnd; piece should measure approx 19"/48.5 cm from CO.

Next rnd: Work RT with last st of previous rnd and first st of new rnd, replacing m between 2 sts just worked; work in patt to one st before right side m; work LT with sts before and after m, replacing m between 2 sts just worked; work in patt to end.

Divide for Front and Back/Shape armholes:
Armhole Dec row (RS): K1, k2tog, work in patt to 3 sts before right-side marker, ssk, k1—2 sts dec'd. Turn and continue to work rem 60 (68, 76, 84, 92, 100, 108) Front sts only (remove m and place 62 [70, 78, 86, 94, 102, 110] Back sts on holder).

Armhole Dec row (WS): P1, ssp, purl to 3 sts before end, p2tog, p1—2 sts dec'd.

Rep these two rows 0 (0, 0, 0, 1, 2, 4) more times, then rep RS dec row 1 (3, 5, 7, 7, 9, 9) more times (work even in patt on WS rows)—56 (60, 64, 68, 72, 72, 72) sts.

Work even for 33 (31, 29, 29, 29, 25, 25) more rows, ending after a WS row.

Next row (RS): BO all sts in patt and break yarn, leaving 30"/75 cm long tail.

Back

Place 62 (70, 78, 86, 94, 102, 110) Back sts on needle and join yarn to work RS.

Armhole Dec row (RS): K1, k2tog, work in patt to 3 sts before right-side marker, ssk, k1—2 sts dec'd.

Armhole Dec row (WS): P1, ssp, purl to 3 sts before end, p2tog, p1—2 sts dec'd.

Rep these two rows 0 (1, 2, 3, 4, 5, 7) more times, then rep RS dec row 6 (8, 10, 11, 11, 14, 14) more times (work even in patt on WS rows), then rep RS dec row every 4th row 4 (3, 2, 2, 2, 1, 1) more times—38 (40, 42, 44, 48, 48, 48) sts.

Work even for 7 (7, 7, 7, 7, 5, 5) more rows, ending after a WS row.

Next row (RS): BO all sts in patt and break yarn, leaving 30"/75 cm long tail.

Finishing

With right sides facing, use one of long yarn tails and tapestry needle to sew last 7 (7, 8, 8, 9, 9, 9) BO sts of Front to first 7 (7, 8, 8, 9, 9, 9) BO sts of Back. Repeat for last 7 (7, 8, 8, 9, 9, 9) BO sts of Back and first 7 (7, 8, 8, 9, 9, 9) BO sts of Front.

Weave in ends and block to finished measurements.

Finished Measurements

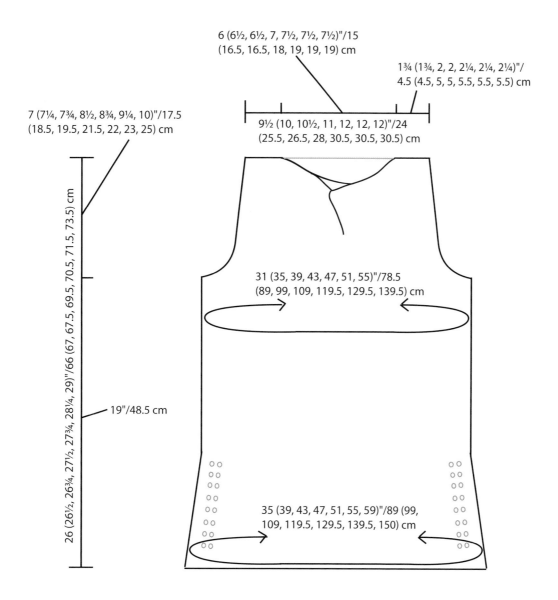

6 (6½, 6½, 7, 7½, 7½, 7½)"/15 (16.5, 16.5, 18, 19, 19, 19) cm

1¾ (1¾, 2, 2, 2¼, 2¼, 2¼)"/ 4.5 (4.5, 5, 5, 5.5, 5.5, 5.5) cm

7 (7¼, 7¾, 8½, 8¾, 9¼, 10)"/17.5 (18.5, 19.5, 21.5, 22, 23, 25) cm

9½ (10, 10½, 11, 12, 12, 12)"/24 (25.5, 26.5, 28, 30.5, 30.5, 30.5) cm

31 (35, 39, 43, 47, 51, 55)"/78.5 (89, 99, 109, 119.5, 129.5, 139.5) cm

26 (26½, 26¾, 27½, 27¾, 28¼, 29)"/66 (67, 67.5, 69.5, 70.5, 71.5, 73.5) cm

19"/48.5 cm

35 (39, 43, 47, 51, 55, 59)"/89 (99, 109, 119.5, 129.5, 139.5, 150) cm

I-cord (make 2)

Using dpns, CO 2 sts. *K2, then without turning work, slide sts to opposite end of needle. Rep from * until cord measures 24–30"/60–75 cm long. BO sts, break yarn and weave in ends.

*Starting on RS, pass ends of I-cord through top eyelets to WS, then through next pair of eyelets to RS. Rep from * 3 more times.

Optional: Use tapestry needle and length of yarn to sew top of I-cord to Body, 4–5 rows above top pairs of eyelets.

Gather sides along I-cords to desired length, then tie I-cord ends in a bow or knot.

Monterey

This empire-waisted tank showcases a flirty textured lace skirt, paired with a flattering overlapped deep V-neck. Wear it over another layer, or on its own if you are feeling adventurous.

SKILL LEVEL

Intermediate: Skills include reading charts, lace knitting, short rows, and three-needle bind-off. See Techniques section beginning on page 146 for a photo tutorial on working short rows.

SIZES

Women's XS (S, M, L, 1X, 2X, 3X)

FINISHED MEASUREMENTS

Bust: 31¼ (34, 36¾, 39¾, 45¼, 50, 53½)"/79.5 (86.5, 93.5, 100.5, 115, 127, 136) cm. *Shown in size S with -1"/2.5 cm ease. Intended to fit with -2"/5 cm to +2"/5 cm ease at bust.*

YARN

720 (800, 880, 960, 1110, 1240, 1330) yd/665 (740, 810, 895, 1020, 1140, 1225) m fine weight #2 yarn; shown in #27-09 Lavender; Premier Yarns Cotton Fair; 52% cotton, 48% acrylic; 317 yd/290 m per 3½ oz/100 g skein, 3 (3, 3, 4, 4, 5, 5) skeins

NEEDLES

US 6/4.0 mm 24–40"/60–100 cm circular needle, depending on selected garment size, for Body and Neck edging; 16–20"/40–50 cm circular needle, for armhole edgings. *Adjust needle size if necessary to obtain correct gauge.*

NOTIONS

- Stitch markers
- Stitch holders
- Tapestry needle

GAUGE

23 sts and 28 rnds in St st = 4"/10 cm square, blocked; 22 sts and 28 rnds in lace patt = 4"/10 cm, blocked

PATTERN NOTES

- Worked in the round to the end of the ribbed band
- Neck and armhole edgings are added after shoulders are joined using three-needle bind-off
- Instructions for hem ruffle pattern are given in written and chart form
- Instructions for lace pattern are given in chart form only

CUSTOMIZING FIT

- Lace "skirt" length can easily be changed in increments of 24 rows (full repeat of lace pattern) or 3½"/8.5 cm.
- It is important for proper fit that the ribbed band lies under the bust. See Bodice section for instructions for customizing for different bra cup sizes.
- Purchase extra yarn if working modifications for larger bra cup sizes.

SPECIAL STITCHES

Knitted Cast-on: Turn work to WS and using working yarn, *K1 st, then return st to left-hand needle, taking care not to twist it: 1 st cast on. Rep from * until required number of sts has been cast on.

Body

Using longer circular needle, CO 360 (396, 432, 468, 504, 540, 576) sts. Pm for side/beg of rnd and join, taking care not to twist sts.

Ruffle Rnd 1: [K7, s2kp, k8] 20 (22, 24, 26, 28, 30, 32) times to end of rnd—40 (44, 48, 52, 56, 60, 64) sts dec'd, 320 (352, 384, 416, 448, 480, 512) sts rem.

Ruffle Rnds 2, 4, 6, and 8: Knit.

Ruffle Rnd 3: [K6, s2kp, k7] 20 (22, 24, 26, 28, 30, 32) times—40 (44, 48, 52, 56, 60, 64) sts dec'd, 280 (308, 336, 364, 392, 420, 448) sts rem.

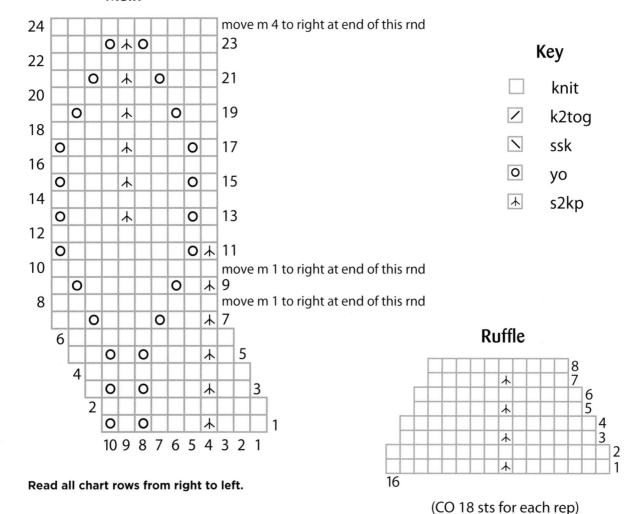

Main

move m 4 to right at end of this rnd (row 23/24)
move m 1 to right at end of this rnd (row 9/10)
move m 1 to right at end of this rnd (row 7/8)

Read all chart rows from right to left.

Key

□	knit
╱	k2tog
╲	ssk
⊙	yo
⋏	s2kp

Ruffle

(CO 18 sts for each rep)

Ruffle Rnd 5: [K5, s2kp, k6] 20 (22, 24, 26, 28, 30, 32) times—40 (44, 48, 52, 56, 60, 64) sts dec'd, 240 (264, 288, 312, 336, 360, 384) sts rem.

Ruffle Rnd 7: [K4, s2kp, k5] 20 (22, 24, 26, 28, 30, 32) times—40 (44, 48, 52, 56, 60, 64) sts dec'd, 200 (220, 240, 260, 280, 300, 320) sts rem.

Next rnd (Est lace patt): Work Row 1 of Main chart 20 (22, 24, 26, 28, 30, 32) times to end of rnd.

Cont to work patt as est until all 24 rows of Main chart have been completed. *Note:* At the end of rnds using chart Rows 8 and 10, stop 1 st before end of rnd, place new beg of rnd m, then beg next rnd (remove old beg of rnd m). At the end of rnds using chart Row 24, stop 4 sts before end of rnd, place new beg of rnd m, then beg next rnd (remove old beg of rnd m).

Work in patt as est for 58 more rnds, ending with chart Row 10; piece should measure approx 13"/33 cm from CO.

Next rnd (Dec rnd):

SIZES XS, S, M, AND L ONLY
[S2kp, k7] 20 (22, 24, 26, -, -, -) times to end of rnd—40 (44, 48, 52, -, -, -) sts dec'd, 160 (176, 192, 208, -, -, -) sts rem.

SIZE 1X ONLY
S2kp, k7, *s2kp, yo, k7, yo, [s2kp, k7] 3 times**; rep from * to ** twice more; s2kp, yo, k7, yo, s2kp, k7; rep from * to ** 3 more times; s2kp, yo, k7, yo— - (-, -, -, 40, -, -) sts dec'd, - (-, -, -, 240, -, -) sts rem.

SIZE 2X ONLY
*S2kp, k7, [s2kp, k7, s2kp, yo, k7, yo] 3 times**; rep from * to ** 2 more times; s2kp, k7, [s2kp, yo, k7, yo] 2 times, [s2kp, k7, s2kp, yo, k7, yo] 3 times— - (-, -, -, -, 32, -) sts dec'd, - (-, -, -, -, 268, -) sts rem.

SIZE 3X ONLY
[S2kp, k7, s2kp, yo, k7, yo] - (-, -, -, -, -, 16) times to end of rnd— - (-, -, -, -, -, 32) sts dec'd, - (-, -, -, -, -, 288) sts rem.

Ribbed Band

SIZES XS, S, M, L, 1X, AND 3X ONLY
[K1, p1] 40 (44, 48, 52, 60, -, 72) times, k1, place removable m for right side, [p1, k1] 39 [43, 47, 51, 59, -, 71) times, p1, place removable m for left side—81 (89, 97, 105, 121, -, 145) sts in Front, 79 (87, 95, 103, 119, -, 143) sts in Back.

SIZE 2X ONLY
[K1, p1] - (-, -, -, -, 66, -) times, k1, place removable m for right side, [p1, k1] - [-, -, -, -, 67, -) times, p1, place removable m for left side— - (-, -, -, -, 133, -) sts in Front, - (-, -, -, -, 135, -) sts in Back.

ALL SIZES
Work 4 more rnds in k1, p1 rib as est, then BO all sts in patt. Break yarn and weave end through first BO st so that BO edge appears unbroken.

Bodice

Using longer circular needle, with RS facing, leaving 36"/90 cm long tail, and beg 33 (36, 38, 39, 47, 52, 58) sts after left side m, pick up and knit one st for every BO st by inserting needle through the center of each st just below BO edge, then turn work and CO 15 (17, 21, 27, 27, 29, 29) sts using knitted cast-on—175 (193, 213, 235, 267, 297, 317) sts, 48 (53, 59, 66, 74, 81, 87) sts in each front section, 79 (87, 95, 103, 119, 135, 143) sts in Back. Do not join.

Next row (WS): Purl.

Note: Choose only one of three Inc row options (for A/B Cup, C Cup, or D Cup) below!

Inc row for A/B Cup (as shown):

SIZES XS, S, AND M ONLY
RS: Ssk, k16 (21, 25, -, -, -, -), *[M1R, k3] 3 times, [M1L, k3] twice, M1L**, k15 (15, 17, -, -, -, -), sm, inc 8 sts evenly spaced across Back sts, sm, k15 (15, 17, -, -, -, -), rep from * to **, k16 (21, 25, -, -, -, -), k2tog—1 st dec'd at each neck edge, 6 sts inc'd in each Front section, 8 sts inc'd in Back.

SIZES L, 1X, 2X, AND 3X ONLY
RS: Ssk, k - (-, -, 25, 31, 36, 40), *[M1R, k4] 3 times, [M1L, k4] twice, M1L**, k - (-, -, 19, 21, 23, 25), sm, inc 8 sts evenly spaced across Back sts, sm, k - (-, -, 19, 21, 23, 25), rep from * to **, k - (-, -, 25, 31, 36, 40), k2tog—1 st dec'd at each neck edge, 6 sts inc'd in each Front section, 8 sts inc'd in Back.

Inc row for C Cup:

SIZES XS, S, AND M ONLY
RS: Ssk, k16 (21, 25, -, -, -, -), *[M1R, k2] 5 times, [M1L, k2] 4 times, M1L**, k12 (12, 14, -, -, -, -), sm, inc 8 sts evenly spaced across Back sts, sm, k12 (12, 14, -, -, -, -), rep from * to **, k16 (21, 25, -, -, -, -), k2tog—1 st dec'd at each neck edge, 10 sts inc'd in each Front section, 8 sts inc'd in Back.

SIZES L, 1X, 2X, AND 3X ONLY
RS: Ssk, k - (-, -, 26, 32, 37, 41), *[M1R, k2, M1R, k3] twice, M1R, k2, [M1L, k3, M1L, k2] twice, M1L**, k - (-, -, 16, 18, 20, 22), sm, inc 8 sts evenly spaced across Back sts, sm, k - (-, -, 16, 18, 20, 22), rep from * to **, k - (-, -, 25, 32, 36, 40), k2tog—1 st dec'd at each neck edge, 10 sts inc'd in each Front section, 8 sts inc'd in Back.

Inc row for D Cup:

ALL SIZES
RS: Ssk, k10 (15, 19, 24, 30, 35, 39), *[M1R, k2] 7 times, [M1L, k2] 6 times, M1L**, k10 (10, 12, 14, 16, 18, 20), sm, inc 8 sts evenly spaced across Back sts, sm, k10 (10, 12, 14, 16, 18, 20), rep from * to **, k10 (15, 19, 24, 30, 35, 39), k2tog—1 st dec'd at each neck edge, 14 sts inc'd in each Front section, 8 sts inc'd in Back.

ALL SIZES/CUP SIZES
Work 2 rows even in St st.

Neck Dec row (WS): P2tog, work in patt to last 2 sts, ssp—1 st dec'd at each neck edge.
Work 2 rows even in St st.
Neck Dec row (RS): Ssk, work in patt to last 2 sts, k2tog—1 st dec'd at each neck edge.
Cont to alternate WS and RS Neck Dec rows every 3rd row; AT THE SAME TIME, on 28th (30th, 32nd, 34th, 34th, 34th, 34th) Bodice row, divide for Front and Back (RS): Work in patt to 3 (4, 5, 6, 8, 10, 12) sts before m, BO 5 (7, 9, 11, 15, 19, 23) sts (remove m), work in patt to 2 (3, 4, 5, 7, 9, 11) sts before m, BO 5 (7, 9, 11, 15, 19, 23) sts (remove m), work in patt to end. Turn and cont to work Left Front sts only (place rem sts on holder for Back and Right Front).

Left Front

Note: Continue to work Neck Dec row every 3rd row.

Armhole Dec row (WS): Work in patt to last 3 sts, p2tog, p1.
Armhole Dec row (RS): K1, k2tog, work in patt to end.

A/B CUP ONLY
Rep these 2 rows 0 (0, 1, 1, 4, 6, 8) more times.

C CUP ONLY
Rep these 2 rows 2 (2, 3, 3, 6, 8, 10) more times.

D CUP ONLY
Rep these 2 rows 4 (4, 5, 5, 8, 10, 12) more times.

ALL CUP SIZES
Rep Armhole Dec row (RS) every RS row 10 (12, 10, 10, 8, 8, 8) more times (work even at armhole edge on WS rows), then work even at armhole edge (cont to work Neck Dec row every 3rd row) until a total of 42 (46, 50, 54, 58, 62, 64) Left Front rows have been worked after armhole BO row, ending after a RS row.

Beg short row (SR) shoulder shaping (cont to work Neck dec every 3rd row as needed):
SR 1 (WS): Work in patt to last 5 (5, 6, 7, 7, 7, 7) sts, W&T.
SR 2 (RS): Work in patt to end.
SR 3 (WS): Work 4 (4, 5, 6, 6, 6, 6) sts in patt, W&T.

SR 4 (RS): Work in patt to end.

Next row (WS): Work in patt to end, picking up wraps and working tog with wrapped sts.

Work one more row in patt, then break yarn and place rem 13 (14, 17, 20, 21, 21, 21) sts on holder.

Right Front

Join yarn to work WS of Right Front (continue to work Neck dec every 3rd row).

Armhole Dec row (WS): P1, ssp, work in patt to end.

Armhole Dec row (RS): Work in patt to last 3 sts, ssk, k1.

A/B CUP ONLY

Rep these 2 rows 0 (0, 1, 1, 4, 6, 8) more times.

C CUP ONLY

Rep these 2 rows 2 (2, 3, 3, 6, 8, 10) more times.

D CUP ONLY

Rep these 2 rows 4 (4, 5, 5, 8, 10, 12) more times.

ALL CUP SIZES

Rep Armhole Dec row (RS) every RS row 10 (12, 10, 10, 8, 8, 8) more times (work even at armhole edge on WS rows), then work even at armhole edge (cont to work Neck Dec row every 3rd row) until a total of 43 (47, 51, 55, 59, 63, 65) Right Front rows have been worked after armhole BO row, ending after a WS row.

Beg short row shoulder shaping:

SR 1 (RS): Work in patt to last 5 (5, 6, 7, 7, 7, 7) sts, W&T.

SR 2 (WS): Work in patt to end.

SR 3 (RS): Work 4 (4, 5, 6, 6, 6, 6) sts in patt, W&T.

SR 4 (WS): Work in patt to end.

Next row (RS): Work in patt to end, picking up wraps and working tog with wrapped sts. Break yarn, leaving 30"/75 cm long tail for three-needle bind-off, and place rem 13 (14, 17, 20, 21, 21, 21) sts on holder.

Back

Join yarn to work WS of Back.

Dec row (WS): P1, ssp, work in patt to last 3 sts, p2tog, p1—2 sts dec'd.

Dec row (RS): K1, k2tog, work in patt to last 3 sts, ssk, k1—2 sts dec'd.

Rep these 2 rows 0 (0, 1, 1, 4, 6, 8) more times, then rep Dec row (RS) every RS row 8 (10, 8, 8, 9, 8, 6) more times—63 (65, 71, 77, 81, 81, 81) sts rem.

Work even until a total of 42 (46, 50, 54, 58, 62, 64) Back rows have been worked, ending on a RS row.

SR 1 (WS): Work in patt to last 5 (5, 6, 7, 7, 7, 7) sts, W&T.

SR 2 (RS): Work in patt to last 5 (5, 6, 7, 7, 7, 7) sts, W&T.

SR 3 (WS): Work in patt to 4 (5, 6, 7, 8, 8, 8) sts before last wrapped st, W&T.

SR 4 (RS): Work in patt to 4 (5, 6, 7, 8, 8, 8) sts before last wrapped st, W&T.

Next row (WS): Work in patt to end, picking up wraps and working tog with wrapped sts.

Next row (RS): Work 13 (14, 17, 20, 21, 21, 21) sts in patt, BO next 37 (37, 37, 37, 39, 39, 39) sts, work rem 13 (14, 17, 20, 21, 21, 21) in patt, picking up wraps and working tog with wrapped sts. Break yarn, leaving 30"/75 cm long tail for three-needle bind-off.

Finishing

Turn work inside out and place Front and Back sts for right shoulder on two needles or on opposite ends of circular needle, with points of needle(s) at armhole edge of shoulder.

Join shoulders using three-needle bind-off: Insert a third needle into first st on each of these 2 needles and knit these 2 sts together, using long yarn tail from Front. *Knit next st on each needle the same way, then pass first st on right-hand needle over second st—1 st bound off. Repeat from * until 1 st is left on the right-hand needle, then pull yarn tail through last st.

Repeat for left shoulder, using long yarn tail from Back.

Using tapestry needle, pass long yarn tail from start of Bodice to WS, and use it to tack knitted-on sts at base of Left Front to top edge of ribbed band. Weave in ends and block to finished measurements.

Armhole Edging

Using shorter circular needle, with RS facing and starting at shoulder seam, pick up and knit

Finished Measurements

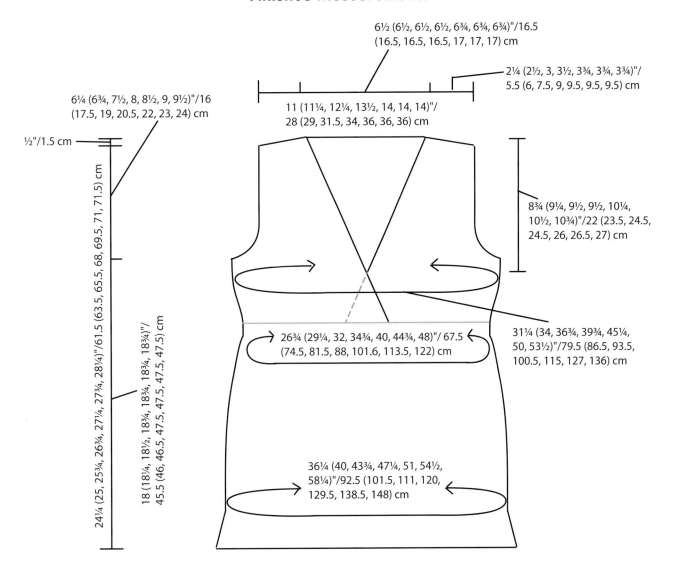

6½ (6½, 6½, 6½, 6¾, 6¾, 6¾)"/16.5 (16.5, 16.5, 17, 17, 17) cm

2¼ (2½, 3, 3½, 3¾, 3¾, 3¾)"/ 5.5 (6, 7.5, 9, 9.5, 9.5, 9.5) cm

11 (11¼, 12¼, 13½, 14, 14, 14)"/ 28 (29, 31.5, 34, 36, 36, 36) cm

6¼ (6¾, 7½, 8, 8½, 9, 9½)"/16 (17.5, 19, 20.5, 22, 23, 24) cm

½"/1.5 cm

8¾ (9¼, 9½, 9½, 10¼, 10½, 10¾)"/22 (23.5, 24.5, 24.5, 26, 26.5, 27) cm

24¼ (25, 25¾, 26¾, 27¼, 27¾, 28¼)"/61.5 (63.5, 65.5, 68, 69.5, 71, 71.5) cm

18 (18¼, 18½, 18¾, 18¾, 18¾, 18¾)"/ 45.5 (46, 46.5, 47.5, 47.5, 47.5, 47.5) cm

26¾ (29¼, 32, 34¾, 40, 44¾, 48)"/ 67.5 (74.5, 81.5, 88, 101.6, 113.5, 122) cm

31¼ (34, 36¾, 39¾, 45¼, 50, 53½)"/79.5 (86.5, 93.5, 100.5, 115, 127, 136) cm

36¼ (40, 43¾, 47¼, 51, 54½, 58¼)"/92.5 (101.5, 111, 120, 129.5, 138.5, 148) cm

1 st at seam; 37 (40, 43, 46, 49, 52, 55) sts to underarm BO sts (approx 4 sts per 5 rows); 1 st for each BO st (5 [7, 9, 11, 15, 19, 23] sts); 37 (40, 43, 46, 49, 52, 55) sts to shoulder seam—80 (88, 96, 104, 114, 124, 134) sts. Pm and join.

Work 1 rnd in k1, p1 rib, dec'ing 1 st on either side of underarm BO sts—78 (86, 94, 102, 112, 122, 132) sts.

Next 3 rnds: [K1, p1] to end of rnd. BO all sts loosely in patt.

Neck Edging

Using longer circular needle, with RS facing and starting at bottom of Right Front neck edge, pick up and knit 59 (64, 69, 73, 76, 79, 81) sts to shoulder seam (approx 4 sts per 5 rows); 2 sts across seam; 1 st for each BO st (37 [37, 37, 37, 39, 39, 39] sts); 2 sts across seam; 59 (64, 69, 73, 76, 79, 81) sts to bottom of Left Front neck edge—159 (169, 179, 187, 195, 201, 205) sts.

Work 1 row (WS) in p1, k1 rib (beg and end with p1), dec'ing 6 sts evenly spaced across Back Neck—153 (163, 173, 181, 189, 195, 199) sts.

Next row (RS): [K1, p1] to last st, k1.

Next row (WS): [P1, k1] to last st, p1.

Work 1 more row in rib as est, then BO all sts loosely in patt.

Weave in ends, using yarn tails to tack side edges of neck ribbing to top edge of band ribbing. Block again as needed.

Odessa

This tunic showcases a lightly variegated ribbon yarn.
The yarn's colors and textures display differently in the lace and
stockinette sections, adding visual interest. A twisted cord
belt allows the wearer to easily adjust fit and length.

SKILL LEVEL

Intermediate: Skills include reading charts, lace knitting, short rows, and seaming. See Techniques section beginning on page 146 for a photo tutorial on working short rows.

SIZES

Women's XS (S, M, L, 1X, 2X)

FINISHED MEASUREMENTS

Bust: 32 (36½, 41¼, 45¾, 50¼, 54¾)"/81.5 (93, 104.5, 116, 127.5, 139.5) cm. *Shown in size S with +2½"/6.5 cm ease. Intended to fit with -2"/5 cm to +3"/7.5 cm ease at bust.*

YARN

830 (960, 1060, 1180, 1320, 1430) yd/765 (885, 975, 1085, 1215, 1315) m medium weight #4 yarn; shown in #1350 Maize, Classic Elite Yarns Sanibel; 58% viscose, 42% cotton; 125 yd/115 m per 1¾ oz/50 g skein, 7 (8, 9, 10, 11, 12) skeins

NEEDLES

US 8/5.0 mm 24"/60 cm or longer circular needle, to accommodate large number of sts. *Adjust needle size if necessary to obtain correct gauge.*

NOTIONS

- Stitch markers
- Stitch holders
- Tapestry needle

GAUGE

18 sts and 28 rows in St st or lace pattern = 4"/10 cm square, blocked

PATTERN NOTES

- Worked sideways in four pieces, from center front and center back out to sides
- Instructions for lace panels are given in written and chart form
- Because all edges are self-finished, new yarn is best joined not at edge of piece, but at transition from stockinette stitch to lace

CUSTOMIZING FIT

There is no waist shaping, so tunic length is easily changed: add/subtract stitches to stockinette stitch section and/or repeats to lace section.

SPECIAL STITCHES

Lace patt (worked over 6 sts and 8 rows):
Row 1 (RS): Yo, ssk, k1, k2tog, yo, k1.
Rows 2, 4, 6, and 8 (WS): Purl.
Row 3 (RS): K1, yo, s2kp, yo, k2.
Row 5 (RS): K2tog, yo, k1, yo, ssk, k1.
Row 7: (RS): Yo, k3, yo, s2kp.

Lace

6 5 4 3 2 1

Key

☐	knit on RS, purl on WS
╱	k2tog
╲	ssk
○	yo
⅄	s2kp
☐	patt repeat

Left Front

CO 122 (126, 126, 128, 128, 128) sts.
Set-up row (WS): P67 (71, 71, 73, 73, 73), pm, p55.
Row 1 (RS): K1, work Row 1 of Lace patt 9 times, sm, knit to last 4 sts, turn work (do not wrap next st).
Rows 2, 4, 6, and 8 (WS): Purl.
Row 3 (RS): K1, work Row 3 of Lace patt 9 times, sm, knit to last 2 sts, yo, k2tog.
Row 5 (RS): K1, work Row 5 of Lace patt 9 times, sm, knit to last 4 sts, turn work.
Row 7 (RS): K2tog, work Row 7 of Lace patt 8 times, yo, k3, yo, ssk, sm, knit to last 2 sts, yo, k2tog.
Rep last 8 rows 1 (2, 2, 2, 2, 2) more times, then work 4 (0, 0, 0, 0, 0) more rows in patt.

Shape neck:
Cont to work patt as est above and AT THE SAME TIME inc 1 st on each of the next 10 (10, 10, 10, 12, 12) RS rows as follows—132 (136, 136, 138, 140, 140) sts:
Inc row (RS Patt Rows 1 and 5): Work in patt to last 6 sts, M1R, k2, turn work—1 st inc'd.
Inc row (RS Patt Rows 3 and 7): Work in patt to last 6 sts, M1R, work in patt to end—1 st inc'd.

Shape shoulder:
After completing all Inc rows, work one WS row in patt (purl).
Next row (RS): Work to m in patt, sm, knit to end.
Next row (WS): Purl.
Dec row (RS): Work to m in patt, sm, knit to last 8 sts, k2tog, k6—1 st dec'd.
Rep Dec row every RS row 2 (2, 4, 5, 4, 5) more times—129 (133, 131, 132, 135, 134) sts.
Next row (WS): Purl.

Shape armhole:
Short row (SR) 1 (RS): Work 105 (115, 117, 121, 128, 133) sts in patt, W&T.
SR 2 (WS): Work in patt to end.
SR 3 (RS): Work to 4 (6, 6, 6, 6, 6) sts before last wrapped st, W&T.
SR 4 (WS): Work in patt to end.
SR 5 (RS): Work to 2 (4, 4, 4, 4, 4) sts before last wrapped st, W&T.
SR 6 (WS): Work in patt to end.

SR 7 (RS): Work to 2 (2, 4, 4, 4, 4) sts before last wrapped st, W&T.

SR 8 (WS): Work in patt to end.

SIZES S, M, L, 1X, AND 2X ONLY

SR 9 (RS): Work to - (2, 2, 2, 4) sts before last wrapped st, W&T.

SR 10 (WS): Work in patt to end.

SR 11 (RS): Work to 2 sts before last wrapped st, W&T.

SR 12 (WS): Work in patt to end. Rep last 2 rows - (2, 5, 8, 11) more times.

ALL SIZES

Next row (RS): BO all sts knitwise (for wrapped sts, pick up wrap and work tog with wrapped st, then BO). Break yarn.

Right Front

CO 122 (126, 126, 128, 128, 128) sts.

Set-up row (WS): P55, pm, p67 (71, 71, 73, 73, 73).

Row 1 (RS): Ssk, yo, knit to m, sm, k1, work Row 1 of Lace patt 9 times.

Rows 2 and 6 (WS): Purl to last 4 sts, turn work (do not wrap next st).

Row 3 (RS): Knit to m, sm, k1, work Row 3 of Lace patt 9 times.

Rows 4 and 8 (WS): Purl to end.

Row 5 (RS): Ssk, yo, knit to m, sm, k1, work Row 5 of Lace patt 9 times.

Row 7 (RS): Knit to m, sm, k2tog, work Row 7 of Lace patt 8 times, yo, k3, yo, ssk.

Rep last 8 rows 1 (2, 2, 2, 2, 2) more times, then work 4 (0, 0, 0, 0, 0) more rows in patt.

Shape neck:

Cont to work patt as est above and AT THE SAME TIME inc 1 st on each of the next 10 (10, 10, 10, 12, 12) RS rows as follows—132 (136, 136, 138, 140, 140) sts:

Inc row (RS Patt Rows 1 and 5): Ssk, yo, k4, M1L, work in patt to end—1 st inc'd.

Inc row (RS Patt Rows 3 and 7): K2, M1L, work in patt to end—1 st inc'd.

Shape shoulder:

After completing all Inc rows, work one WS row in patt (purl).

Next row (RS): Knit to m, sm, work in Lace patt as est to end.

Next row (WS): Purl.

Dec row (RS): K6, ssk, knit to m, sm, work in Lace patt as est to end—1 st dec'd.

Rep Dec row every RS row 2 (2, 4, 5, 4, 5) more times—129 (133, 131, 132, 135, 134) sts.

Shape armhole:

SR 1 (WS): Work 105 (115, 117, 121, 128, 133) sts in patt, W&T.

SR 2 (RS): Work in patt to end.

SR 3 (WS): Work to 4 (6, 6, 6, 6, 6) sts before last wrapped st, W&T.

SR 4 (RS): Work in patt to end.

SR 5 (WS): Work to 2 (4, 4, 4, 4, 4) sts before last wrapped st, W&T.

SR 6 (RS): Work in patt to end.

SR 7 (WS): Work to 2 (2, 4, 4, 4, 4) sts before last wrapped st, W&T.

SR 8 (RS): Work in patt to end.

SIZES S, M, L, 1X, AND 2X ONLY

SR 9 (WS): Work to - (2, 2, 2, 2, 4) sts before last wrapped st, W&T.

SR 10 (RS): Work in patt to end.

SR 11 (WS): Work to 2 sts before last wrapped st, W&T.

SR 12 (RS): Work in patt to end. Rep last 2 rows 0 (2, 5, 8, 11) more times.

ALL SIZES

Next row (WS): Purl, picking up wraps and working tog with wrapped sts.

Next row (RS): BO all sts knitwise (for wrapped sts, pick up wrap and work tog with wrapped st, then BO). Break yarn.

Right Back

CO 116 (118, 118, 120, 122, 122) sts.

Set-up row (WS): P61 (63, 63, 65, 67, 67), pm, p55.

Row 1 (RS): K1, work Row 1 of Lace patt 9 times, sm, knit to last 4 sts, turn work (do not wrap next st).

Rows 2, 4, 6, and 8 (WS): Purl.

Row 3 (RS): K1, work Row 3 of Lace patt 9 times, sm, knit to last 2 sts, yo, k2tog.

Row 5 (RS): K1, work Row 5 of Lace patt 9 times, sm, knit to last 4 sts, turn work.

Row 7 (RS): K2tog, work Row 1 of Lace patt 8 times, yo, k3, yo, ssk, sm, knit to last 2 sts, yo, k2tog.

Shape neck:

Next row: Cont to work patt as est above and AT THE SAME TIME inc 1 st on each of the next 16 (18, 18, 18, 18, 18) RS rows as follows—132 (136, 136, 138, 140, 140) sts.

Inc row (RS, Patt rows 1 and 5): Work in patt as est to last 6 sts, M1R, k2, turn work—1 st inc'd.

Inc row (RS Patt Rows 3 and 7): Work in patt to last 6 sts, M1R, work in patt to end—1 st inc'd.

Work rem of Right Back as for Left Front.

Left Back

CO 116 (118, 118, 120, 122, 122) sts.

Set-up row (WS): P55, pm, p61 (63, 63, 65, 67, 67).

Row 1 (RS): Ssk, yo, knit to m, sm, k1, work Row 1 of Lace patt 9 times.

Rows 2 and 6 (WS): Purl to last 4 sts, turn work (do not wrap next st).

Row 3 (RS): Knit to m, sm, k1, work Row 3 of Lace patt 9 times.

Rows 4 and 8 (WS): Purl to end.

Row 5 (RS): Ssk, yo, knit to m, sm, k1, work Row 5 of Lace patt 9 times.

Row 7 (RS): Knit to m, sm, k2tog, work Row 7 of Lace patt 8 times, yo, k3, yo, ssk.

Shape neck:

Next row: Cont to work patt as est above and AT THE SAME TIME inc 1 st on each of the next 16 (18, 18, 18, 18, 18) RS rows as follows—132 (136, 136, 138, 140, 140) sts.

Inc row (RS, Patt rows 1 and 5): Ssk, yo, k4, M1L, work in patt to end—1 st inc'd.

Inc row (RS Patt Rows 3 and 7): K2, M1L, work in patt to end—1 st inc'd.

Work rem of Left Back as for Right Front.

Finishing

Weave in ends and block pieces to finished measurements. Sew Left and Right Back pieces together at center back by whipstitching CO edges together, taking care to match top and bottom edges and stitch patterns (see photo below). Repeat for Left and Right Front, then sew side seams from lace/St st junction to underarm (leave lower sides open). Sew shoulder seams. Block again as needed.

Finished Measurements

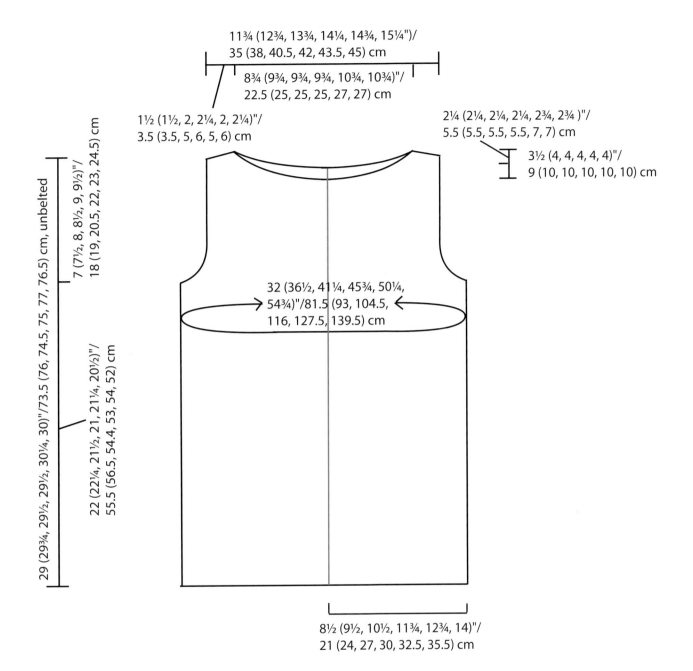

11¾ (12¾, 13¾, 14¼, 14¾, 15¼")/
35 (38, 40.5, 42, 43.5, 45) cm

8¾ (9¾, 9¾, 9¾, 10¾, 10¾)"/
22.5 (25, 25, 25, 27, 27) cm

1½ (1½, 2, 2¼, 2, 2¼)"/
3.5 (3.5, 5, 6, 5, 6) cm

2¼ (2¼, 2¼, 2¼, 2¾, 2¾)"/
5.5 (5.5, 5.5, 5.5, 7, 7) cm

3½ (4, 4, 4, 4, 4)"/
9 (10, 10, 10, 10, 10) cm

7 (7½, 8, 8½, 9, 9½)"/
18 (19, 20.5, 22, 23, 24.5) cm

29 (29¾, 29½, 29½, 30¼, 30)"/73.5 (76, 74.5, 75, 77, 76.5) cm, unbelted

22 (22¼, 21½, 21, 21¼, 20½)"/
55.5 (56.5, 54.4, 53, 54, 52) cm

32 (36½, 41¼, 45¾, 50¼,
54¾)"/81.5 (93, 104.5,
116, 127.5, 139.5) cm

8½ (9½, 10½, 11¾, 12¾, 14)"/
21 (24, 27, 30, 32.5, 35.5) cm

Twisted Cord Belt

Cut 4 strands of yarn, each 12 (12, 14, 16, 18, 20) yds/11 (11, 13, 15, 17, 19) m long. Knot the strands together close to one end and loop tied ends over chair leg or other fixed/heavy object to hold them in place. Knot opposite ends of yarn, insert a knitting needle, and twist the yarn by rotating needle while applying light tension, until entire length is twisted tightly and starts to kink when tension is relaxed. Fold yarn in half, applying light tension while allowing it to twist evenly on itself, and remove cord from chair leg. Remove knitting needle and knot both ends, leaving 2–3"/5–7.5 cm outside knots, and trim ends (removing original end knots). Beginning and ending at center front, thread cord through top row of lace eyelets.

Roanoke

This tank showcases a highly variegated linen yarn for the front and back diamond panels, with a more subtly variegated version of the yarn used for the body and straps. The body is worked down with regular increases, which give it an A-line shape. Instructions for two different lengths are given: hip length as shown, and tunic length (approximately 5"/12.5 cm longer). The drape and texture of this linen yarn benefit from machine washing and drying.

SKILL LEVEL

Easy to intermediate: Skills include working in the round, picking up stitches, knitted cast-on, and three-needle bind-off. See Techniques section beginning on page 146 for photo tutorials on picking up stitches and knitted cast-on.

SIZES

Women's XS (S, S-M, M, M-L, L-1X)

FINISHED MEASUREMENTS

Bust: 30 (32¾, 35¼, 38¾, 41¼, 43¼)"/76 (83, 89.5, 98.5, 105, 110) cm. *Shown in hip length in size S with +1¼"/3 cm ease. Intended to fit with -1½"/4 cm to +1½"/4 cm ease at bust.*

YARN

- **Color A (Diamonds):** 110 yd/100 m sport weight #2 yarn; shown in Collards & Grits, Claudia Hand Painted Yarns Drama; 100% linen; 270 yd/248 m per 3½ oz/100 g skein, 1 skein
- **Color B (Body), Hip length:** 610 (640, 700, 750, 810, 840) yd/560 (590, 645, 690, 745, 775) m sport weight #2 yarn; shown in Silver Shimmer, Claudia Hand Painted Yarns Drama; 100% linen; 270 yd/248 m per 3½ oz/100 g skein, 3 (3, 3, 3, 4, 4) skeins
- **Color B (Body), Tunic length:** 770 (820, 880, 950, 1020, 1060) yd/710 (755, 810, 875, 940, 975) m sport weight #2 yarn; shown in Silver Shimmer, Claudia Hand Painted Yarns Drama; 100% linen; 270 yd/248 m per 3½ oz/100 g skein, 3 (4, 4, 4, 4, 5) skeins

Note: This yarn may be machine dried, which softens the fabric.

NEEDLES

US 2/2.75 mm 24"/60 cm circular and double-pointed needles (dpns) for diamonds; US 5/3.75 mm 24–40"/60–100 cm circular needle, depending on selected garment size, for Body; dpns or straight needles, for straps. *Adjust needle size if necessary to obtain correct gauge.*

NOTIONS

- Stitch markers
- Stitch holders
- Tapestry needle

GAUGE

Using larger needle, 24 sts and 32 rnds in St st = 4"/10 cm square, machine washed and dried.

PATTERN NOTES

- Front and back diamonds are worked first, in the round.
- Stitches for front and back are picked up from bottom edges of diamonds and worked down; short rows shape front and back to diamonds.
- After front and back are joined at underarms, body is worked down in the round.
- Stitches for straps are then picked up from top edges of diamonds and worked up.

CUSTOMIZING FIT

Both hip and tunic length instructions are included. In addition, body length can easily be customized further: since body is worked down, the garment can be tried on when partially completed, to check length. If changing length, continue to work body increases at same interval to preserve A-line.

Back Diamond

Using smaller circular needle and A, [CO 35, pm] 3 times, CO 35—140 sts. Pm and join for working in the rnd, taking care not to twist sts.
Rnd 1: Purl to last 2 sts.
Rnd 2: *Sl 2 tog knitwise wyib, remove m, k1, pass 2 sl sts over st just knit, replace m, knit to 2 before next m; rep from * 3 more times, k1, p1—8 sts dec'd.
Rep last 2 rnds until 4 sts rem (change to dpns as needed). Do not BO sts; break yarn, thread through rem sts and fasten on WS.

Back

Using smaller circular needle and B and starting at a corner of Diamond, pick up and knit 35 sts along one edge; 1 st at corner; 35 sts along next edge—71 sts. Change to larger needle.

Note: Short rows (SR) are worked without wrapping sts; just turn work to opposite side at end of each short row.

SR 1 (WS): P3; turn.
SR 2 (RS): Knit to last st, M1R, k1—1 st inc'd.
SR 3 (WS): Purl sts from last row, p2; turn.
Rep last 2 rows until all 35 sts along edge have been worked, then rep SR 2 once more—52 sts.
Next row (WS): Purl to end.
SR 1 (RS): K1, M1L, k2; turn.
SR 2 (WS): Purl to end.
SR 3 (RS): K1, M1L, knit sts from last row, k2.
Rep last 2 rows until all 35 sts along edge have been worked—52 sts.
Rep SR 2 once more.
Next row (RS): Knit to end—105 sts.

SIZES S-M, M, M-L, AND L-1X ONLY

WS: Purl.
Inc row (RS): K1, M1L, knit to last st, M1R, k1—2 sts inc'd.
Rep last 2 rows - (-, 2, 2, 4, 4) more times— - (-, 111, 111, 115, 115) sts.

ALL SIZES

Turn work to WS and CO 0 (8, 10, 18, 22, 28) sts using knitted cast-on. Break yarn and place 105 (113, 121, 129, 137, 143) Back sts on holder.

Front Diamond

Using smaller circular needle and A, [CO 25, pm] 3 times, CO 25—100 sts. Pm and join for working in the rnd, taking care not to twist sts.
Rnd 1: Purl to last 2 sts.
Rnd 2: *Sl 2 tog knitwise wyib, remove m, k1, pass 2 sl sts over st just knit, replace m, knit to 2 sts before next m; rep from * 3 more times, k1, p1—8 sts dec'd.
Rep last 2 rnds until 4 sts rem (change to dpns as needed). Do not BO sts; break yarn, thread through rem sts and fasten on WS.

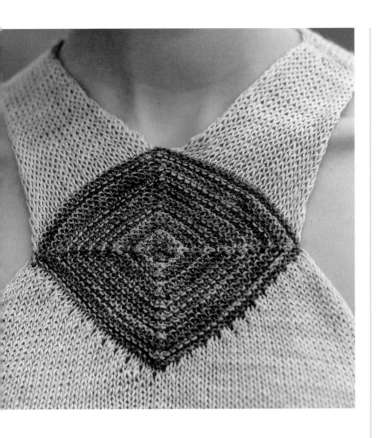

Front

Using smaller circular needle and B and starting at a corner of Diamond, pick up and knit 25 sts along one edge; 1 st at corner; 25 sts along next edge—51 sts. Change to larger needle.

Note: Short rows (SR) are worked without wrapping sts; just turn work to opposite side at end of each short row.

SR 1 (WS): P3; turn.
SR 2 (RS): Knit to last st, M1R, k1—1 st inc'd.
SR 3 (WS): Purl sts from last row, p2; turn.
Rep last 2 rows until all 25 sts along edge have been worked, then rep SR 2 once more—37 sts.
Next row (WS): Purl to end.
SR 1 (RS): K1, M1L, k2; turn.
SR 2 (WS): Purl to end.
SR 3 (RS): K1, M1L, knit sts from last row, k2.
Rep last 2 rows until all 25 sts along edge have been worked—37 sts.
Rep SR 2 once more.
Next row (RS): Knit to end—75 sts.

SIZES S-M, M, M-L, AND L-1X ONLY
WS: Purl.
Inc row (RS): K1, M1L, knit to last st, M1R, k1—2 sts inc'd.
Rep last 2 rows - (-, 2, 4, 6, 6) more times— - (-, 81, 85, 89, 89) sts.

ALL SIZES
Turn work to WS and CO 0 (8, 10, 18, 22, 28) sts using knitted cast-on—75 (83, 91, 103, 111, 117) sts. Do not break yarn.

Body

SIZE XS ONLY
Join Front and Back (RS): Place Back sts on opposite end of needle holding Front sts, with RS facing. Using working yarn and needle from Front, knit Back sts, pm for side, knit Front sts, pm for side/beg of rnd—180 sts.

SIZES S, S-M, M, M-L, AND L-1X ONLY
Join Front and Back (RS): Place Back sts on opposite end of needle holding Front sts, with RS facing. Using working yarn and needle from Front, knit Back sts, knit - (4, 5, 9, 11, 14) CO sts, pm for side, knit - (4, 5, 9, 11, 14) CO sts, knit Front sts, knit - (4, 5, 9, 11, 14) CO sts, pm for side/beg of rnd, knit - (4, 5, 9, 11, 14) CO sts— - (196, 212, 232, 248, 260) sts. Work to end of rnd in St st.

ALL SIZES
Work 12 (11, 11, 11, 11, 11) more rnds even in St st.
Inc rnd: *K5, M1L, work in patt to 5 sts before m, M1R, k5**, rep from * to **—4 sts inc'd.

HIP LENGTH ONLY
Rep Inc rnd every 14th rnd 7 more times—212 (228, 244, 264, 280, 292) sts.

TUNIC LENGTH ONLY
Rep Inc rnd every 14th rnd 10 more times—224 (240, 256, 276, 292, 304) sts.

BOTH LENGTHS
Work 14 more rnds even in patt, then BO all sts loosely knitwise.

Straps

I recommend pinning straps at shoulders and ensuring that neck opening is large enough to pass over head before joining shoulders; if neck opening is too small, work a few more rows on each strap and retry.

Left Front Strap

Using smaller needle and B and with RS facing, pick up and knit 24 sts along top left side of Front Diamond (side that will be worn on left side of body), starting just above side corner of Diamond and ending just before top corner. Change to larger needle and work 3 rows even in St st.
Dec row (RS): K2tog, work in patt to last 2 sts, ssk—2 sts dec'd.
Rep Dec row every 4th row 4 more times—14 sts rem.
Work 2 rows even, then break yarn, leaving 36"/90 cm long tail, and place sts on holder.

Right Front Strap

Using smaller needle and B and with RS facing, pick up and knit 24 sts along top right side of Front Diamond (side that will be worn on right side of body), starting just after top corner of Diamond and ending just before side corner. Change to larger needle and work as for Left Front Strap.

Left Back Strap

Using smaller needle and B and with RS facing, pick up and knit 34 sts along top left side of Back Diamond, starting just after top corner of Diamond and ending just before side corner. Change to larger needle and work 1 row (WS) even in St st.
Dec row 1 (RS): Work in patt to last 2 sts, ssk—1 st dec'd.
Next row (WS): Work even in patt.
Dec row 2 (RS): K2tog, work in patt to last 2 sts, ssk—2 sts dec'd.
Next row (WS): Work even in patt.
Rep last 4 rows 3 more times—22 sts rem.
Rep Dec row 2, 4 more times (work even on WS rows)—14 sts rem. Break yarn, leaving 36"/90 cm long tail, and place sts on holder.

Right Back Strap

Using smaller needle and B and with RS facing, pick up and knit 34 sts along top right side of Back Diamond, starting just above side corner of Diamond and ending just before top corner. Change to larger needle and work 1 row (WS) even in St st.
Dec row 1 (RS): K2tog, work in patt to end—1 st dec'd.
Next row (WS): Work even in patt.
Dec row 2 (RS): K2tog, work in patt to last 2 sts, ssk—2 sts dec'd.
Next row (WS): Work even in patt.
Rep last 4 rows 3 more times—22 sts rem.
Rep Dec row 2, 4 more times (work even on WS rows)—14 sts rem. Break yarn, leaving 36"/90 cm long tail. Leave sts on needle.

Finished Measurements

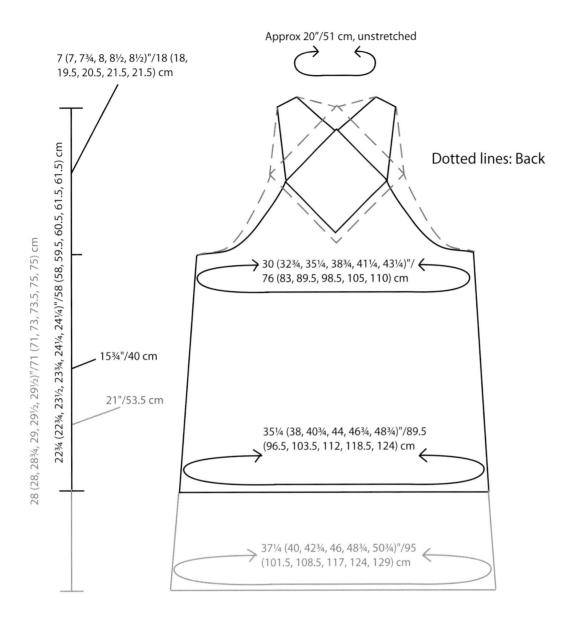

7 (7, 7¾, 8, 8½, 8½)"/18 (18, 19.5, 20.5, 21.5, 21.5) cm

Approx 20"/51 cm, unstretched

Dotted lines: Back

30 (32¾, 35¼, 38¾, 41¼, 43¼)"/ 76 (83, 89.5, 98.5, 105, 110) cm

15¾"/40 cm

21"/53.5 cm

35¼ (38, 40¾, 44, 46¾, 48¾)"/89.5 (96.5, 103.5, 112, 118.5, 124) cm

28 (28, 28¾, 29, 29½, 29½)"/71 (71, 73, 73.5, 75, 75) cm

22¾ (22¾, 23½, 23¾, 24¼, 24¼)"/58 (58, 59.5, 60.5, 61.5, 61.5) cm

37¼ (40, 42¾, 46, 48¾, 50¾)"/95 (101.5, 108.5, 117, 124, 129) cm

Solid gray lines/figures: Tunic length

Finishing

Turn garment inside out. Place held Right Front Strap sts on 2nd needle.

Right shoulder:
Use three-needle bind-off to join Front and Back straps: Insert a third needle into first st on each of these 2 needles and knit these 2 sts together, using one of long yarn tails. *Knit next st on each needle the same way, then

pass first st on right-hand needle over second st—1 st bound off. Repeat from * until 1 st is left on the right-hand needle, then pull yarn tail through last st.

Left shoulder:
Place held Left Back Strap and Left Front Strap sts on 2 needles and join as for Right shoulder.
    Weave in ends and block to finished measurements (machine dry if using suggested yarn, then press or steam lightly as needed).

This sleeveless shell uses a textured stitch pattern for the wide hem and the shoulder panels. Short rows shape the centers of the upper front and back into shallow triangles; textured shoulder panels are worked from the top edges of these triangles. The angles created by the short rows create a shallow V-neck, front and back.

SKILL LEVEL

Intermediate: Skills include working in the round, reading charts, twisted stitches, short rows, and three-needle bind-off. See Techniques section beginning on page 146 for a photo tutorial on working short rows.

SIZES

Women's XS (S, M, L, 1X, 2X)

FINISHED MEASUREMENTS

Bust: 31 (34¾, 38¼, 42¾, 47¼, 50¾)"/79 (88, 97, 108.5, 119.5, 129) cm. *Shown in Size S with +¾"/2 cm ease at bust. Intended to fit with -2"/5 cm to +2"/5 cm ease at bust.*

YARN

500 (560, 620, 700, 770, 840) yd/460 (515, 570, 645, 710, 775) m heavy worsted weight #4 yarn; shown in #513 Anemone, Quince & Co. Kestrel; 100% organic linen; 76 yd/70 m per 1¾ oz/50 g skein, 7 (8, 9, 10, 11, 12) skeins

NEEDLES

US 9/5.5 mm 24–40"/60–100 cm circular needle, depending on selected garment size, for Body; circular or straight needles, for shoulder panels. *Adjust needle size if necessary to obtain correct gauge.*

NOTIONS

- Stitch markers
- Stitch holders
- Tapestry needle

GAUGE

18 sts and 24 rnds in St st = 4"/10 cm square, blocked; 21 sts in Textured patt = 4"/10 cm, blocked

PATTERN NOTES

- Worked in the round to armholes
- Textured shoulder panels are worked flat, then joined at the shoulders with three-needle bind-off
- Waist is shaped with decreases at top of textured border, creating a subtle peplum effect, and then with side increases
- Instructions for textured pattern are given in chart form only

CUSTOMIZING FIT

Depth of textured border can be easily changed in increments of 4 rows (full repeat of pattern). Waist shaping decreases occur all at once at top of textured border; back waist length can be adjusted by changing length from waist decreases to underarm shaping (but side waist increase frequency may also need to be changed).

SPECIAL STITCHES

LT (Left Twist, worked over 2 sts):

RS: Knit 2nd stitch on the left-hand needle through the back loop, leaving it on the needle, then knit first stitch and drop both stitches off needle.

WS (creates Right Twist with knit stitches on the RS): Purl 2nd stitch on the left-hand needle through the back loop, leaving it on the needle, then purl first stitch and drop both stitches off needle.

RT (Right Twist, worked over 2 sts):

RS: Knit 2nd stitch on the left-hand needle, leaving it on the needle, then knit first stitch and drop both stitches off needle.

WS (creates Right Twist with knit stitches on the RS): Purl 2nd stitch on the left-hand needle, leaving it on the needle, then purl first stitch and drop both stitches off needle.

M1L (worked from WS): With left needle tip, lift strand between needles from front to back and purl lifted loop through back, twisting created stitch (creates left-leaning knit stitch on RS).

M1R (worked from WS): With left needle tip, lift strand between needles from back to front and purl lifted loop through front, twisting created stitch (creates right-leaning knit stitch on RS).

Body

Using circular needle, *CO 96 (108, 120, 132, 144, 156) sts**, pm for side, rep once more from * to **—192 (216, 240, 264, 288, 312) sts. Pm for beg of rnd and join, taking care not to twist sts.

Est texture patt:

Rnd 1: Work Row 1 of Hem chart 16 (18, 20, 22, 24, 26) times to end of rnd.

Rnd 2: Work Row 2 of Hem chart 16 (18, 20, 22, 24, 26) times to end of rnd.

Cont to work in patt as est until 7 reps of all 4 rows of Hem chart have been completed, then work 3 more rnds in patt as est.

Next rnd: Dec rnd: [K1b, k2, ssk, p1, k2tog, k2, k1b, p1] 16 (18, 20, 22, 24, 26) times to end of rnd—32 (36, 40, 44, 48, 52) sts dec'd, 160 (180, 200, 220, 240, 260) sts rem.

Next rnd: Knit.

Hem

(also used for Left Back and Right Front for sizes L, 1X, and 2X)

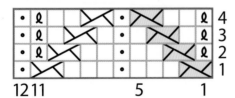

Shoulder Panel

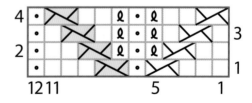

Key

☐	knit on RS, purl on WS
·	purl on RS, knit on WS
⧅	RT
⧄	LT
☐	patt repeat
ℚ	knit into back of st on RS, purl into back of st on WS

SIZES XS, S, AND M ONLY

Dec rnd: [K3, sk2p, k4] 16 (18, 20, -, -, -) times to end of rnd—32 (36, 40, -, -, -) sts dec'd. 128 (144, 160, -, -, -) sts rem.

SIZE L ONLY

Dec rnd: *[K3, sk2p, k4] 5 times, k10, [K3, sk2p, k4] 5 times**, rep once more from * to **— - (-, -, 40, -, -) sts dec'd, - (-, -, 180, -, -) sts rem.

SIZES 1X AND 2X ONLY

Dec rnd: *K10, [K3, sk2p, k4] - (-, -, -, 10, 11) times, k10**; rep once more from * to **— - (-, -, -, 40, 44) sts dec'd, - (-, -, -, 200, 216) sts rem.

ALL SIZES

Work 13 (13, 13, 15, 15, 15) rnds even in St st.

Inc rnd: *K5, M1L, work in patt to 6 sts before m, M1R, k6**; rep once more from * to **—4 sts inc'd.

Rep inc rnd every 12th (12th, 12th, 10th, 8th, 8th) rnd 2 more times—140 (156, 172, 192, 212, 228) sts.

Work 9 (9, 7, 7, 9, 7) rnds even, stopping 1 st before end of last rnd; piece should measure approx 13¾ (13¾, 13¼, 13, 12¾, 12¼)"/34.5 (34.5, 34, 33, 32, 31.5) cm from CO.

Next rnd: LT with last st of rnd and first st of next rnd (replace m between sts), work in patt to 1 st before m, RT (replace m between sts), work in patt to end.

Divide for Front and Back/shape Armholes:

Place 70 (78, 86, 96, 106, 114) sts from beg of rnd to side m on holder for Front (remove m). Turn garment to work WS of rem 70 (78, 86, 96, 106, 114) sts for Back.

Back

Dec row (WS): P2, ssp, work in patt to 4 sts before end of row, p2tog, p2—2 sts dec'd.

Dec row (RS): K2, k2tog, work in patt to 4 sts before end of row, ssk, k2—2 sts dec'd.

Rep these 2 rows 3 (4, 6, 7, 9, 10) more times— 54 (58, 58, 64, 66, 70) sts rem.

Begin short row (SR) shaping:

SR 1 (WS): Work in patt to last 3 (5, 5, 4, 5, 3) sts, W&T.

SR 2 (RS): Work in patt to last 3 (5, 5, 4, 5, 3) sts, W&T.

SR 3 (WS): Work in patt to 4 sts before last wrapped st, W&T.

SR 4 (RS): Work in patt to 4 sts before last wrapped st, W&T.

Rep last 2 rows 4 (4, 4, 5, 5, 6) more times, then rep SR 3 once more.

Next row (RS): K1, W&T.

Next row (WS): Work in patt to end of row, picking up wraps and working tog with wrapped sts.

Next row (RS): Work in patt to end of row, picking up wraps and working tog with wrapped sts.

Inc row (WS): Inc 16 (12, 12, 18, 16, 12) sts evenly spaced, using M1R (worked from WS) for first 8 (6, 6, 9, 8, 6) inc and M1L (worked from WS) for rem inc—70 (70, 70, 82, 82, 82) sts.

Divide for Left and Right Back:

Leave last 35 (35, 35, 41, 41, 41) sts worked on needle and place rem 35 (35, 35, 41, 41, 41) sts on holder for Left Back.

Right Back

Est texture patt:

Row 1 (RS): Work Row 1 of Shoulder Panel chart 2 (2, 2, 3, 3, 3) times, then work Sts 1–11 (1–11, 1–11, 1–5, 1–5, 1–5) once more.

Row 2 (WS): Work Sts 11–1 (11–1, 11–1, 5–1, 5–1, 5–1) of Row 2 once, then work entire Row 2 of Shoulder Panel chart 2 (2, 2, 3, 3, 3) more times.

Cont to work in patt as est until 7 reps of all 4 rows of Shoulder Panel chart have been completed, then work 3 more rows in patt as est.

SIZES XS, S, AND M ONLY
Dec row (WS): [Ssp, p2, p1b, k1, p1b, p2, p2tog, k1] 3 times, ending last rep p2tog—29 sts rem.

SIZES L, 1X, AND 2X ONLY
Dec row (WS): P1b, p2, p2tog, [k1, ssp, p2, p1b, k1, p1b, p2, p2tog] 3 times—34 sts rem.

ALL SIZES
Break yarn and place sts on holder for Right shoulder.

Left Back

Place held Left Back sts on circular or straight needle and join yarn to work RS.

SIZES XS, S, AND M ONLY
Work as for Right Back.

SIZES L, 1X, AND 2X ONLY
Est texture patt:
Row 1 (RS): Work Row 1 of *Hem* chart 3 times, then work Sts 1–5 once more.
Row 2 (WS): Work Sts 5–1 of Row 2 of *Hem* chart once, then work entire Row 2 of *Hem* chart 3 more times.
Cont to work in patt as est until 7 reps of all 4 rows of Hem chart have been completed, then work 3 more rows in patt as est.
Dec row (WS): Ssp, p2, p1b, [k1, P1b, p2, p2tog, k1, ssp, p2, p1b] 3 times—34 sts rem.

ALL SIZES
Break yarn, leaving 36"/90 cm long tail for three-needle bind-off, and place sts on holder for left shoulder.

Front

Place held Front sts on circular needle and join yarn to work WS. Front is worked same as Back; Left Front is worked same as Right Back; Right Front is worked same as Left Back, except that once completed, sts are left on needle (break yarn, leaving 36"/90 cm long tail for three-needle bind-off).

Finished Measurements

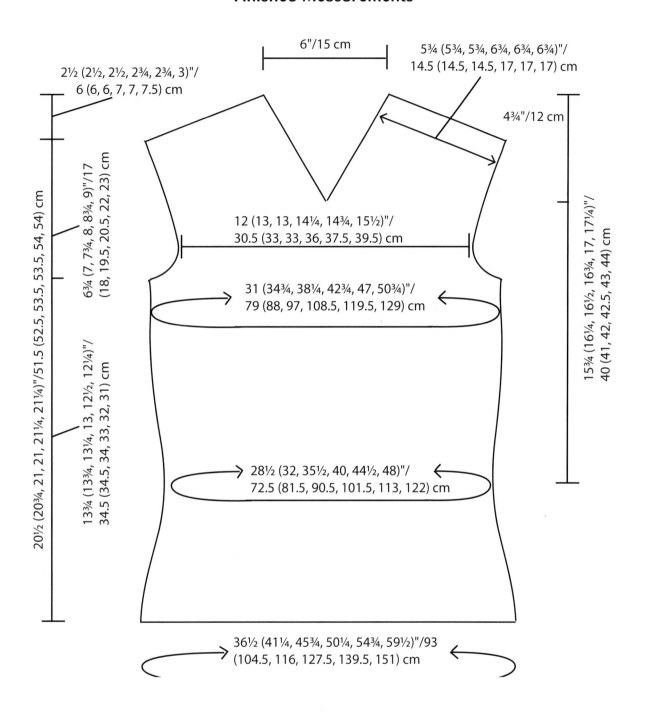

6"/15 cm

5¾ (5¾, 5¾, 6¾, 6¾, 6¾)"/
14.5 (14.5, 14.5, 17, 17, 17) cm

2½ (2½, 2½, 2¾, 2¾, 3)"/
6 (6, 6, 7, 7, 7.5) cm

4¾"/12 cm

12 (13, 13, 14¼, 14¾, 15½)"/
30.5 (33, 33, 36, 37.5, 39.5) cm

6¾ (7, 7¾, 8, 8¾, 9)"/17
(18, 19.5, 20.5, 22, 23) cm

31 (34¾, 38¼, 42¾, 47, 50¾)"/
79 (88, 97, 108.5, 119.5, 129) cm

15¾ (16¼, 16½, 16¾, 17, 17¼)"/
40 (41, 42, 42.5, 43, 44) cm

20½ (20¾, 21, 21, 21¼, 21¼)"/51.5 (52.5, 53, 53.5, 54, 54) cm

13¾ (13¾, 13¼, 13, 12½, 12¼)"/
34.5 (34.5, 34, 33, 32, 31) cm

28½ (32, 35½, 40, 44½, 48)"/
72.5 (81.5, 90.5, 101.5, 113, 122) cm

36½ (41¼, 45¾, 50¼, 54¾, 59½)"/93
(104.5, 116, 127.5, 139.5, 151) cm

Finishing

Turn work inside out and place Back sts for right shoulder on 2nd needle or on opposite end of circular needle.

Join shoulders using three-needle bind-off: Insert a third needle into first st on each of these 2 needles and knit these 2 sts together, using long yarn tail. *Knit next st on each needle the same way, then pass first st on right-hand needle over second st—1 st bound off. Repeat from * until 1 st is left on the right-hand needle, then pull yarn tail through last st.

Place Front and Back left shoulder sts on 2 needles or on opposite ends of circular needle, with needle tips pointing in same direction. Join as for right shoulder.

Weave in ends and block to finished measurements.

Sayre

With its slightly cropped length (the hem hits slightly above the widest part of the hips), body-skimming fit, lace yoke, and not-quite-halter styling, this tank makes the most of a relatively small amount of yarn.

SKILL LEVEL
Easy to intermediate: skills include reading lace charts, lace knitting, decreasing and increasing, and three-needle bind-off.

SIZES
Women's XS (S, M, L, 1X, 2X, 3X)

FINISHED MEASUREMENTS
Bust: 29½ (33¾, 37, 41¼, 45½, 49¾, 53)"/75 (85.5, 94, 105, 115.5, 126, 135) cm. *Shown in Size S with -¼"/.5 cm ease. Intended to fit with -2"/5 cm to +2"/5 cm ease at bust.*

YARN
420 (460, 500, 560, 600, 670, 710) yd/390 (425, 460, 520, 555, 620, 665) m medium weight #4 yarn; shown in #16 Mineral Green, Valley Yarns Southwick; 52% pima cotton, 48% bamboo viscose; 105 yd/96 m per 1¾ oz/50 g skein, 5 (5, 5, 6, 6, 7, 7) skeins.

Note: More yarn may be required if working optional short row bust shaping.

NEEDLES
US size 7/4.5 mm circular needle 24–40"/60–100 cm, depending on selected garment size, for Body; straight or set of double-pointed needles (dpns) for straps. *Adjust needle size if necessary to obtain the correct gauge.*

NOTIONS
- Stitch markers
- Stitch holders
- Tapestry needle

GAUGE
19 sts and 24 rnds in St st = 4"/10 cm square, blocked

PATTERN NOTES
- Worked in the round from the bottom up to the armholes
- Lace pattern is given in chart form only

CUSTOMIZING FIT
- Options are given for short row bust shaping, for high or low back (low back has same neck drop as front), and for strap width. Read through all directions before starting each section, and highlight or circle directions for chosen options. The yoke with higher back has been designed to cover a crossback or racerback bra in most sizes; the yoke with lower back may still cover bra straps (yoke width measurements may be helpful in determining whether a particular bra will be covered).
- Body length may be changed as desired; if length is increased, I recommend adding one or two waist decreases (and casting on 4 additional stitches to compensate for each additional waist decrease) at intervals of 6 to 8 rounds. This is because the hem circumference was calculated for a length that hits above the widest part of the hip.

SPECIAL STITCHES
Knit front and back (kfb): Knit into front of stitch, then knit into the back of the same stitch (1 stitch increased).

Body

Using circular needle, *CO 74 (84, 92, 102, 112, 122, 130) sts**, pm for right side, rep from * to **—148 (168, 184, 204, 224, 244, 260) sts. Pm for beg of rnd/left side and join for working in the rnd, taking care not to twist sts.
Rnds 1, 3, and 5: Purl.

Lace Pattern Chart

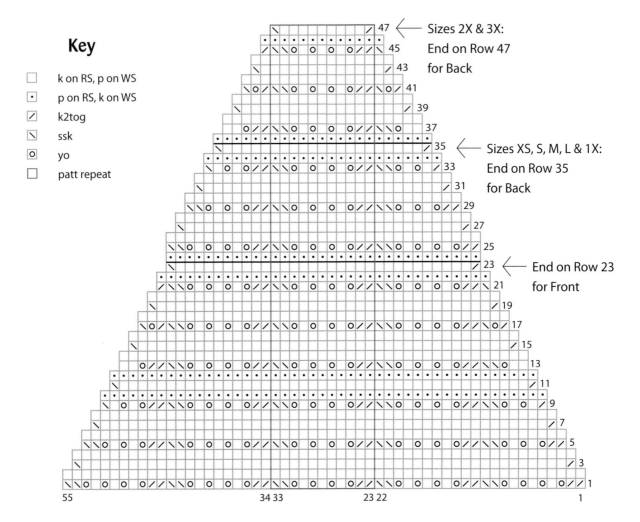

Key
- ☐ k on RS, p on WS
- ⬚ p on RS, k on WS
- ☑ k2tog
- ◹ ssk
- ⊙ yo
- ☐ patt repeat

Sizes 2X & 3X:
End on Row 47
for Back

Sizes XS, S, M, L & 1X:
End on Row 35
for Back

End on Row 23
for Front

Rnds 2 and 4: Knit.
Dec rnd: *K3, k2tog, knit to 5 before m, ssk, k3;
    rep from *—4 sts dec'd. Rep dec rnd every
    6th rnd 5 more times (work even in St st on
    other rnds)—124 (144, 160, 180, 200, 220,
    236) sts rem.
Work even for 11 rnds.
Inc rnd: *K3, M1R, knit to 3 before m, M1L, k3;
    rep from *—4 sts inc'd.
Rep inc rnd every 8th rnd 3 more times—140
    (160, 176, 196, 216, 236, 252) sts.

IF WORKING OPTIONAL SHORT ROWS
C (D, DD) Cup: *K to 3 sts before right side m,
    W&T, p to 3 sts before left side m, W&T.
Next row: Work to 3 sts before last wrapped
    stitch, W&T.
Repeat last row until 4 sts on each side have
    been wrapped (8 rows).
RS: Work one rnd, picking up wraps and
    working tog with wrapped sts**. Rep from * to
    ** 0 (1, 2) times.
Work 13 (12, 11) rnds even, stopping 3 (4, 5, 6, 7,
    8, 9) sts before end of final rnd.

IF NOT WORKING SHORT ROWS
Work 14 rnds even, stopping 3 (4, 5, 6, 7, 8, 9)
sts before end of final rnd.

ALL KNITTERS
Pm for new beg of rnd/beg underarm sts.
Next rnd: *P3 (4, 5, 6, 7, 8, 9), remove m, p3
    (4, 5, 6, 7, 8, 9), pm for end underarm sts,
    p64 (72, 78, 86, 94, 102, 108)**, pm for beg
    underarm sts; rep from * to **.

Next rnd: Underarm dec rnd/Lace set-up rnd
(underarm dec compensates for tendency of
garter st to spread sideways; each size also has
dec OR inc in Front and Back, to set up proper
number of sts for Lace patt):

SIZE XS ONLY
K2, k2tog, k2; knit Front sts while inc 2 sts
evenly spaced; k2, k2tog, k2; knit Back sts
while inc 2 sts evenly spaced—5 sts rem each
underarm, 66 sts each in Front and Back.

SIZES S, M, L, AND 1X ONLY
*K - (1, 2, 1, 2, -, -), ssk, [k2, k2tog] - (1, 1, 2,
2, -, -) times, k - (1, 2, 1, 2, -, -), **; knit Front
sts while - (dec 6, dec 1, inc 2, dec 6, -, -) sts
evenly spaced; rep from * to **; knit Back
sts while - (dec 6, dec 1, inc 2, dec 6, -, -) sts
evenly spaced— - (6, 8, 9, 11, -, -) sts rem in
each underarm, - (66, 77, 88, 88, -, -) sts each in
Front and Back.

SIZES 2X AND 3X ONLY
*K - (-, -, -, -, 1, 2), [ssk, k2] twice, k2tog, k2,
k2tog, k - (-, -, -, -, 1, 2)**; knit Front sts while
dec - (-, -, -, -, 3, 9) sts evenly spaced; rep from
* to **; knit Back sts while dec - (-, -, -, -, 3, 9)
sts evenly spaced— - (-, -, -, -, 12, 14) sts rem
each underarm, - (-, -, -, -, 99, 99) sts each in
Front and Back.

ALL SIZES

Note: Extra st created by kfb is BO to
strengthen transition from Front or Back to
underarm sts.

Next rnd: Purl to last st, kfb—1 st inc'd.
Divide for Front/Back: *BO 2nd st of kfb
    and rem 5 (6, 8, 9, 11, 12, 14) underarm sts
    knitwise**, knit to last Front st, kfb, rep from *
    to **, knit to end. Turn and cont to work Back
    sts only (place Front sts on holder or leave
    on needle).

Back
WS: Knit.
Est Lace patt (RS): Work Sts 1–22 of Row 1 of
    chart once, Sts 23–33 2 (2, 3, 4, 4, 5, 5) times,
    and Sts 34–55 once.

IF WORKING HIGH BACK (AS SHOWN)
Cont to work Lace patt as est until all 35 (35,
35, 35, 35, 47, 47) rows of chart have been
completed—34 (34, 45, 56, 56, 55, 55) sts rem.

Beg straps (WS): K11 (11, 11, 11, 11, 10, 10), kfb, BO
    2nd st of kfb and next 10 (10, 21, 32, 32, 33,
    33) sts, k to end—12 (12, 12, 12, 12, 11, 11) sts rem
    each strap. Turn and cont to work Right Back
    strap sts only (place Left Back strap sts on
    holder or leave on needle).

SIZES XS, S, M, L, AND 1X ONLY
Next row (RS): K5, k2tog, k5—11 sts.
Next row (WS): Knit.

For strap as shown:
Next row (RS): K2tog, k7, ssk—9 sts.

For slightly wider strap:
Next row (RS): Knit (cont to work 11 sts).

SIZES 2X AND 3X ONLY
For strap as shown:
Next row (RS): K2tog, k7, ssk—9 sts.

For slightly wider strap:
Next row (RS): Knit (cont to work 11 sts).
Work 2 rows in garter st.

ALL SIZES
Work 1 (3, 5, 9, 13, 3, 7) more rows in garter st, ending after a WS row. Break yarn, leaving 24"/60 cm long tail for three-needle bind-off, and place sts on holder.

Left Back strap:
Join yarn to work RS. Work as for Right Back strap.

IF WORKING BACK SAME AS FRONT
Cont to work lace patt as est until 23 rows of chart have been completed—44 (44, 55, 66, 66, 77, 77) sts rem.

Beg straps (WS): K10, kfb, BO 2nd st of kfb, BO next 22 (22, 33, 44, 44, 55, 55) sts, k to end—11 sts rem each strap. Turn and cont to work Right Back strap sts only (place Left Back strap sts on holder or leave on needle).

For strap as shown:
Next row (RS): K2tog, k7, ssk—9 sts.

For slightly wider strap:
Next row (RS): Knit (cont to work 11 sts).
Work even in garter st for 15 (17, 19, 23, 27, 29, 33) more rows, ending after a WS row. Break yarn, leaving 24"/60 cm long tail for three-needle bind-off, and place sts on holder.

Left Back strap:
Join yarn to work RS. Work as for Right Back strap.

Front
Join yarn to work WS. Knit 1 row.
Est Lace patt (RS): Work as for Back until 23 rows of chart have been completed—44 (44, 55, 66, 66, 77, 77) sts rem.
Beg straps (WS): K10, kfb, BO 2nd st of kfb, BO next 22 (22, 33, 44, 44, 55, 55) sts, k to end—11 sts rem each strap. Turn and cont to work Left Front strap sts only (place Right Front strap sts on holder or leave on needle).

Note: To best assess strap length, it may be necessary to block garment before completing Front straps. After blocking, try on garment and pin Front straps to Back straps, then adjust Front strap length as needed.

Finished Measurements

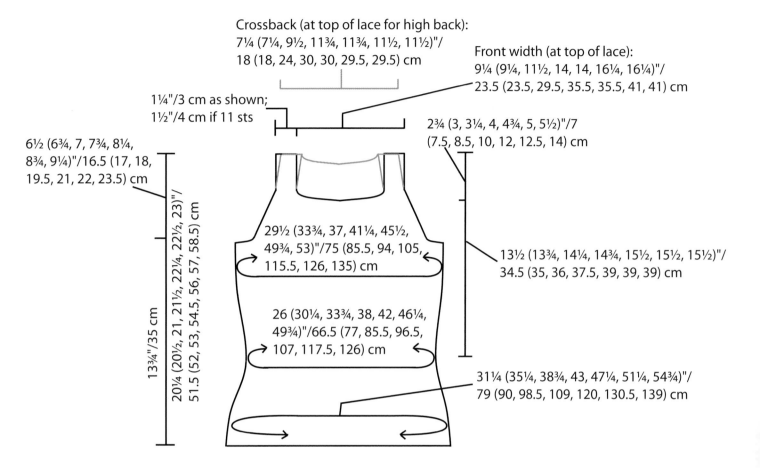

Crossback (at top of lace for high back):
7¼ (7¼, 9½, 11¾, 11¾, 11½, 11½)"/
18 (18, 24, 30, 30, 29.5, 29.5) cm

Front width (at top of lace):
9¼ (9¼, 11½, 14, 14, 16¼, 16¼)"/
23.5 (23.5, 29.5, 35.5, 35.5, 41, 41) cm

1¼"/3 cm as shown;
1½"/4 cm if 11 sts

6½ (6¾, 7, 7¾, 8¼, 8¾, 9¼)"/16.5 (17, 18, 19.5, 21, 22, 23.5) cm

2¾ (3, 3¼, 4, 4¾, 5, 5½)"/7 (7.5, 8.5, 10, 12, 12.5, 14) cm

20¼ (20½, 21, 21½, 22¼, 22½, 23)"/ 51.5 (52, 53, 54.5, 56, 57, 58.5) cm

13¾"/35 cm

29½ (33¾, 37, 41¼, 45½, 49¾, 53)"/75 (85.5, 94, 105, 115.5, 126, 135) cm

13½ (13¾, 14¼, 14¾, 15½, 15½, 15½)"/
34.5 (35, 36, 37.5, 39, 39, 39) cm

26 (30¼, 33¾, 38, 42, 46¼, 49¾)"/66.5 (77, 85.5, 96.5, 107, 117.5, 126) cm

31¼ (35¼, 38¾, 43, 47¼, 51¼, 54¾)"/
79 (90, 98.5, 109, 120, 130.5, 139) cm

Left Front Strap

For strap as shown:
Next row (RS): K2tog, k7, ssk—9 sts.

For slightly wider strap:
Next row (RS): Knit (cont to work 11 sts).
Work even in garter st for 15 (17, 19, 23, 27, 29, 33) more rows, ending after a WS row. Break yarn, leaving 24"/60 cm long tail for three-needle bind-off, and place sts on holder.

Right Front Strap

Join yarn to work RS. Work as for Left Front strap.

Finishing

Turn work inside out and place Right Front and Right Back strap sts on two needles or on opposite ends of circular needle, with points of needle(s) at armhole edges of shoulder.

Three-needle bind-off: Insert a third needle into first st on each of these 2 needles and knit these 2 sts together, using one of long yarn tails. *Knit next st on each needle the same way, then pass first st on right-hand needle over second st—1 st bound off. Repeat from * until 1 st is left on the right-hand needle, then pull yarn tail through last st.

Repeat for left straps.

Weave in ends and block to finished measurements.

Sedalia

A floral lace pattern adorns the upper front and back of this sleeveless tank, and the flower "stems" are carried into the body of the tank, creating flattering vertical lines. All edgings are self-finished; underarm gussets allow the armhole edgings to continue unbroken from underarm to shoulder, while keeping the armholes from being too deep.

SKILL LEVEL

Intermediate to advanced: Skills include reading lace charts, lace knitting, decreasing and increasing, short row shaping, and three-needle bind-off. See Techniques section beginning on page 146 for a photo tutorial on working short rows.

SIZES

Women's XS (S, M, L, 1X, 2X, 3X)

FINISHED MEASUREMENTS

Bust: 30½ (34¼, 38½, 42¼, 46½, 50¼, 54½)"/77.5 (87, 98, 107, 118, 127.5, 138.5) cm. *Shown in Size S with -¾"/2 cm ease. Intended to fit with -2"/5 cm to +2"/5 cm ease at bust.*

YARN

600 (680, 770, 860, 950, 1040, 1150) yd/545 (620, 710, 790, 865, 950, 1055) m light weight #3 yarn; shown in #5846 Island Blue, Classic Elite Yarns Provence; 100% mercerized Egyptian cotton; 102 yd/94 m per 1¾ oz/50 g skein, 6 (7, 8, 9, 10, 11, 12) skeins

NEEDLES

US 6/4.0 mm 24–40"/60–100 cm circular needle, depending on selected garment size. *Adjust needle size if necessary to obtain the correct gauge.*

NOTIONS

- Stitch markers
- Stitch holders
- Tapestry needle

GAUGE

22 sts and 29 rnds in St st = 4"/10 cm square, blocked

PATTERN NOTES

- Worked in the round to the armholes
- Lace pattern is given in chart form only
- To work short row shoulder and neck shaping, use both charts and written instructions
- Shown with boat neck in back and shallow scoop neck in front; may be reversed
- All edgings are self-finished

CUSTOMIZING FIT

Tank as shown is slightly shorter than hip length. Body length can be adjusted in increments of two rounds; if change in length is substantial, side waist decrease and/or increase frequency may need to be changed.

SPECIAL STITCHES

LT (Left Twist, worked over 2 sts):
RS: Knit 2nd stitch on the left-hand needle through the back loop, leaving it on the needle, then knit first stitch and drop both stitches off needle.

RT (Right Twist, worked over 2 sts):
RS: Knit 2nd stitch on the left-hand needle, leaving it on the needle, then knit first stitch and drop both stitches off needle.

Sixes XS, S, and M

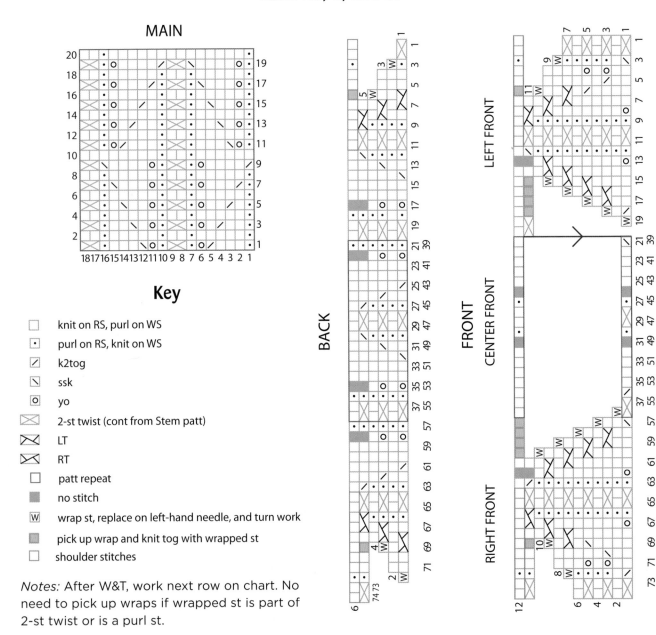

MAIN

Key

☐	knit on RS, purl on WS
·	purl on RS, knit on WS
╱	k2tog
╲	ssk
○	yo
⊠	2-st twist (cont from Stem patt)
⊠	LT
⊠	RT
☐	patt repeat
▨	no stitch
W	wrap st, replace on left-hand needle, and turn work
▨	pick up wrap and knit tog with wrapped st
☐	shoulder stitches

Notes: After W&T, work next row on chart. No need to pick up wraps if wrapped st is part of 2-st twist or is a purl st.

BACK

FRONT

CENTER FRONT

LEFT FRONT

RIGHT FRONT

Sizes L, 1X, 2X, and 3X

MAIN

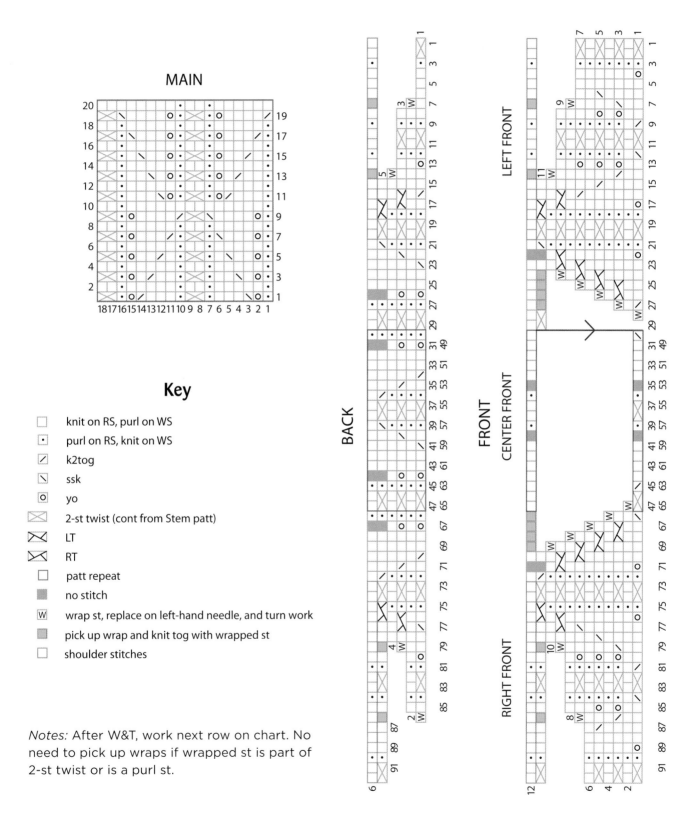

Key

□	knit on RS, purl on WS
·	purl on RS, knit on WS
⟋	k2tog
⟍	ssk
⚬	yo
⊠	2-st twist (cont from Stem patt)
⋈	LT
⋈	RT
□	patt repeat
▨	no stitch
W	wrap st, replace on left-hand needle, and turn work
▨	pick up wrap and knit tog with wrapped st
□	shoulder stitches

Notes: After W&T, work next row on chart. No need to pick up wraps if wrapped st is part of 2-st twist or is a purl st.

BACK

FRONT

CENTER FRONT

LEFT FRONT

RIGHT FRONT

Stem Panel (worked over 4 sts and 4 rnds or rows):

In the round:
Rnd 1: P1, RT, p1.
Rnds 2 and 4: P1, k2, p1.
Rnd 3: P1, LT, p1.
Rep Rnds 1–4 for pattern.

Worked flat:
Row 1 (RS): P1, RT, p1.
Rows 2 and 4 (WS): K1, p2, k1.
Row 3 (RS): P1, LT, p1.
Rep Rows 1–4 for pattern.

Body

CO 176 (196, 220, 240, 264, 284, 308) sts. Pm for beg of rnd/left side and join for working in the rnd, taking care not to twist sts.

Set-up rnd: *Work Rnd 1 of Stem panel over 4 sts, k13 (9, 6, 11, 8, 13, 10), [work Rnd 1 of Stem panel over 4 sts, k5] 6 (8, 10, 10, 12, 12, 14) times, work Rnd 1 of Stem panel over 4 sts, k13 (9, 6, 11, 8, 13, 10)**; pm for right side; rep from * to **. Note that actual sides of garment fall 2 sts after m, in center of Stem panel.

Work 5 (7, 7, 9, 9, 11, 11) more rnds even in patt as est (cont to work sts between Stem panels in St st).

Dec rnd: *Work 4 sts in patt, ssk, work to 2 sts before m, k2tog; rep from *—4 sts dec'd. Rep Dec rnd every 8th rnd 4 more times—156 (176, 200, 220, 244, 264, 288) sts rem.

Work 11 rnds even.

Inc rnd: *Work 5 sts in patt, M1R, work to 1 st before m, M1L, k1; rep from *—4 sts inc'd.

Rep Inc rnd every 14th (14th, 14th, 14th, 12th, 12th, 12th) rnd 2 more times—168 (188, 212, 232, 256, 276, 300) sts.

Work 16 (14, 14, 12, 12, 10, 10) rnds even, OR until garment is ¾ (1, 1, 1, 1, 1, 1)"/2 (3, 3, 3, 3, 3, 3) cm shorter than desired length to underarm, ending after Rnd 1 or Rnd 3 of Stem panel.

Beg gussets/armhole shaping:

Set-up rnd: *P1, M1R, k2, M1L, work in patt to m; rep from *—4 sts inc'd, 172 (192, 216, 236, 260, 280, 304) sts.

Note: In all odd-numbered gusset rnds and in RS rows, work "2-st twist" as in Stem panel: i.e., if on this rnd Stem panel rnd or row calls for LT or RT, follow patt as est.

Rnd 1: *P1, 2-st twist, pm for beg gusset, M1L, pm for end gusset, 2-st twist, p1, ssk, work to 2 sts before side m, k2tog; rep from *—1 st in each gusset, 4 sts dec'd in Body.

Rnd 2: *P1, k2, sm, k1, sm, k2, p1, ssk, work to 2 sts before side m, k2tog; rep from *—4 sts dec'd in Body.

Rnd 3: *P1, 2-st twist, sm, M1P, k1, M1P, sm, 2-st twist, p1, ssk, work to 2 sts before side m, k2tog; rep from *—3 sts in each gusset, 4 sts dec'd in Body.

Rnd 4: *P1, k2, sm, p1, k1, p1, sm, k2, p1, ssk, work to 2 sts before side m, k2tog; rep from *—4 sts dec'd in Body.

Rnd 5: *P1, 2-st twist, sm, M1L, p1, k1, p1, M1R, sm, 2-st twist, p1, ssk, work to 2 sts before side m, k2tog; rep from *—5 sts in each gusset, 4 sts dec'd in Body.

Rnd 6: *P1, k2, sm, [k1, p1] twice, k1, sm, k2, p1, ssk, work to 2 sts before side m, k2tog; rep from *—4 sts dec'd in Body.

SIZE XS ONLY

148 sts rem in Body, 5 sts in each gusset.

Divide for Front and Back: *P1, 2-st twist, remove m, M1L, BO st just created and next 4 sts loosely in patt, remove m, M1R, BO1, reposition next 2 sts for twist but place them back on left-hand needle without working them, move st on right-hand needle to left-hand needle and k2tog, k1, p1, work to side m, remove m; rep from *; p1, k2—74 sts rem each in Front and Back. Turn and cont to work Back sts only (place Front sts on holder).

SIZES S, M, L, 1X, 2X, AND 3X ONLY

Rnd 7: *P1, 2-st twist, sm, M1P, [k1, p1] twice, k1, M1P, sm, 2-st twist, p1, ssk, work to 2 sts before side m, k2tog; rep from *—7 sts in each gusset, 4 sts dec'd in Body.

Rnd 8: *P1, k2, sm, [p1, k1] 3 times, p1, sm, k2, p1, ssk, work to 2 sts before side m, k2tog; rep from *—4 sts dec'd in Body, - (160, 184, 204, 228, 248, 272) sts rem in Body, 7 sts in each gusset.

Divide for Front and Back: *P1, 2-st twist, remove m, M1L, BO st just created and next 6 sts loosely in patt, remove m, M1R, BO1, reposition next 2 sts for twist but place them back on left-hand needle without working

them, move st on right-hand needle to left-hand needle and k2tog, k1, p1, ssk, work to 2 sts before m, k2tog, remove m; rep from *; p1, k2—2 sts dec'd each in Front and Back. - (78, 90, 100, 112, 122, 134) sts rem each in Front and Back. Turn and cont to work Back sts only (place Front sts on holder).

Back (Boat Neck)

SIZE XS ONLY

Next row (WS): Knit k sts and purl p sts.

Next row (RS): 2-st twist, [p1, k5, p1, 2-st twist] 8 times to end of row.

Work 5 more rows even in patt as est, ending after a WS row.

SIZES S AND L ONLY

WS: Knit k sts and purl p sts.

Dec row (RS): 2-st twist, p1, ssk, work to last 5 sts, k2tog, p1, 2-st twist—2 sts dec'd.

Rep last 2 rows - (1, -, 3, -, -, -) more times— - (74, -, 92, -, -, -) sts rem.

Work - (3, -, 7, -, -, -) more rows even in patt, ending after a WS row.

SIZES M, 1X, 2X, AND 3X ONLY

Dec row (WS): P2, k1, p2tog, knit k sts and purl p sts to last 5 sts, ssp, k1, p2—2 sts dec'd.

Dec row (RS): 2-st twist, p1, ssk, work to last 5 sts, k2tog, p1, 2-st twist—2 sts dec'd.

Rep last 2 rows - (-, 2, -, 0, 3, 7) more times, then rep Dec row (RS) every RS row - (-, 2, -, 8, 7, 5) more times (on WS rows, knit k sts and purl p sts) — - (-, 74, -, 92, 92, 92) sts rem. Work 1 more row even (WS).

ALL SIZES

Beg Lace patt:

Row 1 (RS): 2-st twist; work Row 1 of Main chart 4 (4, 4, 5, 5, 5, 5) times.

Row 2 (WS): Work Row 2 of Main chart 4 (4, 4, 5, 5, 5, 5) times; 2-st twist.

Cont patt as est for chart Rows 3–20, then rep Rows 1–14.

Short row (SR) shoulder shaping:

SIZES XS, S, AND M ONLY (USE BACK CHART FOR SIZES XS, S, AND M)

SR 1 (RS): Work Sts 1–72 of Row 1 of Back chart (making sure it is for the correct size) (after returning wrapped st to left-hand needle, there will be 3 sts rem on left-hand needle). Turn work to WS.

SR 2 (WS): Work Sts 71–3 of Row 2 of chart (after returning wrapped st to left-hand needle, there will be 3 sts rem on left-hand needle). Turn work to RS.

SR 3 (RS): Work Sts 4–69 of Row 3 (after returning wrapped st to left-hand needle, there will be 6 sts rem on left-hand needle). Turn work to WS.

SR 4 (WS): Work Sts 68–6 of Row 4 (after returning wrapped st to left-hand needle, there will be 6 sts rem on left-hand needle). Turn work to RS.

SR 5 (RS): Work Sts 7–74 of Row 5—68 sts rem.

Row 6 (WS): Work Sts 74–64 of Row 6 in patt and place 11 sts just worked on holder for left shoulder; BO Sts 63–12 (46 sts) in patt; work Sts 11–1 in patt and place these 11 sts on holder for right shoulder.

SIZES L, 1X, 2X, AND 3X ONLY (USE BACK CHART FOR SIZES L, 1X, 2X, AND 3X)

SR 1 (RS): Work Sts 1–86 of Row 1 of Back chart (making sure it is the correct size) (after returning wrapped st to left-hand needle, there will be 7 sts rem on left-hand needle). Turn work to WS.

SR 2 (WS): Work Sts 85–7 of Row 2 of chart (after returning wrapped st to left-hand needle, there will be 7 sts rem on left-hand needle). Turn work to RS.

SR 3 (RS): Work Sts 8–79 of Row 3 (after returning wrapped st to left-hand needle, there will be 14 sts rem on left-hand needle). Turn work to WS.

SR 4 (WS): Work Sts 78–14 of Row 4 (after returning wrapped st to left-hand needle, there will be 14 sts rem on left-hand needle). Turn work to RS.

SR 5 (RS): Work Sts 15–92 of Row 5—86 sts rem.

Row 6 (WS): Work Sts 92–73 of Row 6 in patt and place 20 sts just worked on holder for left shoulder; BO Sts 72–21 (46 sts) in patt; work

Sts 20–1 in patt and place these 20 sts on holder for right shoulder.

ALL SIZES

Break yarn, leaving 36"/90 cm long tail.

Front (Shallow Scoop Neck)

Place 74 (78, 90, 100, 112, 122, 134) held Front sts on needle and join yarn to work WS.

Work as for Back until Rows 1–20, then Rows 1–8 of Main chart are complete: 74 (74, 74, 92, 92, 92, 92) sts.

Short-row neck and shoulder shaping:

SIZES XS, S, AND M ONLY (BEGIN FRONT CHART FOR SIZES XS, S, AND M)

Left front:

SR 1 (RS): Work Sts 1–19 of Row 1 of Left Front chart (making sure it is the correct size). Turn work to WS.

SR 2 (WS): Work Sts 18–1 of Row 2 of Left Front. Turn work to RS.

SR 3–10: Cont to work Left Front as charted.

Transition to Right Front (RS): Work Sts 7–20 of Row 11 of Left Front chart; Sts 21–56 of Row 1 of Center Front chart (note chart repeat here); Sts 57–74 of Row 1 of Right Front chart—69 sts rem. Turn work to WS.

Right front (continued):

SR 2 (WS): Work Sts 74–56 of Right Front chart Row 2. Turn work to RS.

SR 3–11: Cont to work Right Front as charted— 68 sts rem.

Row 12 (WS): Work Sts 74–64 of Row 12 in patt and place on holder for right shoulder; BO Sts 63–12 in patt; work Sts 11–1 in patt and leave on needle for left shoulder.

SIZES L, 1X, 2X, AND 3X ONLY (USE FRONT CHART FOR SIZES L, 1X, 2X, AND 3X)

Left front:

SR 1 (RS): Work Sts 1–28 of Row 1 of Left Front chart (making sure it is the correct size). Turn work to WS.

SR 2 (WS): Work Sts 27–1 of Row 2 of Left Front. Turn work to RS.

SR 3–10: Cont to work Left Front as charted.

Transition to Right Front (RS): Work Sts 15–29 of Row 11 of Left Front chart; Sts 30–65 of

Finished Measurements

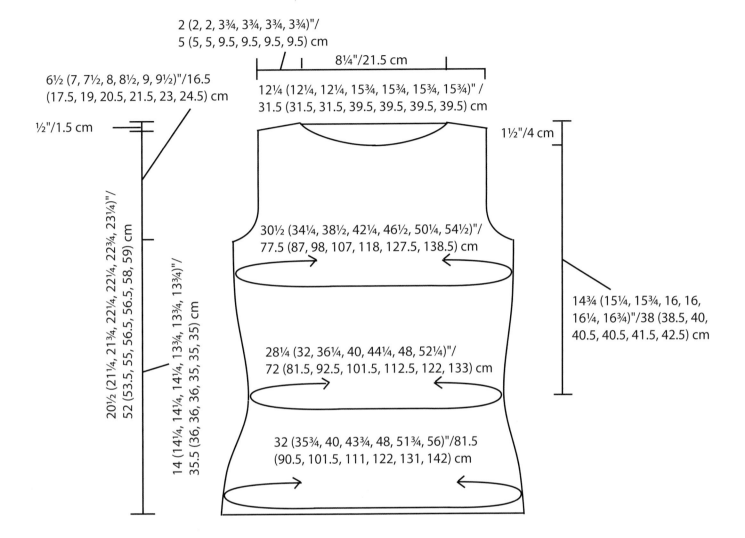

2 (2, 2, 3¾, 3¾, 3¾, 3¾)"/
5 (5, 5, 9.5, 9.5, 9.5, 9.5) cm

8¼"/21.5 cm

6½ (7, 7½, 8, 8½, 9, 9½)"/16.5
(17.5, 19, 20.5, 21.5, 23, 24.5) cm

12¼ (12¼, 12¼, 15¾, 15¾, 15¾, 15¾)" /
31.5 (31.5, 31.5, 39.5, 39.5, 39.5, 39.5) cm

½"/1.5 cm

1½"/4 cm

20½ (21¼, 21¾, 22¼, 22¼, 22¾, 23¼)" /
52 (53.5, 55, 56.5, 56.5, 58, 59) cm

14 (14¼, 14¼, 14¼, 13¾, 13¾, 13¾)" /
35.5 (36, 36, 36, 35, 35, 35) cm

30½ (34¼, 38½, 42¼, 46½, 50¼, 54½)"/
77.5 (87, 98, 107, 118, 127.5, 138.5) cm

14¾ (15¼, 15¾, 16, 16,
16¼, 16¾)"/38 (38.5, 40,
40.5, 40.5, 41.5, 42.5) cm

28¼ (32, 36¼, 40, 44¼, 48, 52¼)"/
72 (81.5, 92.5, 101.5, 112.5, 122, 133) cm

32 (35¾, 40, 43¾, 48, 51¾, 56)"/81.5
(90.5, 101.5, 111, 122, 131, 142) cm

Row 1 of Center Front chart (note chart repeat here); Sts 66–92 of Row 1 of Right Front chart—87 sts rem. Turn work to WS.

Right front (continued):
SR 2 (WS): Work Sts 92–65 of Right Front chart Row 2. Turn work to RS.
SR 3–11: Cont to work Right Front as charted—86 sts rem.
Row 12 (WS): Work Sts 92–73 of Row 12 in patt and place on holder for right shoulder; BO Sts 72–21 in patt; work Sts 20–1 in patt and leave on needle for left shoulder.

ALL SIZES
Break yarn, leaving 36"/90 cm tail.

Finishing

Turn work inside out and place left back shoulder sts on 2nd needle or on opposite end of circular needle, with points of needle(s) at armhole edge of shoulder. Insert a third needle into first st on each of these 2 needles and knit these 2 sts together, using long yarn tail from Front. *Knit next st on each needle the same way, then pass first st on right-hand needle over second st—1 st BO; rep from * until 1 st is left on the right-hand needle, then pull yarn tail through last st.

Repeat for right shoulder, using long yarn tail from Back.

Weave in ends and block to finished measurements.

Sheridan

With a deep scoop neck, this tank can be layered over another tank or blouse, or worn on its own. Unusual cables create highly textured panels on front and back.

SKILL LEVEL
Intermediate: Skills include reading charts, cables, short rows, and three-needle bind-off. See Techniques section beginning on page 146 for a photo tutorial on working short rows.

SIZES
Women's XS (S, M, L, 1X, 2X, 3X)

FINISHED MEASUREMENTS
Bust: 30¼ (34, 38¼, 42, 45½, 50, 53½)"/77 (86.5, 97.5, 106.5, 116, 127, 136) cm. *Shown in Size S with 0"/0 cm ease. Intended to fit with -2"/5 cm to +2"/5 cm ease at bust.*

YARN
630 (700, 790, 860, 980, 1080, 1150) yd/580 (645, 730, 790, 905, 995, 1060) m light weight #3 yarn; shown in #04 Silver, Cascade Yarns Anchor Bay; 50% cotton, 50% superwash merino wool; 262 yd/240 m per 3½ oz/100 g skein, 3 (3, 4, 4, 4, 5, 5) skeins

NEEDLES
US 6/4.0 mm 24–40"/60–100 cm circular needle, depending on selected garment size, for Body and Neckline edging; 16–20"/40–50 cm circular needle, for Armhole edging. *Adjust needle size if necessary to obtain correct gauge.*

NOTIONS
- Stitch markers
- Cable needle
- Removable stitch marker
- Stitch holders
- Tapestry needle

GAUGE
22 sts and 30 rnds in St st = 4"/10 cm square, blocked; 31 sts and 30 rnds in textured cable patt = 4"/10 cm square, blocked

Chart shows textured panel sections of front, back, and straps;
St st sections not shown. Follow written directions as well as chart.

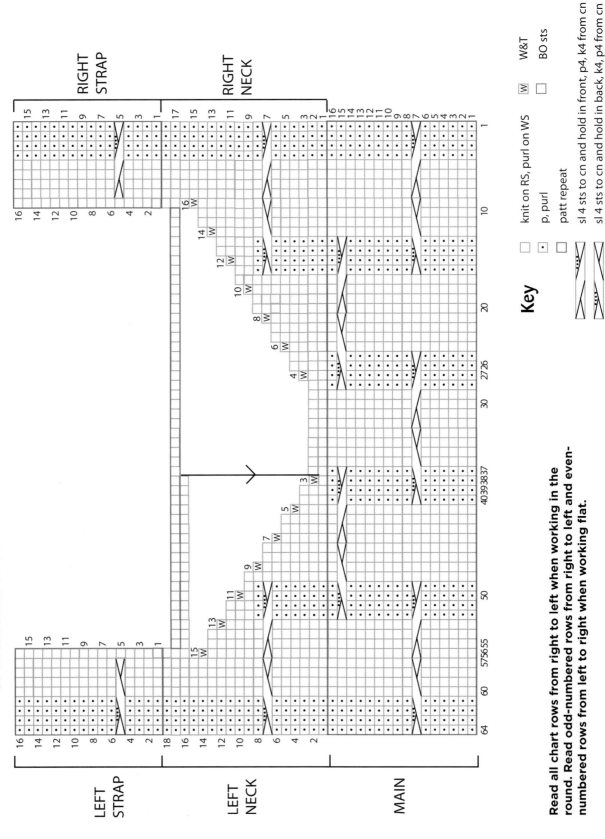

Key

☐	knit on RS, purl on WS
•	p, purl
☐	patt repeat
▨	sl 4 sts to cn and hold in front, p4, k4 from cn
▨	sl 4 sts to cn and hold in back, k4, p4 from cn
W	W&T
☐	BO sts

Read all chart rows from right to left when working in the
round. Read odd-numbered rows from right to left and even-
numbered rows from left to right when working flat.

PATTERN NOTES

- Worked in the round to the armholes
- Short rows shape neckline and shoulders
- Neck and armhole edgings are added after shoulders are joined
- Instructions for textured panel stitch pattern are given in chart form only; neckline short rows are also charted

CUSTOMIZING FIT

- Body length can be changed in increments of 8 rounds (half repeat of textured pattern); if length is changed by 8 rounds, begin the Main chart on Row 1 (1, 1, 1, 9, 9, 9) so that the division for front and back occurs on the chart row specified in the instructions (ensuring that the Main pattern still flows properly into the Neck and Strap charts). If length is changed by 16 rounds, begin the Main chart as instructed below. Side waist decrease and/or increase frequency may also need to be changed if changing body length.
- Strap length can also be changed as desired: this will change neck drop and armhole depth as well as overall length.

Body

Using longer circular needle, CO 216 (236, 260, 280, 300, 324, 344) sts. Pm for side/beg of rnd and join for working in the rnd, taking care not to twist sts.

Set-up rnd: *K22 (27, 33, 38, 43, 49, 54), pm for beg textured panel, [p4, k8] 5 times, p4, pm for end textured panel, k22 (27, 33, 38, 43, 49, 54)**; pm for side; rep from * to **.

Work in patt as est for 5 (5, 5, 5, 5, 7, 7) more rnds.

Est patt: *Knit to beg panel m, work Main chart Row 9 (9, 9, 9, 1, 1, 1) over 64 sts, knit to side m; rep from * to end of rnd.

Next rnd: Knit to beg panel m, work Main chart Row 10 (10, 10, 10, 2, 2, 2) over 64 sts, knit to side m; rep from * to end of rnd.

Begin waist shaping:

Dec rnd: *K5, k2tog, work in patt as est to 7 sts before side m, ssk, k5; rep from * to end of rnd—4 sts dec'd.

Charted panels are worked AT THE SAME TIME as waist shaping: Read through entire section before continuing.

SIZES XS, S, M, AND L ONLY

Work Main chart Rows 12–16 as est on subsequent rnds.

SIZES 1X, 2X, AND 3X ONLY

Work Main chart Rows 4–16 as est on subsequent rnds.

ALL SIZES

Work 96 more rnds, using Main chart Rows 1–16, 6 more times as est.

AT THE SAME TIME, rep Dec rnd every 6th rnd 5 more times—192 (212, 236, 256, 276, 300, 320) sts.

Work even for 13 more rnds.

Inc rnd: *K5, M1L, work in patt to 5 sts before side m, M1R, k5; rep from * to end of rnd—4 sts inc'd.

Rep Inc rnd every 14th rnd 2 more times—204 (224, 248, 268, 288, 312, 332) sts. Work even for 27 (27, 23, 21, 23, 21, 17) more rnds, stopping 3 (4, 5, 6, 7, 8, 9) sts before end of final rnd; piece should measure approx 14½ (14½, 13¾, 13½, 13¾, 13¾, 14, 13¼)"/36.5 (36.5, 35, 34.5, 35, 35, 34) cm from CO. Next chart row should be Main chart Row 15 (15, 11, 9, 3, 1, 13).

Divide for Front and Back: *BO 6 (8, 10, 12, 14, 16, 18) sts** (remove beg of rnd m), work to 3 (4, 5, 6, 7, 8, 9) sts before side m; rep from * to ** (remove side m), work to end. Turn and cont to work 96 (104, 114, 122, 130, 140, 148) Back sts only (place 96 [104, 114, 122, 130, 140, 148] Front sts on holder).

Back

Cont to follow charts as est. Armhole shaping and neck shaping are worked AT THE SAME TIME: Read through entire Back section before continuing.

After completing all reps of Main chart as instructed above, beg Neck chart.

Beg armhole shaping on first row after divide for front and back:

Dec row (WS): P1, ssp, work in patt to last 3 sts, p2tog, p1—2 sts dec'd.

Dec row (RS): K1, k2tog, work in patt to last 3 sts, ssk, k1—2 sts dec'd.

Rep last 2 rows 0 (0, 2, 3, 6, 7, 9) more times—92 (100, 102, 106, 102, 108, 108) sts. Next chart row should be Neck Row 2.

Next row: Beg short row neck shaping (see below) AND cont armhole shaping: Work dec at Left armhole edge on every row as directed above for 4 (4, 2, 2, 0, 2, 2) more rows, then on RS rows only 5 (7, 8, 9, 9, 10, 10) more times—11 (13, 16, 19, 23, 28, 32) sts dec'd at Left armhole edge, 5 (7, 9, 10, 10, 10, 10) sts rem between edge and end panel m.

Short row Left neck shaping (WS): Work in patt to end panel m; work Sts 64–38 of Left Neck chart Row 2 (last st should be wrapped); turn work.

Next row (RS): Work Sts 39–64 of Left Neck chart Row 3; work in patt to end.

Cont to work short rows as est (each wrapped st should fall 3 sts before last wrapped st) through Left Neck chart Row 15: a total of 7 sts have been wrapped.

Next row (WS): Work in patt to end panel m; work Sts 64-38 of Left Neck chart Row 16, picking up wraps and working them tog with wrapped sts; work Sts 37–1 of Right Neck chart Row 2; work in patt to end of row.

Cont armhole shaping: Work dec at Right armhole edge on every row for 4 (4, 2, 2, 0, 2, 2) more rows, then on RS rows only 5 (7, 8, 9, 9, 10, 10) more times—11 (13, 16, 19, 23, 28, 32) sts dec'd at Right armhole edge, 5 (7, 9, 10, 10, 10, 10) sts rem between edge and end panel m.

AT THE SAME TIME, begin Short row Right neck shaping (RS): Work in patt to beg panel m;

work Sts 1–27 of Right Neck chart Row 3 (last st should be wrapped); turn work.

Next row (WS): Work Sts 26–1 of Right Neck chart Row 4; work in patt to end.

Cont to work short rows as est (each wrapped st should fall 3 sts before last wrapped st) through Right Neck chart Row 16: a total of 7 sts have been wrapped.

Next row (RS): Work in patt to beg panel m; work Sts 1–9 of Row 17 of Right/Left Neck chart, picking up wrap; BO Sts 10–55, picking up wraps; work Sts 56–64, picking up wrap; work in patt to end.

Next row (WS): Work in patt to end panel m; work Sts 64–56 of Row 18 of Left Neck chart.

Left Strap (RS): Work Row 1 of Left Strap chart; work in patt to end. Place removable marker in row just worked and cont patt as est (after armhole shaping is completed, 14 [16, 18, 19, 19, 19, 19] sts rem) until strap is 28 (28, 28, 30, 28, 30, 30) rows long (or ¾"/2 cm less than desired final length), ending after a WS row.

Beg short row (SR) shoulder shaping:

SR 1 (RS): Work in patt to last 5 (5, 6, 7, 7, 7, 7) sts, wrap next st and turn work.

SR 2 (WS): Work in patt to end.

SR 3 (RS): Work 4 (5, 5, 5, 5, 5, 5) sts in patt, W&T.

SR 4 (WS): Work in patt to end.

Next row (RS): Work in patt to end, picking up wrap of knit st(s) and working tog with wrapped st (no need to pick up wrap of purl st).

Work 1 more row in patt. Break yarn, leaving 30"/75 cm long tail for three-needle bind-off, and place sts on holder.

Right Strap: Join yarn to work WS of Right Neck. Work Sts 9–1 of Row 18 of Right Neck chart.

Next row (RS): Work in patt to beg panel m; work Row 1 of Right Strap chart.

Cont patt as est (after armhole shaping completed, 14 [16, 18, 19, 19, 19, 19] sts rem) until strap is 29 (29, 29, 31, 29, 31, 31) rows long (or ¾"/2 cm less than desired final length), ending after a RS row.

Beg short row shoulder shaping:

SR 1 (WS): Work in patt to last 5 (5, 6, 7, 7, 7, 7) sts, wrap next st and turn work.

SR 2 (RS): Work in patt to end.

SR 3 (WS): Work 4 (5, 5, 5, 5, 5, 5) sts in patt, W&T.

SR 4 (RS): Work in patt to end.

Next row (WS): Work in patt to end, picking up wrap of purl st(s) and working tog with wrapped st (no need to pick up wrap of knit st). Break yarn, leaving 30"/75 cm long tail for three-needle bind-off, and place sts on holder.

Front

Join yarn to work WS of Front. Front is worked same as Back (note that Left and Right on chart refer to Front sts with RS facing, not side of garment when worn).

Finishing

Turn work inside out and place Front and Back sts for right shoulder on two needles or on opposite ends of circular needle, with points of needle(s) at armhole edge of shoulder.

Join shoulders using three-needle bind-off: Insert a third needle into first st on each of these 2 needles and knit these 2 sts together, using long yarn tail. *Knit next st on each needle the same way, then pass first st on right-hand needle over second st—1 st bound off. Repeat from * until 1 st is left on the right-hand needle, then pull yarn tail through last st.

Repeat for left shoulder.

Weave in ends and block to finished measurements.

Finished Measurements

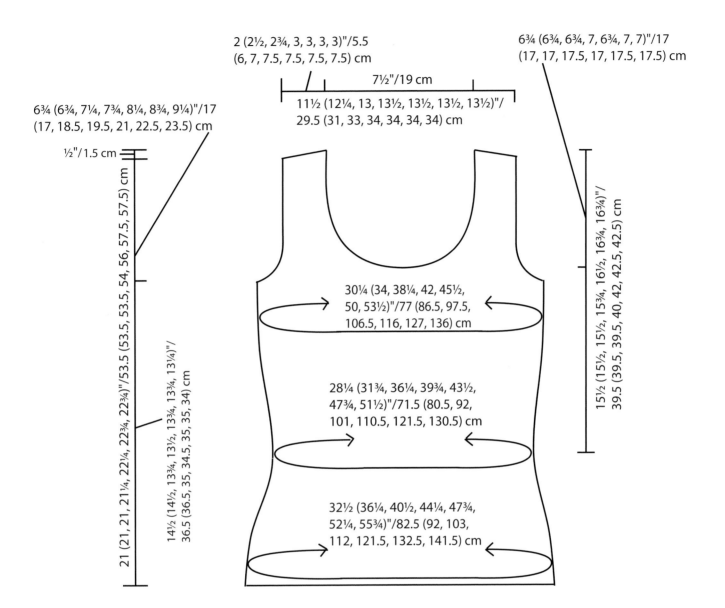

2 (2½, 2¾, 3, 3, 3, 3)"/5.5 (6, 7, 7.5, 7.5, 7.5, 7.5) cm

7½"/19 cm

11½ (12¼, 13, 13½, 13½, 13½, 13½)"/ 29.5 (31, 33, 34, 34, 34, 34) cm

6¾ (6¾, 6¾, 7, 6¾, 7, 7)"/17 (17, 17, 17.5, 17, 17.5, 17.5) cm

6¾ (6¾, 7¼, 7¾, 8¼, 8¾, 9¼)"/17 (17, 18.5, 19.5, 21, 22.5, 23.5) cm

½"/1.5 cm

21 (21, 21, 21¼, 22¼, 22¾, 22¾)"/53.5 (53.5, 53.5, 54, 56, 57.5, 57.5) cm

14½ (14½, 13¾, 13½, 13¾, 13¾, 13¼)"/ 36.5 (36.5, 35, 34.5, 35, 35, 34) cm

30¼ (34, 38¼, 42, 45½, 50, 53½)"/77 (86.5, 97.5, 106.5, 116, 127, 136) cm

28¼ (31¾, 36¼, 39¾, 43½, 47¾, 51½)"/71.5 (80.5, 92, 101, 110.5, 121.5, 130.5) cm

32½ (36¼, 40½, 44¼, 47¾, 52¼, 55¾)"/82.5 (92, 103, 112, 121.5, 132.5, 141.5) cm

15½ (15½, 15½, 15¾, 16½, 16¾, 16¾)"/ 39.5 (39.5, 39.5, 40, 42, 42.5, 42.5) cm

Neck Edging

Using longer needle, with RS facing and starting at one shoulder seam, *pick up and knit 30 sts along curved neck edge; 1 st for each BO st (46 sts); 30 sts to shoulder seam. Rep from *—212 sts. Pm and join. Knit 5 rnds, then BO all sts loosely in patt.

Armhole Edging

Using shorter needle, with RS facing and starting at center of underarm, pick up and knit 1 st for each BO st (3 [4, 5, 6, 7, 8, 9] sts); 39 (39, 43, 46, 49, 52, 55) sts (approx 4 sts per 5 rows) to shoulder seam; 39 (39, 43, 46, 49, 52, 55) sts to BO underarm sts; 1 st for each BO st (3 [4, 5, 6, 7, 8, 9] sts)—84 (86, 96, 104, 112, 120, 128) sts. Pm and join. Knit 5 rnds, then BO all sts loosely in patt.

Weave in rem ends and block again as needed.

Tequesta

A bulky weight yarn and simple lace pattern ensure that this project progresses quickly. The empire waist "skirt" is worked from the top down to show the popular Vine Lace stitch pattern from a different angle. A twisted cord tie under the bust is threaded through the top round of eyelets.

SKILL LEVEL
Easy to Intermediate: Skills include working in the round, keeping track of multiple increases and decreases, simple lace knitting, sewing seams *or* grafting live stitches to finished edge stitches, and twisted cord.

SIZES
Women's XS (S, M, L, 1X, 2X, 3X)

FINISHED MEASUREMENTS
Bust: 29¼ (33¼, 37¼, 41¼, 45¼, 49¼, 53¼)"/74.5 (84.5, 95, 105, 115, 125.5, 135.5) cm. *Shown in size S with -1¾"/4.5 cm ease at bust. Intended to fit with -2"/5 cm to +2"/5 cm ease at bust.*

YARN
410 (480, 550, 620, 700, 790, 870) yd/380 (445, 505, 570, 645, 730, 800) m bulky weight #5 to super bulky weight #6 yarn; shown in #0005 Apfel, Schoeller & Stahl Veneta; 100% cotton; 71 yd/65 m per 1¾ oz/50 g skein, 6 (7, 8, 9, 10, 12, 13) skeins

NEEDLES
US 13/9 mm 24–40"/60–100 cm circular needle, depending on selected garment size, for Body; circular or straight needles, for shoulder straps. *Adjust needle size if necessary to obtain correct gauge.*

NOTIONS
- Stitch markers
- Stitch holders
- Tapestry needle

GAUGE

12 sts and 17 rnds in St st = 4"/10 cm square, blocked; 13 sts and 16 rows in Vine Lace patt = 4"/10 cm, blocked

PATTERN NOTES

- Upper Front and Back are worked separately down to the underarms, where they are joined
- Body is worked in the round down to the hem
- Stitches for shoulder straps are picked up from top edge of back; straps are worked flat
- Straps angle out when worn so crossback measurement on schematic is for the base of the straps.
- Strap ends are grafted or sewn to top of front
- Instructions for lace pattern are given in chart and written form

CUSTOMIZING FIT

- Lace skirt length can be changed in increments of 4 rounds or approximately 1"/2.5 cm.
- It is important for proper fit that the underbust cord sits comfortably under the bust; I recommend trying on garment in progress to make sure that the bodice is long enough to comfortably cover the bust before working underbust decreases (lengthening the bodice will not affect the armhole depth, but it may affect the overall length of the garment). When measured flat, this top is hip length from sizes XS–M, close to tunic length for sizes 2X and 3X, and in between for sizes L and 1X, but when worn with the cord tied under the bust, the top as shown will be approximately hip length for all sizes. Length of lace straps can also be changed in increments of 4 rounds or approximately 1"/2.5 cm; changing strap length will change neck drop *and* armhole depth as well as overall length.

SPECIAL STITCHES

M1L (worked from WS): With left needle tip, lift strand between needles from front to back and purl lifted loop through back, twisting created stitch (creates left-leaning knit stitch on RS).

M1R (worked from WS): With left needle tip, lift strand between needles from back to front and purl lifted loop through front, twisting created stitch (creates right-leaning knit stitch on RS).

Vine Lace (worked over 9 sts and 4 rnds)
Rnds 1 and 3: Knit.
Rnd 2: K1, yo, k2, ssk, k2tog, k2, yo.
Rnd 4: Yo, k2, ssk, k2tog, k2, yo, k1.

Vine Lace

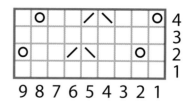

9 8 7 6 5 4 3 2 1

Key

☐   knit on RS, purl on WS
☑   k2tog
◣   ssk
⊡   yo
☐   patt repeat

Read all chart rows from right to left.

Upper Back

Using circular needle, CO 40 (42, 46, 48, 48, 50, 50) sts.
Row 1 (RS): Knit.
Row 2 (WS): Purl.
Work 6 (6, 6, 6, 4, 4, 2) more rows even in St st.
Inc row (RS): K1, M1L, work in patt to last st, M1R, k1—2 sts inc'd, 42 (44, 48, 50, 50, 52, 52) sts.

SIZES M AND L ONLY

Next row (WS): Work even in patt as est.
Next row: Rep Inc row (RS) once more— - (-, -, 50, 52, -, -, -) sts.

SIZES 1X, 2X, AND 3X ONLY

Next row (WS): Work even in patt as est.
Rep last 2 rows - (-, -, -, 1, 1, 2) more times, then rep Inc row (RS) once more— - (-, -, -, 54, 56, 58) sts.

ALL SIZES

Inc row (WS): P1, M1R, work in patt to last st, M1L, p1—2 sts inc'd.

Rep last 2 rows 0 (1, 1, 2, 3, 4, 5) more times—44 (50, 56, 62, 68, 74, 80) sts.

Break yarn and place sts on holder.

Upper Front

Work Upper Front as for Upper Back, but do not break yarn. Work one more RS row even, stopping 1 st before end.

Join Front and Back

Place final Front st on holder and hold in back of work; place held Upper Back sts on opposite end of circular needle, with RS facing. Using working yarn and needle from Upper Front, knit first st of Upper Back, pm for side, knit held st from Upper Front, then knit to last st of Upper Back. Hold this st in front of work, knit first st of Upper Front, pm for beg of rnd, knit held st—88 (100, 112, 124, 136, 148, 160) sts.

Body

Cont to work in St st to end of rnd, then work 8 (10, 12, 14, 16, 18, 20) more rnds even in patt (or until body is long enough to comfortably cover bust).

Underbust Dec rnd:

SIZES XS, S, AND M ONLY

K6 (9, 10, -, -, -, -), [k2tog, k3] twice, k2tog, k8 (8, 12, -, -, -, -), [ssk, k3] twice, ssk, k6 (9, 10, -, -, -, -), sm, k11 (14, 15, -, -, -, -), k2tog, k18 (18, 22, -, -, -, -), ssk, k11 (14, 15, -, -, -, -)—8 sts dec'd.

SIZES L AND 1X ONLY

K- (-, -, 10, 12, -, -), [k2tog, k4] twice, k2tog, k- (-, -, 14, 16, -, -), [ssk, k4] twice, ssk, k- (-, -, 10, 12, -, -), sm, k- (-, -, 16, 18, -, -), k2tog, k- (-, -, 26, 28, -, -), ssk, k- (-, -, 16, 18, -, -)—8 sts dec'd.

SIZES 2X AND 3X ONLY

K- (-, -, -, -, 13, 14), [k2tog, k5] twice, k2tog, k- (-, -, -, -, 16, 20), [ssk, k5] twice, ssk, k- (-, -, -, -, 13, 14), sm, k- (-, -, -, -, 20, 21), k2tog,

k- (-, -, -, -, 30, 34), ssk, k- (-, -, -, -, 20, 21)—8 sts dec'd.

ALL SIZES

80 (92, 104, 116, 128, 140, 152) sts rem: 38 (44, 50, 56, 62, 68, 74) sts in Front and 42 (48, 54, 60, 66, 72, 78) sts in Back. Work 1 rnd even.

Lace Inc rnd:

SIZE XS ONLY

*M1L, k1, [yo, k1, yo, k6] 5 times, [yo, k1] twice, M1R**, remove m, k2, rep from * to **, k2—28 sts inc'd, 108 sts. Remove beg of rnd m, k3, place new beg of rnd m—m moved 3 sts to left.

SIZE S ONLY

K1, *[yo, k1, yo, k5] 3 times, yo, k1, yo, k2, M1L, k2, [yo, k1, yo, k5] 3 times, yo, k1, yo**, k1, remove m, k3, rep from * to **, k2, place new beg of rnd m (remove old beg of rnd m after work first st of next rnd)—m moved 1 st to right, 34 sts inc'd, 126 sts.

SIZE M ONLY

K2, *[yo, k1, yo, k3, M1L, k2, yo, k1, yo, k6] twice, [yo, k1, yo, k2, M1R, k3, yo, k1, yo, k6] twice** (remove m), rep from * to **, ending last rep k4 instead of k6—40 sts inc'd, 144 sts. Remove beg of rnd m, k3, place new beg of rnd m—m moved 3 sts to left.

SIZE L ONLY

K2, *yo, k1, yo, k6, yo, k2tog, yo, k6, [yo, k1, yo, k6] 4 times, yo, ssk, yo, k6, yo, k1, yo, k6**

(remove m), rep from * to **, ending last rep k4 instead of k6—28 sts inc'd, 144 sts. Remove beg of rnd m, k3, place new beg of rnd m—m moved 3 sts to left.

SIZE 1X ONLY

Yo, k6, [yo, k1, yo, k6] 10 times (remove m), yo, k2tog, yo, k6, [yo, k1, yo, k6] 4 times, yo, ssk, yo, k6, yo, k1, yo, k6, yo, place new beg of rnd m (remove old beg of rnd m after work first st of next rnd)—m moved 1 st to right, 34 sts inc'd, 162 sts.

SIZE 2X ONLY

K2, *[yo, k1, yo, k6] 10 times** (remove m), rep from * to **, ending last rep k4 instead of k6—40 sts inc'd, 180 sts. Remove beg of rnd m, k3, place new beg of rnd m—m moved 3 sts to left.

SIZE 3X ONLY

K2, *[yo, k2tog, yo, k6, yo, k1, yo, k6] twice, yo, k2tog, yo, k6, [yo, ssk, yo, k6, yo, k1, yo, k6] twice, yo, ssk, yo, k6** (remove m), rep from * to **, ending last rep k4 instead of k6—28 sts inc'd, 180 sts. Remove beg of rnd m, k3, place new beg of rnd m—m moved 3 sts to left.

ALL SIZES

Est Vine Lace patt:
Rnd 1: Work Rnd 1 of Vine Lace patt 12 (14, 16, 16, 18, 20, 20) times to end of rnd.
Rnd 2: Work Rnd 2 of Vine Lace patt 12 (14, 16, 16, 18, 20, 20) times to end of rnd.
Work 2 more rnds in patt as est using subsequent patt rnds, then rep these 4 rnds 11 more times or to desired garment length, ending on patt Rnd 4.
Next rnd: BO all sts loosely knitwise.

Straps

Note: Loose ends of straps will be joined to CO edge of Front. After each strap is worked, it is recommended to try on the garment and check strap length before breaking yarn; strap can be lengthened or shortened in increments of 4 rows.

Right Strap

With RS of Back facing, pick up and knit 11 sts from CO edge, beg at right armhole edge.

Est patt:
Rows 1 and 3 (WS): Purl.
Row 2 (RS): K2, yo, k2, ssk, k2tog, k2, yo, k1.
Row 4 (RS): K1, yo, k2, ssk, k2tog, k2, yo, k2.
Rep Rows 1–4, 7 more times, then work 1 more row in patt (WS). Break yarn, leaving 24"/60 cm long tail, and place sts on holder (OR if sewing strap to front, BO all sts loosely and break yarn, leaving 24"/60 cm long tail).

Left Strap

With RS of Back facing, pick up and knit 11 sts from CO edge, beg 11 sts from left armhole edge.

Est patt:
Rows 1 and 3 (WS): Purl.
Row 2 (RS): K1, yo, k2, ssk, k2tog, k2, yo, k2.
Row 4 (RS): K2, yo, k2, ssk, k2tog, k2, yo, k1.
Rep Rows 1–4, 7 more times, then work 1 more row in patt (WS). Break yarn, leaving 24"/60 cm long tail, and place sts on holder (OR if sewing strap to front, BO all sts loosely and break yarn, leaving 24"/60 cm long tail).

Finishing

If grafting live sts of strap ends to Front:
Hold garment with RS of Front and Right strap facing, and live sts of Right strap on dpn, held below and parallel to CO edge of Front; right edge of strap should line up with right armhole edge of Front. Using tapestry needle and yarn tail, graft live sts of strap to row of sts just above CO edge of Front:

Insert tapestry needle through center of live stitch with long yarn tail from WS to RS, then pass needle under both legs of edge stitch of top piece. Pull yarn through (leave loose), then insert needle into center of stitch with long yarn tail from RS to WS.

1. Graft yarn has been passed through center of live side edge stitch on bottom piece from RS to WS, then through center of adjacent live stitch from WS to RS; tapestry needle shown passing under both legs of corresponding stitch just above BO edge of top piece.

2. Yarn has been pulled through on top piece; tapestry needle is inserted through center of

live stitch from RS to WS on bottom piece (after yarn pulled through, this completes graft of one knit stitch).

3. Tapestry needle is inserted from WS to RS through the center of first stitch still on the dpn. After yarn is pulled through, this completes graft of previous stitch, and stitch on dpn can be slipped off while continuing graft, without fear of dropping it.

Continue until all strap stitches have been grafted, then repeat for Left strap, lining up left edge of strap with left armhole edge of Front, and beginning 11 sts in from left armhole edge.

Weave in ends and block to finished measurements.

If sewing BO strap ends to Front:
Hold garment with RS of Front and Right strap facing, and BO edge of strap parallel to top edge of Front; right edge of strap should line up with right armhole edge of Front. Using yarn needle and yarn tail, sew strap end to row of sts just above CO edge of Front, using the invisible horizontal method (see photo tutorial on page 152).

Repeat for Left strap, lining up left edge of strap with left armhole edge of Front, and beginning 11 sts in from left armhole edge.

Weave in ends and block to finished measurements.

Twisted Cord Belt

Finished belt should be underbust circumference *plus* 36"/90 cm. Cut 3 strands of yarn, each 3 times longer than total length needed. Knot the strands together close to one end and

Finished Measurements

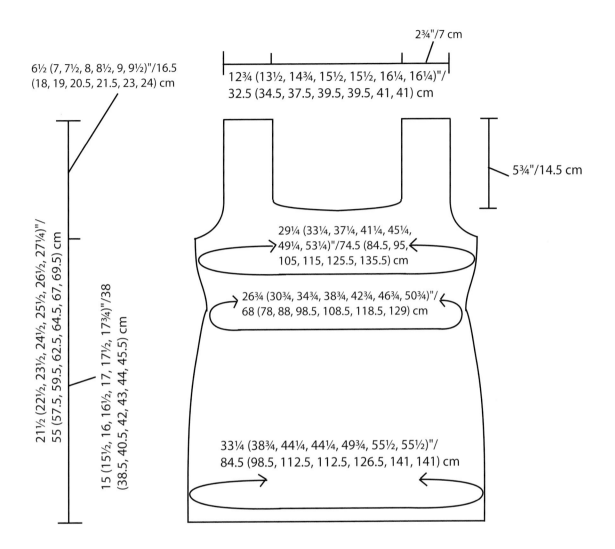

6½ (7, 7½, 8, 8½, 9, 9½)"/16.5 (18, 19, 20.5, 21.5, 23, 24) cm

2¾"/7 cm

12¾ (13½, 14¾, 15½, 15½, 16¼, 16¼)"/ 32.5 (34.5, 37.5, 39.5, 39.5, 41, 41) cm

5¾"/14.5 cm

29¼ (33¼, 37¼, 41¼, 45¼, 49¼, 53¼)"/74.5 (84.5, 95, 105, 115, 125.5, 135.5) cm

26¾ (30¾, 34¾, 38¾, 42¾, 46¾, 50¾)"/ 68 (78, 88, 98.5, 108.5, 118.5, 129) cm

21½ (22½, 23½, 24½, 25½, 26½, 27¼)"/ 55 (57.5, 59.5, 62.5, 64.5, 67, 69.5) cm

15 (15½, 16, 16½, 17, 17½, 17¾)"/38 (38.5, 40.5, 42, 43, 44, 45.5) cm

33¼ (38¾, 44¼, 44¼, 49¾, 55½, 55½)"/ 84.5 (98.5, 112.5, 112.5, 126.5, 141, 141) cm

loop tied ends over chair leg or other fixed/heavy object to anchor them in place. Knot opposite ends of yarn, insert a knitting needle, and twist the yarn by rotating needle while applying light tension, until entire length is twisted tightly and starts to kink when tension is relaxed. Fold yarn in half, applying light tension while allowing it to twist evenly on itself, and remove cord from anchor. Remove knitting needle and knot both ends, leaving 2–3"/5–7.5 cm outside knots, and trim ends (removing original end knots). Starting and ending at center front, pass one end of cord through pairs of eyelets just below bust.

Yuma

The mirrored lace stitch patterns used in this tunic cause the fabric to bias in opposite directions, creating the diagonal hem and one-shouldered bodice.

SKILL LEVEL

Easy to intermediate: Skills include reading lace charts, simple shaping, and seaming.

SIZES

Women's XS (S, M, L, 1X, 2X, 3X)

FINISHED MEASUREMENTS

Bust: 34 (36¾, 42½, 45¼, 50¾, 53½, 56½)"/86.5 (93.5, 107.5, 115, 129, 136, 143.5) cm. *Shown in size S with +2¾"/7 cm ease. Intended to fit with -2"/5 cm to +3"/7.5 cm ease at bust.*

YARN

580 (620, 700, 740, 810, 850, 900) yd/540 (570, 645, 680, 745, 780, 830) m fine weight #2 to light weight #3 yarn; shown in #7743 Bronze, Classic Elite Yarns Firefly; 75% viscose, 25% linen; 155 yd/142 m per 1¾ oz/50 g skein, 4 (5, 5, 5, 6, 6, 6) skeins

NEEDLES

US 7/4.5 mm 24–40"/60–100 cm circular needle, depending on selected garment size, for Body. *Adjust needle size if necessary to obtain correct gauge.*

NOTIONS

- Stitch markers
- Tapestry needle

GAUGE

20 sts and 25 rnds in lace patt st = 4"/10 cm square, blocked (note that bias of fabric will cause row gauge to decrease on long side of garment)

PATTERN NOTES

- Worked in the round to the armhole
- All edgings are self-finished and are worked along with the body; do not join new balls of yarn at edge of piece
- Instructions for lace stitch pattern are given in written and chart form

CUSTOMIZING FIT

- In addition to bust circumference, measure one-shouldered circumference (around neck and under opposite arm) and compare to circumference of top edge of garment to check fit for your size.
- There is no waist shaping, so body length can be easily increased or decreased in increments of 12 rounds (full repeat of lace pattern).

SPECIAL STITCHES

Lace Pattern A (worked over 7 sts and 12 rnds or rows)

Rnd 1 and all odd-numbered rnds (RS): Knit.

Row 1 and all odd-numbered rows (WS): Purl.

Rnd or Row 2 (RS): Yo, k5, k2tog.

Rnd or Row 4 (RS): K1, yo, k4, k2tog.

Rnd or Row 6 (RS): K2, yo, k3, k2tog.

Rnd or Row 8 (RS): K3, yo, k2, k2tog.

Rnd or Row 10 (RS): K4, yo, k1, k2tog.

Rnd or Row 12 (RS): K5, yo, k2tog.

Lace Pattern B (worked over 7 sts and 12 rnds or rows)

Rnd 1 and all odd-numbered rnds (RS): Knit.

Row 1 and all odd-numbered rows (WS): Purl.

Rnd or Row 2 (RS): Ssk, k5, yo.

Rnd or Row 4 (RS): Ssk, k4, yo, k1.

Rnd or Row 6 (RS): Ssk, k3, yo, k2.

Rnd or Row 8 (RS): Ssk, k2, yo, k3.

Rnd or Row 10 (RS): Ssk, k1, yo, k4.

Rnd or Row 12 (RS): Ssk, yo, k5.

Lace Charts

Key

☐	knit on RS, purl on WS
☑	k2tog
◺	ssk
⊙	yo
☐	patt rep

When working in the round, read all chart rows from right to left. When working flat, read odd (WS) rows from left to right and even (RS) rows from right to left.

Body

CO 170 (184, 212, 226, 254, 268, 282) sts. Pm for beg of rnd and join, taking care not to twist sts.

Est patts:

Rnd 1: K1, M1L; pm, work Row 1 of Lace chart A 12 (13, 15, 16, 18, 19, 20) times, pm, work Row 1 of Lace chart B 12 (13, 15, 16, 18, 19, 20) times, pm; M1R, k1—2 sts inc'd.

Rnd 2: Ssk; sm, work next row of Lace chart A 12 (13, 15, 16, 18, 19, 20) times, sm, work next row of Lace chart B 12 (13, 15, 16, 18, 19, 20) times, sm; k2tog—2 sts dec'd.

Rnd 3: K1, M1L; sm, work in patt as est to last st, sm; M1R, k1—2 sts inc'd.

Rep last 2 rnds for patt.

Work in patts as est for a total of 84 (80, 78, 74, 64, 60, 56) rnds from CO, ending after an even-numbered Lace chart row.

Divide for armhole:

Turn to work WS and remove beg of rnd m.

Dec row 1 (WS): P1, M1R; sm, p2tog, work in patt to last 3 sts, ssp, sm; M1L, p1—2 sts dec'd in Body, 1 st inc'd in each edge.

Dec row 2 (RS): Ssk; sm, ssk, work in patt to last 4 sts, k2tog, sm; k2tog—2 sts dec'd in Body, 1 st dec'd in each edge.

Rep these 2 rows 2 (2, 6, 6, 6, 6, 6) more times.

Next row (WS): Work even in Body but work [p1, M1R] at beg and [M1L, p1] at end of row.

Rep Dec row 2 (RS) every RS row 8 (8, 7, 7, 7, 7, 7) more times (work WS rows as above)—28 (28, 42, 42, 42, 42, 42) sts dec'd in Body, 142 (156, 170, 184, 212, 226, 240) total sts rem.

Work even in patts as est (including edge sts) for 24 (28, 24, 28, 30, 34, 38) more rows, ending on a RS row.

Shoulder shaping: Work Dec row 1 (WS) and Dec row 2 (RS) 7 (7, 7, 7, 11, 11, 11) times, for a total of 14 (14, 14, 14, 22, 22, 22) rows—28 (28, 28, 28, 44, 44, 44) sts dec'd in Body, 114 (128, 142, 156, 168, 182, 196) total sts rem.

Next row: BO all sts loosely purlwise and break yarn, leaving 30"/75 cm long tail.

Finished Measurements

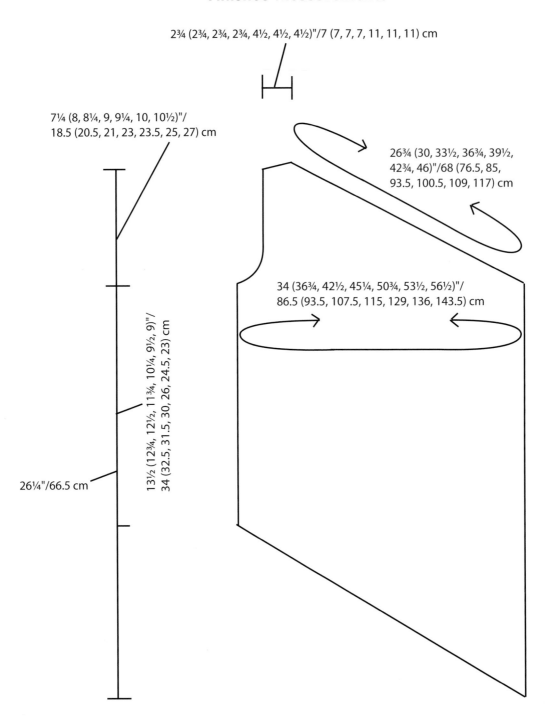

2¾ (2¾, 2¾, 2¾, 4½, 4½, 4½)"/7 (7, 7, 7, 11, 11, 11) cm

7¼ (8, 8¼, 9, 9¼, 10, 10½)"/
18.5 (20.5, 21, 23, 23.5, 25, 27) cm

26¾ (30, 33½, 36¾, 39½,
42¾, 46)"/68 (76.5, 85,
93.5, 100.5, 109, 117) cm

34 (36¾, 42½, 45¼, 50¾, 53½, 56½)"/
86.5 (93.5, 107.5, 115, 129, 136, 143.5) cm

13½ (12¾, 12½, 11¾, 10¼, 9½, 9)" /
34 (32.5, 31.5, 30, 26, 24.5, 23) cm

26¼"/66.5 cm

Finishing

Using long yarn tail and tapestry needle and, with RS facing, sew shoulder seam (opposite ends of rows with shoulder shaping decreases) using invisible horizontal seam method (see photo tutorial on page 152).

Weave in ends and block to finished measurements.

Abbreviations

approx	approximately		**p2tog**	purl 2 sts together (1 st dec'd, if worked on WS creates right-leaning dec on RS)
beg	beginning			
BO	bind (bound) off			
cm	centimeter(s)		**rem**	remain(ing)
cn	cable needle		**rep**	repeat
CO	cast on		**rnd**	round
cont	continue		**RS**	right side
dec	decrease		**sk2p**	slip 1 stitch purlwise, k2tog, pass slipped st over (center st on bottom, 2 sts dec'd)
est	establish(ed)			
inc	increase			
k	knit		**sl**	slip
kfb	knit into front and back of same st (1 st inc'd)		**sm**	slip marker
			ssk	[slip 1 stitch knitwise] twice, then knit slipped stitches together through the back loops (left-leaning dec, 1 st dec'd)
k1b	knit into back of stitch, twisting stitch			
k2tog	knit 2 sts together (right-leaning dec, 1 st dec'd)			
			ssp	[slip 1 stitch knitwise] twice, then purl slipped stitches together through the back loops (1 st dec'd, if worked on WS creates left-leaning dec on RS)
m	marker(s)			
M1L	with left needle tip, lift strand between needles from front to back; knit lifted loop through back, twisting created stitch (left-leaning inc, 1 st inc'd)			
			st, sts	stitch, stitches
			St st	stockinette st
M1P	with left needle tip, lift strand between needles from front to back; purl lifted loop through back, twisting created stitch (1 st inc'd)		**s2kp**	slip 2 sts as if to k2tog, knit next st, then pass 2 slipped sts over (center st on top, 2 sts dec'd)
			tbl	through back loop
			tog	together
M1R	with left needle tip, lift strand between needles from back to front; knit lifted loop through front, twisting created stitch (right-leaning inc, 1 st inc'd)		**WS**	wrong side
			wyib	with yarn in back
			wyif	with yarn in front
			W&T	wrap and turn
p	purl		**yd**	yards
patt	pattern		**yo**	yarn over
pm	place marker			
p1b	purl into back of stitch, twisting stitch			

Techniques

Quick Reference

GARTER STITCH
Worked in the round: Alternate one round of all knit stitches with one round of all purl stitches.
Worked flat: Knit all stitches every row.

KNITTED CAST-ON
Turn work to WS and, using working yarn, *knit one stitch, then return stitch to left-hand needle, taking care not to twist it: one stitch cast on. Rep from * until required number of stitches has been cast on.

LT (LEFT TWIST, WORKED OVER 2 STS)
RS: Knit 2nd stitch on the left-hand needle through the back loop, leaving it on the needle, then knit first stitch and drop both stitches off needle.
(WS, creates Left Twist with knit stitches on the RS): Purl 2nd stitch on the left-hand needle through the back loop, leaving it on the needle, then purl first stitch and drop both stitches off needle.

M1L, WORKED FROM WS TO CREATE M1L ON RS
With left needle tip, lift strand between needles from front to back. Purl lifted loop through back, twisting created stitch.

M1R, WORKED FROM WS TO CREATE M1R ON RS
With left needle tip, lift strand between needles from back to front. Purl lifted loop through front, twisting created stitch.

RT (RIGHT TWIST, WORKED OVER 2 STS)
RS: Knit 2nd stitch on the left-hand needle, leaving it on the needle, then knit first stitch and drop both stitches off needle.
(WS, creates Right Twist with knit sts on the RS): Purl 2nd stitch on the left-hand needle, leaving it on the needle, then purl first stitch and drop both stitches off needle.

SLIPPED STITCH EDGE (SSE)—WORKED OVER 3 STITCHES AND 2 ROWS
RS: K1, slip stitch with yarn in front, k1.
WS: Slip stitch with yarn in front, k1, slip stitch with yarn in front.

STOCKINETTE STITCH (ST ST)
Worked in the round: Knit all stitches.
Worked flat: Knit RS rows and purl WS rows.

STURDY KNITTED CAST-ON
Turn work to WS; stitches just worked are now on left-hand needle. *Insert right-hand needle tip between first two stitches on left-hand needle, draw loop of working yarn through, and place loop on left-hand needle, taking care not to twist it: one stitch cast on. Rep from * until required number of stitches has been cast on.

THREE-NEEDLE BIND-OFF
Hold pieces to be joined with right sides together. Place stitches to be bound off on two needles, held parallel. Insert a third needle into first stitch on each of these two needles and knit these two stitches together. *Knit next stitch on each needle the same way, then pass first stitch on right-hand needle over second stitch—one stitch bound off. Repeat from * until one stitch is left on the right-hand needle, then pull yarn tail through last stitch.

Photo Tutorials

KNITTED CAST-ON
Turn work to WS; stitches just worked are now on left-hand needle.

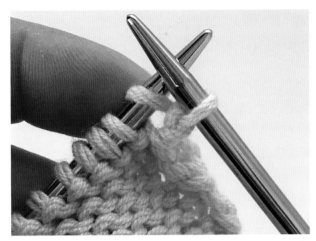

Using working yarn, insert needle into last stitch as if to knit it, and draw yarn through to make new stitch.

Return new stitch to left-hand needle, taking care not to twist it: first stitch cast on. Keep stitch loose to allow needle to pass through it to create next stitch.

*Using working yarn, insert needle into last stitch as if to knit it, and draw yarn through to make new stitch. Return new stitch to left-hand needle** as in previous photo: second stitch cast-on.

Repeat from * to ** until required number of stitches have been cast on. (Note that edge stitch of original piece may be mistaken for first cast-on stitch.)

STURDY KNITTED CAST-ON
Turn work to WS; stitches just worked are now on left-hand needle. Insert right-hand needle tip from front to back between first two stitches on left-hand needle.

Draw loop of working yarn through, from back to front.

Place loop on left-hand needle, taking care not to twist it: first stitch cast on. Keep stitch loose to allow needle to pass behind it to create next stitch.

Insert right-hand needle tip from front to back between first two stitches on left-hand needle.

Draw loop of working yarn through, from back to front.

Place loop on left-hand needle, taking care not to twist it: second stitch cast on.

Six stitches cast on: Note that what appears to be first cast-on stitch is actually edge stitch of original piece.

SHORT ROW SHAPING
Wrap & Turn (W&T)

If stitch before wrapped stitch is knitted: Bring yarn to front of work, slip next stitch purlwise, bring yarn to back of work around base of stitch, then return wrapped stitch to left-hand needle. Turn work to opposite side.

If stitch before wrapped stitch is purled: Slip next stitch purlwise, bring yarn to back of work, then return wrapped stitch to left-hand needle. Turn work to opposite side.

Picking up wraps and working together with wrapped stitches:

If wrapped stitch is knit: Insert right-hand needle tip into wrap from underneath and then into wrapped stitch as if to knit, then knit wrapped stitch and wrap together.

If wrapped stitch is purled: With right-hand needle tip, from back, lift back strand of wrap and place it over left-hand needle, then p2tog.

Short rows starting on knit side (or if last stitch worked before wrap is knit stitch): Work to stitch to be wrapped. Bring yarn to front and slip stitch to be wrapped from left-hand to right-hand needle, purlwise.

To pick up wrap, insert tip of right-hand needle into wrap from front to back.

Bring yarn to back, around base of stitch and between needles.

With wrap on right-hand needle, insert needle tip into wrapped stitch and knit stitch and wrap together.

Short rows starting on purl side (or if last stitch worked before wrap is purl stitch): Work to stitch to be wrapped. Slip stitch to be wrapped from left-hand to right-hand needle, purlwise.

Return wrapped stitch to left-hand needle, turn work to opposite side, and reverse direction, working across last row of stitches in pattern.

Bring yarn to back between needles, around base of stitch.

Return wrapped stitch to left-hand needle, turn work to opposite side, bring yarn between needles to back of work, and reverse direction, working across last row of stitches in pattern.

To pick up wrap, insert tip of right-hand needle under back strand of wrap from back to front and place it over left-hand needle tip. Purl wrapped stitch and wrap together.

ATTACHED I-CORD

Note: Two-stitch I-cord is shown; I-cord may also be worked with three or more stitches.

Turn work to WS and using working yarn, cast on two stitches using knitted cast-on. Slip these two stitches onto left-hand needle, ready to work.

*Knit first stitch on left-hand needle, then ssk next two stitches (2nd stitch of ssk is from original piece).

Return two stitches remaining on right-hand needle to left-hand needle**. Repeat from * to ** until all live stitches from original piece have been worked.

I-cord in progress as shown from RS.

Grafting Ends of I-Cord
After all live stitches from original piece have been worked, two I-cord stitches remain on needle.

Remove needle or holder from two remaining I-cord stitches. Note that yarn tail is coming from lower stitch in photo.

Thread needle with yarn tail and insert needle into other live stitch from underneath, as shown.

To begin graft to first row of I-cord, pass needle under both legs of the knit stitch in this row that is closest to RS of work.

After pulling yarn through (keep it loose for now), insert needle back into same live stitch, this time from the top, and then into remaining live stitch (from which yarn tail originated) from underneath. This live stitch will tend to flip over (as it has in photo, making it appear that the needle is entering it from the top); before inserting needle, ensure that the stitch is oriented so that it appears to be part of the chain of knit stitches forming one column of the I-cord.

Continue graft to first row of I-cord by passing needle under both legs of the knit stitch in this row that is next to stitch previously grafted.

Pull yarn through.

Starting with the last two live I-cord stitches, tighten graft stitches carefully so that tension is even, and graft row blends with rest of I-cord.

INVISIBLE HORIZONTAL SEAM

This seam mimics the appearance of a row of knit stitches. Since bound-off edges of both pieces will be joined, stitches meet head-to-head, so using this method will move one of the pieces one-half stitch to the side (which is not obvious in the finished garment). Set up pieces to be seamed with right sides facing, and edges to be seamed parallel. Thread needle with long yarn tail from one of the pieces.

Insert needle into corner stitch of opposite (top) piece from back to front, then into stitch with long yarn tail from back to front, creating a figure eight. Pull yarn snug enough to close gap.

Pass needle under both legs of knit stitch just above bound-off edge, on edge of top piece.

Insert needle from RS to WS through center of stitch on edge of bottom piece, just below bound-off edge, then insert needle from WS to RS through center of next stitch in same row.

*Pull yarn through and pass needle under both legs of next knit stitch in row just above bound-off edge, on top piece.

Pull yarn through. Insert needle from RS to WS through center of same stitch last worked on bottom piece, then insert needle from WS to RS through center of next stitch in same row**. Repeat from * to ** until all stitches are seamed.

Tighten yarn just enough to hide bound-off edges, while still closely matching stitches in adjacent rows.

At end of seam, repeat figure 8 at garment edges.

PICKING UP STITCHES FROM BOUND-OFF EDGE

Generally one stitch is picked up for each stitch bound off; bound-off edge is hidden by the picked-up stitches.

With yarn held in back, insert needle through center of edge stitch just below bound-off edge and pull loop of yarn through to RS. (Not shown: yarn can be held in front, needle inserted from back to front, and then loop of yarn pulled through to back: this technique leaves the bound-off edge on the RS, creating an accent cord.)

Continue to insert needle through center of each stitch in row just below bound-off edge and pull the yarn through; arrow shows where to insert needle to pick up next stitch.

PICKING UP STITCHES FROM SIDE EDGE

Since knit stitches are wider than they are tall, generally fewer stitches than rows are picked up from the side edge of a piece.

Pick up the first stitch in the space between the edge stitch and the next stitch, just above the cast-on (or below the bound-off) edge.

Pull gently on the side edge to expose the bars of yarn that connect the edge stitches with the adjacent column of stitches. Stitches are picked up through the spaces between these bars; skip some spaces so that you don't pick up too many stitches.

In this swatch, three stitches have been picked up for every four rows; at every fourth (skipped) row, two bars are visible between picked-up stitches.

CONTRAST COLOR DUPLICATE STITCH GRAFTING

This method greatly simplifies grafting of different stitch patterns. Knitters familiar with Kitchener stitch can graft stockinette stitch fabric fairly easily, but grafting more complex stitch patterns can be quite tricky. By using the contrast color duplicate stitch method, you avoid having to create or follow complicated charts for grafting lace and other pattern stitches; in addition, there are no live stitches to drop! The rows of stitches that are adjacent to the graft row are held securely in place by stitches worked in pattern with contrast color waste yarn, making it easy to see how all of the stitches are interconnected. To create the graft, you simply follow the path of contrasting yarn as it passes through the stitches on each side of the graft row, alternating top and bottom. Remember that the stitches of the graft row connect two other rows, one on the top and one on the bottom: for the top side of the graft row, follow just the top loops of waste yarn; for the bottom edge, follow just the bottom loops of waste yarn. The beginning and the end of the row require extra attention, but the middle of the graft progresses much faster than if using a traditional grafting technique. Finally, yarn tension can be adjusted (best to leave yarn fairly loose, then go back and tighten it after completing several stitches) and any mistakes can be redone, without fear of dropping stitches: the contrast color waste yarn is not removed until the graft is completed to your satisfaction.

In this book, only pieces that have been worked in the same direction (for instance, the beginning and end of a loop) are grafted using this method. This allows the stitch patterns to be joined perfectly using grafting, and avoids having to hide the half-stitch jog that occurs when two knitted pieces are grafted end-to-end (such as the toe of a sock).

In preparation for this method of grafting, stitches are cast on using a contrast color waste yarn of similar thickness to the main yarn. A couple of rows are worked in pattern; the last row worked will be the pattern graft row. The waste yarn is broken and main yarn joined, and the stitch pattern continued until the piece is the proper length, stopping at the beginning of a pattern graft row. The main yarn is broken, leaving a tail long enough to complete the graft (very important!). Waste yarn is joined and two more rows worked in pattern, then all stitches are bound off. The example shown is from Galena on page 46.

To set up for grafting, place the bound-off end of the piece below the cast-on end, with edges parallel and RS facing. Thread a needle with yarn tail, which should be at the lower right.

Note that the free end of the waste yarn passes through a loop of the main yarn at the edge of the piece: the first grafting step is to pass the needle through this loop.

Row 7 (graft row)

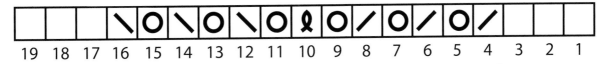

Graft row from Galena chart.

Draw yarn through, then bring it to the cast-on (top) piece and follow the path of the waste yarn as it passes through a loop of main yarn on the side edge, crosses under and then over itself, and then goes under the horizontal bar of a purl stitch (see arrow).

Main yarn shown pulled through loop on side edge and then passed under itself.

Main yarn shown continuing to follow path of waste yarn: over itself, under purl bar, and then back to bound-off (bottom) piece, where it passes the center of the side-edge stitch from top to bottom (this pass is not visible in photo), then through the center of the adjacent stitch from bottom to top. On the bottom piece, each yarn loop passes between two charted stitches, completing the first stitch and beginning the second. On this piece, follow just the bottom loops of the waste yarn.

Main yarn shown following path of waste yarn on top piece, as it passes under the same purl bar shown in the 2nd photo, and then under the purl bar of the adjacent stitch (follow just the top loops of the waste yarn on this piece). The needle is then brought to the bottom piece and passed through the center of same stitch worked last in previous photo, but this time the

Row 7 (graft row)

19   18   17   16   15   14   13   12   11   10   9   8   7   6   5   4   3   2   1

needle is inserted from top to bottom, instead of bottom to top. The needle is then passed through the center of the adjacent stitch from bottom to top.

Yarn has been pulled through stitches shown in previous photo on bottom piece, then under the same purl bar worked last on the upper piece in previous photo. Yarn then passed under the purl bar of the adjacent stitch. The arrow shows the next pass of the needle/yarn as it follows the bottom loop of waste yarn on the bottom piece; this pass goes through three loops of main yarn because it includes the left leg of a knit stitch (Stitch 3 of the graft row), and the right leg of the next stitch, which is a k2tog.

The needle is shown following the top loop of waste yarn as it passes behind the next stitch

on the top piece, creating a knit stitch. Note that on the top piece, each stitch is looped around the stitch directly above it; whether the horizontal bar of this loop sits on top or behind the stitch above determines whether it is a purl or a knit stitch.

Needle is brought back to the bottom piece and enters the same stitch from which it exited on the last pass, exiting this stitch from on the WS.

The knit column that forms the right border of the "wheel" has been grafted; this is a good place to make sure the stitches on top and bottom pieces are lining up correctly. Needle is shown following loop of waste yarn on top piece as it forms a yarn over (Stitch 5 of the graft row).

Row 7 (graft row)

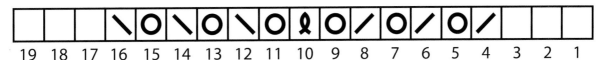

| 19 | 18 | 17 | 16 | 15 | 14 | 13 | 12 | 11 | 10 | 9 | 8 | 7 | 6 | 5 | 4 | 3 | 2 | 1 |

Needle follows path of waste yarn as it completes the yarn over shown in the last photo (Stitch 5 of graft row) and begins a k2tog (Stitch 6 of graft row).

Main yarn shown following path of waste yarn as it forms the top part of Stitch 14 of graft row; needle is following path of waste yarn on bottom piece as it completes the ssk of Stitch 14 and begins the yarn over of Stitch 15.

In this photo we have skipped ahead to Stitch 12 of the graft row; the needle is shown passing behind the stitch on the top piece, creating a knit stitch.

Main yarn shown following path of waste yarn as it forms the top part of Stitch 16 of graft row; needle is following path of waste yarn on bottom piece as it completes the ssk of Stitch 16 and begins Stitch 17 (a knit stitch).

Row 7 (graft row)

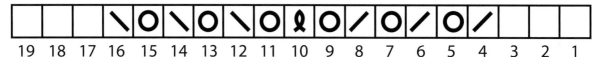

Yarn is shown exiting center of knit Stitch 18 on bottom piece; needle inserted on top piece to begin following loop of waste yarn that forms top of same stitch.

Yarn has been pulled up through the center of Stitch 19 on the bottom piece, then follows the loop of waste yarn as it continues the same stitch on the upper piece.

Yarn has completed loop following waste yarn in top piece; needle inserted through center of Stitch 18 from RS to WS to complete this stitch on bottom piece, then from WS to RS through center of next stitch (final stitch of graft row).

Needle is inserted through the center of Stitch 19 on the bottom piece, from RS to WS, following the final loop of waste yarn and completing the last stitch of the graft row. After yarn is pulled through, the tension of the last few stitches will be adjusted, completing the graft.

After the entire graft has been checked to make sure stitches line up properly and yarn tension is satisfactory, turn the piece to the WS and carefully snip the waste yarn loops that connect to the graft stitches. Main yarn ends can then be trimmed and woven in on the WS.

Row 7 (graft row)

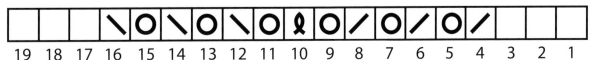

WEAVING IN ENDS

Skimming yarn on WS:

Thread yarn end onto needle and pass needle tip through a diagonal line of four or five stitches on the WS, splitting the yarn in each of these stitches (this avoids creating extra bulk in this area on the RS).

Change directions several times to anchor the yarn end more securely.

The yarn changes direction 180 degrees in the top part of this photo; this anchors the yarn more securely than changing direction by 90 degrees (as in the bottom part of the same photo), but also concentrates more bulk of yarn in a smaller area. Consider yarn weight and likelihood that it will work free (for instance if using a slippery yarn) when deciding which technique to use.

Weaving in end along edge of stitch pattern:

View of WS of work: needle shown passing through knit stitches on edge of cabled pattern. On the RS, these stitches are at the edge of a purl column, and tend to recede behind the adjacent knit column (the edge of an area of reverse stockinette on the WS). In this technique, the needle tip does not split the strands of yarn, but goes under each strand.

Weaving the yarn end on the WS through the back legs of purl stitches can be done in several adjacent columns of stitches without showing through on the RS, because the purl bumps on the RS hide the backs of the stitches (in addition to the fact the purl columns between knit columns are recessed on the RS). In this photo the yarn has been pulled through the stitches from the last photo, and the needle passed through the other legs of the same stitches, in the opposite direction.

Yarn shown making three passes in opposite directions, which anchors the yarn securely.

Similar to weaving an end along the edge of a textured stitch pattern, the edge of a seam, or juncture of seam and edging, is a good place to weave the yarn in opposite directions.

Weaving in end using duplicate stitch:

If yarn is medium or fine weight, end can be woven in by following the path of a row of stitches on the WS, in this case reverse stockinette. Because of multiple direction changes, end will be securely anchored, but may cause extra bulk on RS.

In this photo the yarn follows the path of a row of knit stitches.

Acknowledgments

I had a wonderful time working on the 21 patterns in this book, in large part because Stackpole Books and my editor, Candi Derr, allowed me great freedom in choosing yarns, designs, and even pattern names, as well as welcoming my input on photography, for which I am grateful. I am also grateful to Pam Hoenig, who approached me with the idea for this book, and provided sage advice and some very helpful yarn company contacts.

Many thanks also to Tom Moore, whose photography is stunning, and to his assistant, Christine Alicea, for allowing me to tag along (and even "help") during the photo shoot—a fascinating and eye-opening experience.

Thanks also to Christine for hair and outfit styling, and to models Christine, Lexi Wood, and Alex Andrezen for making all of my designs look so wonderful.

The following companies generously provided yarn support:
Berroco
Blue Sky Fibers
Brown Sheep Company, Inc.
Cascade Yarns
Classic Elite Yarns
Claudia Hand Painted Yarns
Premier Yarns
Quince & Co.
Rowan
Schachenmayr
Schoeller + Stahl / LoveKnitting
Spinrite Yarns
Universal Yarn
Valley Yarns

Finally, thanks to my mother, for teaching me how to knit; to both of my parents, for refraining from any outward signs of concern when I decided to give up my veterinary practice to create knitting patterns; and thanks to Tom, Louis, and Joseph, for watching movies with the lights on, occasional stints as photographers and/or models, and otherwise tolerating and even encouraging the curiously obsessive business of knitwear design—especially to Tom, my most enthusiastic promoter.